KU-578-642

RESPONDING TO HATE CRIME

The case for connecting policy and research

Edited by Neil Chakraborti and Jon Garland

First published in Great Britain in 2014 by

Policy Press
University of Bristol
6th Floor
Howard House
Queen's Avenue
Clifton
Bristol BS8 1SD
UK
t: +44 (0)117 331 5020
pp-info@bristol.ac.uk
www.policypress.co.uk

North America office:
Policy Press
c/o The University of Chicago Press
1427 East 60th Street
Chicago, IL 60637, USA
t: +1 773 702 7700
f: +1 773 702 9756
sales@press.uchicago.edu
www.press.uchicago.edu

© Policy Press 2014

British Library Cataloguing in Publication Data
A catalogue record for this book is available from the British Library

Library of Congress Cataloging-in-Publication Data
A catalog record for this book has been requested

ISBN 978 1 44730 876 8 hardcover

The right of Neil Chakraborti and Jon Garland to be identified as editors of this work has been asserted by them in accordance with the Copyright, Designs and Patents Act 1988.

All rights reserved: no part of this publication may be reproduced, stored in a retrieval system, or transmitted in any form or by any means, electronic, mechanical, photocopying, recording, or otherwise without the prior permission of Policy Press.

The statements and opinions contained within this publication are solely those of the authors and not of the University of Bristol or Policy Press. The University of Bristol and Policy Press disclaim responsibility for any injury to persons or property resulting from any material published in this publication.

Policy Press works to counter discrimination on grounds of gender, race, disability, age and sexuality.

Cover design by Robin Hawes
Printed and bound in Great Britain by CPI Group (UK) Ltd,
Croydon, CR0 4YY
Policy Press uses environmentally responsible print partners

Neil: to my mother and father

Jon: to Sharon, Darren, Isabelle and Isaac

Contents

Acknowledgements

Putting an edited collection together is never an easy task, particularly when its success relies on the goodwill of multiple contributors with their own commitments, workload pressures and deadlines. Nonetheless, our role as editors was made considerably easier by the efforts shown by our co-contributors in producing engaging, thought-provoking chapters for this book. We are grateful to you all. We would like to offer thanks to Karen Bowler for her initial help in getting this project off the ground and to the rest of the Policy Press team for being such a pleasure to work with.

Thanks also to our friends, families and colleagues, and to all of the practitioners, policy leads, fellow academics, activists and unsung heroes who have inspired our thinking around hate crime issues. There are too many of you to thank individually but you all make our worlds much better places.

And a final mention to our old friend 'Death Incarnate' whose response to our last edited book left quite an impression. Your promise to reward us with 'a slow and painful death ... for challenging the white supremacy of the English countryside' was not quite the fan-mail we were hoping for, but we hope you like this book just as much as the last one.

About the contributors

Karen Ainsworth began her career in local government, working in the housing department at Burnley Borough Council, UK, being responsible for managing the sheltered housing service, the lettings team and three neighbourhood offices across Burnley and Padiham. Following this Karen worked in a strategic management role with responsibility for anti-social behaviour and community safety policy. Since October 2010, she has managed Smile Mediation, a volunteer-led organisation based in Burnley that delivers a wide range of mediation services across Lancashire, West Yorkshire and Greater Manchester, including a Hate Crime Awareness project. Karen is the chair of Safenet Domestic Abuse Services and is strongly committed to raising awareness of the dynamics of domestic violence and abuse. She is also a board member of Calico Homes, a stock transfer housing association.

Rosie Campbell OBE has been involved in sex work research, policy development and support service delivery in the UK for two decades. She advocates for policies that enhance the safety and rights of sex workers. She was a founder and former chair of the UK Network of Sex Work Projects (UKNSWP) and has also worked with UKNSWP to set up the pioneering National Ugly Mugs scheme. As coordinator of the Armistead Street Project (a sex work support, information and sexual health promotion service) in Liverpool, she worked with Merseyside Police to introduce the policy of treating crimes against sex workers as hate crime. She is chief executive officer of the Leeds-based sex work project Genesis, is completing her PhD on Merseyside's sex work and hate crime approach (based at Durham University), and is a visiting research fellow at the University of Leeds.

Neil Chakraborti is a reader in criminology at the University of Leicester, UK, and an adjunct professor at the University of Ontario Institute of Technology, Canada. He has published widely within the field of hate crime, and his books include *Islamophobia, Victimisation and the Veil* (with Irene Zempi, Palgrave Macmillan, 2014); *Hate Crime: Concepts, Policy, Future Directions* (Routledge, 2010); *Hate Crime: Impact, Causes and Responses* (with Jon Garland, Sage, 2014 and 2009); and *Rural Racism* (with Jon Garland, Routledge, 2004). Neil is the principal investigator of a project funded by the Economic and Social Research Council exploring victims' experiences of hate crime, and co-investigator of an EU-funded study of populist political discourse and its effects on those 'othered' by such discourse. He has also been appointed as a commissioner by the Howard League for Penal Reform on the first ever inquiry into sex in prisons within England and Wales. He sits on the editorial board of the *British Journal of Criminology*, is chair of research on the board of trustees at the Howard League for Penal Reform, and is director of the Leicester Centre for Hate Studies.

Marian Duggan is a senior lecturer in criminology at Sheffield Hallam University, UK. Her research interests focus on gender, sexuality and hate crime victimisation, including homophobia in Northern Ireland, gendered experiences of hate crime and male engagement in 'violence against women' prevention strategies. Marian is the author of *Queering Conflict: Examining Lesbian and Gay Experiences of Homophobia in Northern Ireland* (Ashgate, 2012) and co-editor (with M. Cowburn, P. Senior and A. Robinson) of *Values in Criminology and Community Justice* (Policy Press, 2013).

D. Ryan Dyck is director of research and policy at Egale Canada Human Rights Trust, Canada's only national LGBT human rights organisation. He leads the organisation's research and policy agenda on matters relating to lesbian, gay, bisexual and trans human rights both in Canada and abroad, with a focus on hate crime, youth suicide, education, families and seniors. Ryan's background lies in policy development, government relations and community engagement, having worked for the Canadian federal government in the areas of security and intelligence, governance, immigration and labour law. He holds an MA in women's studies from York University.

Jon Garland is a reader in criminology in the Department of Sociology at the University of Surrey, UK. His main areas of research are in the fields of hate crime, rural racism, community and identity, policing and victimisation. He is currently working on the Leicester Hate Crime project, a two-year hate crime victimisation study funded by the Economic and Social Research Council. Previously he has researched the effectiveness of police diversity training, examined the issue of racism in football, and investigated the nature and impact of rural racism. He has published four books, including *Racism and Anti-racism in Football* (with Mike Rowe, Palgrave, 2001) and *Hate Crime: Impact, Causes, and Consequences* (with Neil Chakraborti, Sage, 2014 and 2009). He has also had numerous journal articles and reports published on issues of racism, the far right, hate crime, policing, cultural criminology and identity.

Laura Geraghty has worked as both a staff member and volunteer in a diverse range of charitable organisations that support people including the British Red Cross Society and the London Detainee Support Group. She began specialising in hate crime victim support and advocacy five years ago when working on the award-winning Race Hate Awareness and Prevention project. Laura is now a founding director of the Independent Hate Crime Hub CIC, a community interest company that offers specialist advocacy support to people affected by hate crime along with providing training and awareness raising materials.

Paul Giannasi OBE is a police superintendent. Since 2007 he has been responsible for the development of policy regarding hate crime within the UK government and the police. He manages the cross-government Hate Crime programme, which brings all departments and criminal justice agencies together to ensure a coordinated and effective response. Paul is the UK's hate crime 'national point of contact' for international multi-state bodies and has been involved in training and capacity-building initiatives in many countries that have suffered extreme conflict or that are only recently addressing the issue of hate crime. He is a member of the international working group seeking to work with industry bodies to address the challenges of hatred on the internet.

Nathan Hall is a principal lecturer in criminology and policing at the Institute of Criminal Justice Studies at the University of Portsmouth, UK, and has published widely in the field of hate crime. He is a member of the cross-government Hate Crime Independent Advisory Group and the Association of Chief Police Officers Hate Crime Working Group. Nathan has also acted as an independent member of the UK government hate crime delegation to the Organization for Security and Co-operation in Europe, and is a member of the Crown Prosecution Service (Wessex) Independent Strategic Scrutiny and Involvement Panel, Hampshire Constabulary's Strategic Independent Advisory Group, and the Metropolitan Police Service's Hate Crime Diamond Group.

Stevie-Jade Hardy is a research associate for the Leicester Hate Crime project based in the Department of Criminology at University of Leicester, UK. She has previously worked for the Youth Offending Service where she developed strategies to combat anti-social behaviour, and at Victim Support as a hate crime specialist. She is in the process of completing doctoral research exploring the concept of everyday multiculturalism and hate crime motivation, and has an established track record as a trainer, facilitator and researcher in the field of hate studies.

Paul Iganski is professor of criminology and criminal justice in the Lancaster University Law School, UK. For over a decade he has specialised in research, writing, teaching, public engagement and impact activity on hate crime. His books include *Hate Crime and the City* (Policy Press, 2008), *Hate Crimes Against London's Jews* (with Vicky Kielinger and Susan Paterson, Institute for Jewish Policy Research/Metropolitan Police Service, 2005) and the edited volumes *Hate Crime: The Consequences of Hate Crime* (Praeger, 2009), and *The Hate Debate* (Profile, 2002). Most of his research is conducted in collaboration with, or commissioned by, non-governmental organisations and the equalities sector. He has recently served as the project coordinator of the European Network Against Racism's study *Racist Violence in Europe* (2011). He was principal investigator (with David Smith) for the Equality and Human Rights Commission's (EHRC) (Scotland) project on the *Rehabilitation of Hate Crime Offenders* (2011), and principal investigator on projects recently commissioned by the EHRC that analyse data from the British Crime Survey and the Scottish Crime and Justice Survey on equality groups' perceptions and experience of harassment and crime.

Zoë James is an associate professor (senior lecturer) in criminology at the University of Plymouth, UK. Her key research interests lie in policing issues, particularly relating to public order policing, plurality in policing, managing diversity and hate crime. Zoë worked for the Home Office Research and Statistics Directorate in the 1990s and subsequently completed her PhD at the University of Surrey on the policing of New Travellers. Since joining University of Plymouth in 1999, Zoë has gone on to research further issues relating to policing, focusing on Gypsies and Travellers. She leads Teaching and Learning in Criminology at Plymouth and lectures undergraduates and postgraduates on criminology and policing. Zoë's current research explores Gypsies' and Travellers' experiences of hate crime and policing responses to them.

Spiridoula Lagou is a research analyst with H8hurts (www.H8hurts.com), which provides commissioned evaluation research, consultancy, training and public engagement activities concerned with tackling the problem of hate crime, supporting victims and working with offenders. She contributed data analysis for the Equality and Human

Rights Commission's (EHRC) (Scotland) project on the *Rehabilitation of Hate Crime Offenders* (2011), and on projects recently commissioned by the EHRC that analyse data from the British Crime Survey and the Scottish Crime and Justice Survey on equality groups' perceptions and experience of harassment and crime.

Sylvia Lancaster is chief executive of the Sophie Lancaster Foundation, which was set up in response to her daughter Sophie's murder in August 2007. Sophie was targeted solely because of her alternative appearance. The work that Sylvia and the Foundation undertake focuses on challenging the intolerance and prejudice faced by alternative subcultures. Sylvia also campaigns to change hate crime legislation so that it incorporates attacks on alternatives and is a member of the independent Hate Crime Advisory Board. She has devised an educational resource that the Foundation delivers to a host of organisations throughout the UK, including schools, prisons and universities.

JaneMaree Maher is an associate professor and works in the Centre for Women's Studies and Gender Research at Monash University, Australia, and is director of the Social and Political Sciences Graduate Research Program. She is working on an Australian Research Council Linkage project with Professors Sharon Pickering, Gail Mason and Jude McCulloch in conjunction with Victoria Police on prejudice motivated crime. She has recently edited *The Globalization of Motherhood* (with Wendy Chavkin, Routledge, 2010) and is author of *Sex Work: Labour, Mobility and Sexual Services* (with Sharon Pickering and Alison Gerard, Routledge, 2013).

Gail Mason is associate professor in the University of Sydney Law School, Australia. Her research centres on crime, social justice and exclusion, particularly racist and homophobic violence, hate crime law and punishment, and resilience among former refugee communities. Gail is coordinator of the Australian Hate Crime Network and chief investigator on an Australian Research Council project on prejudice motivated crime, with Victoria Police and Professors Sharon Pickering, Jude McCulloch and JaneMaree Maher. She has recently edited *Restorative Justice and Adult Offending: Emerging Practice* (Sydney Institute of Criminology, 2012).

Hannah Mason-Bish is a lecturer in criminology and sociology at the University of Sussex. Her main areas of research are hate crime policy and victimisation with a particular focus on gender and disability. She co-edited (with Alan Roulstone) a comprehensive and interdisciplinary examination of *Disability, Hate Crime and Violence* (Routledge, 2012), exploring its emergence on the policy agenda. Hannah is currently researching intersectionality and hate crime policy and is working on a monograph based on her doctoral thesis.

Jude McCulloch is a criminologist at Monash University, Australia. She is a chief investigator on an Australian Research Council Linkage project with Professors Sharon Pickering, Gail Mason and JaneMaree Maher, working with Victoria Police on prejudice motivated crime. She has recently edited *Crime and Borders* (with Sharon Pickering, Pan Macmillan, 2012) and *State Crime and Resistance* (with Elizabeth Stanley, Routledge, 2013).

Lucy Michael is a lecturer in criminology in the School of Social Sciences at the University of Hull, UK. Her research has an interdisciplinary focus on racisms and crime and she has published in the areas of ethnic leadership, radicalisation and victimisation. She is currently working on an international comparison of student experiences of hate crime using qualitative and quantitative methods.

Nafysa Patel has over 15 years of academic and practical experience in the hate crime field and has extensive links throughout the UK with statutory, voluntary and community sectors in shaping policies to improve services for victims. She also has a great deal of experience in delivering training and awareness to a wide variety of organisations on the impact of hate crime on victims. Nafysa is currently a company director at the Independent Hate Crime Hub CIC, providing specialist support to victims and organisations in relation to hate crime. Prior to this she managed an internationally award winning Race Hate Awareness & Prevention project that won Community Project of the Year 2012 at the European Diversity Awards. She has also worked on local and national hate crime projects in conjunction with the Ministry of Justice, winning awards such as the Compact Advancing Equality Award 2011 and the North West Employer's Recognising Diversity Award 2011.

Barbara Perry is professor and associate dean of social science and humanities at the University of Ontario Institute of Technology, Canada. She has written extensively on hate crime, and among her books are *In the Name of Hate: Understanding Hate Crime* (Routledge, 2001) and *Hate and Bias Crime: A Reader* (Routledge, 2003). She has also published *The Silent Victims: Native American Victims of Hate Crime* (University of Arizona Press, 2008), a study of Native American victimisation and social control, and *Policing Race and Place: Under- and Over-Enforcement in Indian Country* (Lexington Press, 2009) regarding the policing of Native American communities. She was the general editor of a five volume set on hate crime (Praeger), and editor of *Volume 3: Victims of Hate Crime* of that set. Most recently, she has studied anti-Muslim violence, hate crime against LGBTQ communities and the community impacts of hate crime.

Joanna Perry has been a hate crime officer at the Organisation for Security and Cooperation in Europe Office for Democratic Institutions and Human Rights since January 2011. Before that she led on criminal justice policy at Victim Support in the UK, and coordinated hate crime policy and performance at the Crown Prosecution Service. She teaches a Master's module on hate crime at Birkbeck College, University of London. Joanna received her Bachelor's degree in psychology from the University of Bristol and later gained a graduate diploma in law from the College of Law, and a Master's in research in law from Birkbeck College. She is particularly interested in exploring the utility of the disability hate crime concept in efforts to understand and address more structural and pervasive forms of exclusion and discrimination, and the current challenges in achieving a shared concept of hate crime at the international level among policy makers, civil society, practitioners and scholars.

Chih Hoong Sin is director at the Office for Public Management, UK, and head of the Evaluation, Research and Engagement division. He directed the major research project looking at targeted violence and hostility against disabled people for the Equality and Human Rights Commission that contributed to the launch of the formal inquiry into disability-related harassment. He also directed Mencap's 'Stand By Me' campaign, looking at how criminal justice agencies can work more effectively to tackle hate crime against people with learning disabilities. Chih Hoong also convened the national conference No Place For Hate, looking at sharing learning across the hate crime 'strands' and across the different countries of the UK. He edited a special issue of the journal *Safer Communities* to this effect. Chih Hoong was previously head of information and research at the former Disability Rights Commission.

James Treadwell joined Birmingham Law School as a lecturer in January 2013, having previously worked in the Department of Criminology at the University of Leicester. He researches and teaches on topics of professional and organised crime, violent crime and victimisation. He is the author of the best-selling textbook *Criminology: The Essentials* (SAGE, 2013). He is known as an ethnographic researcher who has published articles in a number of leading national and international criminology and criminal justice journals. Alongside work on football violence and the English Defence League he was the first criminologist to undertake empirical research with former military personnel in UK prisons, and is currently researching the nature and character of contemporary forms of riot, violent protest and public disorder.

Mark Austin Walters is a lecturer at the University of Sussex, UK, where he teaches criminal law and criminology. Mark completed his DPhil in law (criminology) at the Centre for Criminology, University of Oxford, in 2011. He has published widely in the field of hate crime, focusing in particular on the criminalisation of hate-motivated offences, the use of restorative justice in hate crime cases, and criminological theories of causation. Mark is author of the book *Hate Crime and Restorative Justice: Exploring Causes, Repairing Harms* (OUP, 2014). He is currently co-investigator of a Leverhulme Trust-funded three-year research project, examining the indirect impacts of hate crime.

Irene Zempi is a PhD student at the Department of Criminology, University of Leicester, UK. Her main research interests include hate crime with a particular focus on victimisation, gender and religion. Irene is a member of the advisory committee for the Measuring Anti-Muslim Attacks Project organised by Faith Matters. She is also a volunteer support worker at Victim Support in Leicester where she works with victims of hate crime and victims of domestic violence.

Introduction and overview

Neil Chakraborti

Signs of progress

Hate crime – the umbrella concept used in its broadest sense to describe acts motivated by prejudice towards an individual's identity or 'difference' – is a term many of us will have become increasingly familiar with in recent years. With problems of bigotry continuing to pose complex challenges for societies across the world, hate crime has become an internationally used term; one that has the capacity to transcend differences in interpretation in order to promote a collective awareness of the harms of hate among a range of different actors, be they law-makers, law-enforcers, non-governmental organisations (NGOs), scholars, students, activists or 'ordinary' citizens.

Hate crime has also become a contentious term with its conceptual, moral and legal basis being a perennial source of conjecture. However, most readers would agree that hate crimes have a particular set of consequences that distinguish them from other types of crime. These are summarised by the Office for Democratic Institutions and Human Rights (2009) who describe the multiple layers of damage caused by hate crimes in terms of their violation of human rights and equality between members of society; the harms inflicted on the individual victim, particular in relation to greater psychological injury and increased feelings of vulnerability; the sense of fear and intimidation transmitted to the wider community or group to whom the victim 'belongs'; and the security and public order problems that ensue from the creation or widening of potentially explosive social tensions.

These problems have been recognised through what at face value appears to be a greater prioritisation and improved understanding of the issues at an academic and policy level. For instance, to avoid becoming side-tracked by the now familiar conceptual ambiguities of hate crime (see, *inter alia*, Jacobs and Potter, 1998; Hall, 2005; Chakraborti and Garland, 2009), Iganski (2008) refers to the merits of thinking of hate crime as both a policy and a scholarly domain: the first domain where elements of the political and criminal justice systems have converged as a result of progressive social movements and campaigns over time to combat bigotry in its various guises; and the second where scholars

– ostensibly from diverse fields of study and disciplines but united in their focus on the synergies and intersections between different forms of marginalisation and discriminatory violence – seek to use their empirical knowledge to inform effective interventions.

Certainly, the pace of change within both domains is indicative of significant progress. Within the United Kingdom alone we have seen a series of laws introduced by successive governments covering different forms of hate crime, as well as a wealth of criminal justice policy and guidance and relentless campaign group activism relating to various spheres of targeted victimisation (Chakraborti and Garland, 2012; Mason-Bish, 2010). These developments have been mirrored across the world, with countries such as the United States, Canada and Australia, along with many states across Western and Eastern Europe, now having their own sets of laws treating hate crime as a substantive offence or a form of penalty enhancement. While the scope and implementation of these laws may vary, the value of their existence – allied with the tireless work in this arena undertaken by NGOs and lobbyists – should not be understated. Equally, the sheer weight of theoretical and empirical developments within the field of hate crime scholarship in recent years has helped to create a significantly more nuanced picture of these multi-layered and complex offences. Put simply, we now know much more about hate crime than ever before – whether in terms of the groups of people victimised; the nature, extent and impact of victimisation; the factors behind the selection of victims; the profile of perpetrators; or the effectiveness, or otherwise, of different interventions. These are just some of the areas where our knowledge has developed, and the continuing growth of hate crime studies will invariably lead to further empirically informed advances.

Faultlines between scholarship and policy

A contributory factor to these developments has been the welcome recognition of the need for national government, local authorities, criminal justice agencies and third sector organisations to work together to improve the way that hate crimes are dealt with (HM Government, 2012). This joined-up working may sometimes involve academic input but it is here that cracks begin to emerge in our collective responses to hate crime. Despite the various developments within the twin domains referred to above, academics and practitioners have often operated on separate lines without having sufficient regard for the benefits of working in tandem.

I would argue that a polarised approach to hate crime scholarship and policy creates and reinforces three significant problems. One of these relates to the perceived usefulness (or otherwise) of hate crime scholarship, and specifically the perception that academic theorising is often too complex, too ethereal and too detached from the everyday realities confronting those who deal with hate crime cases in the 'real world'. This criticism could obviously be extended to other areas of academia more generally, but it is a feeling that practitioners are often quick to share with me and with other scholars working within the field of hate crime. It is also evident within the different ways in which hate crime is conceived of within the two domains: whereas scholars tend to see hate crime as an elusive social construct contingent on a complex set of defining characteristics that they regard as central to its commission,[1] practitioners often adopt a much more straightforward stance that requires few of the machinations evident within academic interpretations. If hate crime scholarship is to have a sustained impact on policy and practice then academic theorising cannot be developed in any meaningful sense without one eye on the practical application of those theoretical ideas.

Secondly, and following on from this point, I would argue that policy that is not empirically driven or based on academic knowledge is likely to have limited effectiveness. Grimshaw and Jefferson's (1987) influential work on police policy and practice refers to the implementation gaps (between what is supposed to happen and what actually happens) that can arise when policing decisions are guided by operational common sense and discretion rather than the requirements of law and managerial supervision. A similar argument could be used to account for implementation gaps in the hate crime environment wherever the policy stage is not informed by academic knowledge. Good practice needs to be informed by good policy, which in turn needs to be informed by good scholarship. Of course these latter two factors do not in themselves guarantee good practice as the dangers of other issues such as occupational bias, the misapplication of discretion, the (un)availability of resources and wilful or unwitting neglect still remain. Nonetheless, the likelihood of correct decisions being taken is far higher with the other two building blocks in place.

Thirdly, and again linked to the first two points, the term hate crime begins to lose credibility in the absence of synergy between scholarship and policy. Some readers will be familiar with, and frustrated by, those more sceptical voices that see the field of hate crime as resembling little more than an 'industry' where the term is used tokenistically, politically or cynically by organisations and individuals as a buzzword *du jour* or as a box to tick. In reality, these claims have little substance in a world where the collective endeavours of practitioners, researchers, activists and other campaigners are as necessary now as they ever have been in the fight against bigotry. However, to silence such claims we must do all we can to make our policies and our scholarship relevant and effective. For instance, the improved understanding of disablist hate crime that has emerged as a result of recent studies has not fully translated to the policy domain where problems of flawed multi-agency working, lip service among statutory organisations and failures to protect victims of disablist harassment are still evident (Equality and Human Rights Commission 2012; Quarmby, 2011). These failings can lead to charges of tokenism and can quickly undo the sense of progress made in this and other spheres of hate crime.

But so too can the failings of academics to use the term hate crime judiciously or with any sense of purpose. To cite one example, I, like other contributors to this book, have been heartened by the increasing numbers of regional, national and international hate crime meetings and events held over recent years but can recall too many instances where the subject matter has either had only tenuous links to our field; or where the term has been interpreted far too narrowly or literally; or where such meetings and events have been used as 'talking shops' by practitioners or academics rather than as springboards for more meaningful dialogue and action within and between both domains. Invariably, and perhaps unfairly, this can create a damaging impression of separatism – or worse still of bandwagon-jumping – within the field of hate crime, and does little to bridge the gap between scholarship and policy.

About the book

The concerns described above are illustrative of the fact that the relationship between hate crime scholarship and policy formation is symbiotic: policy formation needs academic substance in order to be fit for purpose; and scholarship needs to inform policy in order to have any lasting 'real-world' value to responses to hate crime. While there are faultlines between the two, we should also recognise the important work being done to harness and cement the links between scholarship and policy. The relationship between these two domains has rarely been given prominence within the hate crime literature, while the relevance of academic theorising to the work undertaken by policy makers and practitioners has not always been clear.

This book draws from the expertise of leading hate crime scholars, practitioners and activists to put forward the case for connecting policy and research. The important work undertaken by each contributor helps to underline the links between academic knowledge and 'real-world' policy and practice and the scope for further exploration. The book has been split into three distinct sections, each of which draws attention to a series of interconnected themes that can inform our collective endeavours to challenge hate crime more effectively.

Part One – 'Working together: developing shared perspectives' – begins with a personalised account from Nathan Hall documenting his experiences as an academic venturing into the world of hate crime policy making within the context of both policing and central government. Describing himself as an 'accidental' hate crime scholar (for reasons that become clear on reading his account), Hall reflects on the different cultures of academia and policy making, and ways in which real and constructed divides between the two domains can be broken down. Similar thoughts, but from a practitioner's perspective, are then offered in the next chapter from Paul Giannasi, which discusses the way in which relationships between policing, academia and government have evolved within the context of hate crime. Giannasi draws from his experiences within the police service to reflect on underlying factors behind the shift in perception of academics as mistrusted adversaries to valued allies. In doing so, he outlines why and how embedded partnerships between policy and scholarship can be mutually beneficial in the context of responding to hate crime.

Chapter Three takes the form of an 'in conversation' piece with Sylvia Lancaster, founder of the Sophie Lancaster Foundation, a campaigning charitable organisation formed in the wake of her daughter Sophie's tragic murder in 2007. The chapter highlights the multiple successes of the Foundation, not least in generating national and international debate about the intolerance of 'difference', in empowering people who fear being targeted because of their 'alternative' identity, and in encouraging academics and practitioners to formally recognise attacks against members of alternative subcultures as hate crimes. Like those targeted on the basis of their alternative appearance or lifestyles, sex workers too have found themselves on the margins of hate crime frameworks, and in Chapter Four Rosie Campbell examines the practical benefits of treating the targeted victimisation of sex workers as hate crime. In 2006 Merseyside Police became the first force in the UK to respond to crimes against sex workers as hate crimes, and Campbell uses this example to illustrate the progress that can be made through the convergence of local policy development, service provision, national policy advocacy and scholarship within the hate crime arena. Similar themes are raised in the following chapter by Joanna Perry, whose discussion draws attention to the lack of consistency and clarity internationally with regard to the conceptualisation and measurement of hate crime and the use of terminology. By way of addressing these challenges, Perry puts forward a model, or 'triangle', which underlines the importance of interaction between international and national policy and law makers at the first point; activists and civil society at a second point; and academic scholarship at the third.

Part Two of the book – 'Researching key issues: emerging themes and challenges' – moves on to explore the relationship between hate crime research and hate crime policy. It begins with Chapter Six from Marian Duggan, which evaluates collaborative engagements between criminal justice agents, community voluntary workers, public servants and lay citizens of lesbian, gay, bisexual and transgender (LGB&T) communities in South Yorkshire. Duggan's analysis highlights the value of academic insight to the design and delivery of hate crime policy, but calls for greater reflection on the part of scholars with reference to the accessibility and applicability of their recommendations. The next chapter from Chih Hoong Sin presents a 'layers of influence' model to illustrate the ways in which research, policy and practice interact within the context of disablist hate crime. He argues that simply looking at the impact that research on disablist hate crime has, or has not had made, on policy and practice can lead us to merely address the symptoms of the problem, rather than the causes. Instead, Sin suggests that greater priority should be given to the prevention of hate crime, and more specifically to what needs to be done at the various layers within his model to prevent hate crimes from taking place.

The following two chapters, from Irene Zempi and James Treadwell, respectively, examine issues of Islamophobic hate from two different perspectives. Zempi explores links between academic research, policy and practice in relation to the support offered to victims of Islamophobic hate, and calls for a more flexible needs-based approach that facilitates greater communication between statutory and voluntary service providers and community-based Muslim organisations such as mosques, Islamic schools and Islamic community centres. Treadwell, meanwhile, draws from his ethnographic research with the English Defence League (EDL) to identify ways of controlling the threat posed by this street-based protest movement to Muslim communities and to community cohesion more generally. Noting some of the myths and realities associated with EDL supporters and their motivations, Treadwell advocates a policing approach 'that is both gradual and not premised on initial confrontational or forceful public order policing, but nevertheless places restrictions and limitations on the activities of the group'. Related themes are explored within the context of the subsequent chapter from Stevie-Jade Hardy. Using the concept of 'everyday multiculturalism' as a lens through which to explore underlying motivations of hate crime perpetration, Hardy's research highlights that young White-British people's interactions with cultural diversity are contingent on their existing fears, prejudices and frustrations. Correspondingly, she argues, those who express negative and hostile views towards multiculturalism are also most likely to admit to being involved in racist and religiously motivated hate crime.

Young people are again the focus of the subsequent chapter, or more specifically young people who are students of further and higher education. Within this chapter Lucy Michael outlines the case for considering students as a distinct and under-researched victim population within hate crime studies, and uses recent survey findings from the UK to consider gaps within our understanding of the hate crime suffered and perpetrated by student victim groups. The section is rounded off by Hannah Mason-Bish whose chapter focuses on the relevance of gender to hate crime policy and research. Mason-Bish notes that the exclusion of gender from hate crime frameworks – which has arisen primarily because violence against women is perceived as already being dealt with elsewhere under rape and domestic violence policy – has stymied hate crime research and has resulted in the gendered experiences of many hate crime victims being overlooked. Rather than arguing for or against its inclusion as a specific 'strand' to be added to the list of groups protected under hate crime policy, she urges academics and practitioners to focus on the complex harms caused to victims of hate crime, and not simply on victims' membership of a particular identity group.

Part Three of the book – 'Challenging prejudice: combating hate offending' – highlights how those of us working in different spheres can pave the way collectively for more informed responses to hate crime. It starts with Chapter Thirteen from Barbara Perry and D. Ryan Dyck, which outlines the success of an innovative Canadian educational project designed to support victims of homophobic and transphobic hate crime and to reduce future occurrences. Their chapter describes how the project was developed through an active partnership between research, activism and community, and illustrates the multiple benefits that can arise from such a project. These include facilitating greater levels of confidence and reporting within LGB&T communities and dispelling prejudice among young people outside of those communities. The subsequent chapter by Gail Mason, Jude McCulloch and JaneMaree Maher also draws from lessons learned from partnerships between different actors involved in challenging hate crime – in this context, hate crime academics and police in the Australian state of Victoria. Mason, McCulloch and Maher describe how this partnership helped the police to implement their strategic framework for understanding, recording and responding to hate crime, and they underline the importance of research that informs not just academic knowledge but policing practice and policy. Similar themes are raised within the following chapter from Zoë James who focuses on the policing of hate against Gypsies and Travellers. As she notes, these are groups who are commonly thought of as a 'problem' in need of management or assimilation, and whose victimisation is normalised within society to the point that policing agencies do not respond to them appropriately. James makes the case for much greater engagement between the fields of scholarship and policy, not least because this can ensure that policies designed to protect and support Gypsies and Travellers are not negated by policies designed to manage them.

Chapter Sixteen from Paul Iganski and collaborators then draws from evaluations of projects conducted in the north west of England to illustrate how an understanding of the harms of hate crime can be used in work with offenders and potential offenders. Their analysis suggests that non-punitive interventions present a more humanistic approach to managing some hate crime offenders, and to preventing the commission of hate crimes, than the punishments more typically associated with cases of hate crime. This theme is further explored within the last chapter in this section from Mark Walters. Walters discusses ways in which restorative practices have been used to challenge and modify the hate-motivated behaviours of offenders, while simultaneously protecting participants against re-victimisation. He argues that while restorative approaches should not be seen as a panacea for the prevention of hate crime, they do provide 'a more intelligent means through which communities can attempt to challenge, condemn and ultimately transform the behaviours of hate crime offenders'. Finally, within the Conclusion my co-editor Jon Garland revisits some of the recurring messages from preceding chapters to underline the case for making stronger connections between hate crime policy and hate crime research.

This edited collection is by no means an exhaustive description of the many and various ways in which we can collectively challenge hate crime. Nor does it seek to document all of the connections that can be made between each of the different actors involved in challenging various forms of hate crime in various contexts. What this edited collection aims to illustrate is that policy-driven research and research-driven policy hold the key to developing long-term, effective and sustainable responses to hate crime. We hope that you, the reader, are as inspired by the contributions that follow as Jon and I have been as editors.

References

Chakraborti, N. and Garland, J. (2009) *Hate Crime: Impact, Causes and Responses*, London: Sage.

Chakraborti, N. and Garland, J. (2012) 'Reconceptualising Hate Crime Victimization Through the Lens of Vulnerability and 'Difference', *Theoretical Criminology*, 16 (4): 499–514.

Equality and Human Rights Commission (2012) *Out in the Open. Tackling Disability-Related Harassment: A Manifesto for Change*, Manchester: Equality and Human Rights Commission.

Grimshaw, R. and Jefferson, T. (1987) *Interpreting Policework: Policy and Practice in Forms of Beat Policing*, London: HarperCollins.

Hall, N. (2005) *Hate Crime*, Cullompton: Willan.

HM Government (2012) *Challenge It, Report It, Stop It: The Government's Plan to Tackle Hate Crime*, London: HM Government.

Iganski, P. (2008) *'Hate Crime' and the City*, Bristol: The Policy Press.

Jacobs, J. and Potter, K. (1998) *Hate Crimes: Criminal Law and Identity Politics*, Oxford: Oxford University Press.

Mason-Bish, H. (2010) 'Future Challenges for Hate Crime Policy: Lessons from the Past', in N. Chakraborti (ed.) *Hate Crime: Concepts, Policy, Future Directions*, Cullompton: Willan, 58–77.

Office for Democratic Institutions and Human Rights (ODIHR) (2009) *Hate Crime Laws: A Practical Guide*, Warsaw: ODIHR.

Quarmby, K. (2011) *Scapegoat: Why We Are Failing Disabled People*, London: Portobello Books.

PART ONE

Working together: developing shared perspectives

Hate crime is a broad umbrella term that draws focus to the commonalities and distinctions between a diverse range of offences, harms and prejudices. These are complex, multi-layered problems that raise difficult questions for those working within this field. Such problems will invariably be all the more challenging in the context of prevailing economic, social and political factors, whether this be the continued demonisation of 'marginal' communities, the dwindling opportunities for young people across Europe or the prevailing climate of austerity and spending cuts. With this in mind, a collaborative, joined-up response from policy makers, practitioners, scholars and activists would seem to stand the best chance of addressing the problems posed by hate crime.

Part One gives examples of how collaborative thinking and the development of shared perspectives has facilitated improved work within the field of hate crime. Each chapter is written from a different perspective. Nathan Hall begins with a personalised account, documenting his experiences as an academic venturing into the world of hate crime policy making and illustrating ways in which real and constructed divides between the two domains of academia and policy can be bridged. The next chapter by Paul Giannasi draws from his experiences within the police service to examine the evolving relationship between policing, academia and government within the context of hate crime, and outlines why and how embedded partnerships between policy and scholarship can be mutually beneficial. Chapter Three's 'in conversation' piece with Sylvia Lancaster moves on to highlight the value of grassroots campaigning in generating debate about the intolerance of 'difference', in empowering targets of prejudice, and in encouraging greater recognition among academics and practitioners. Related themes are discussed within the next chapter from Rosie Campbell, which uses policy developments in the context of violence against sex workers as an example of the progress that can be made through the convergence of service provision, national policy advocacy and scholarship within the hate crime arena. Finally, Joanna Perry points to the lack of clarity internationally with regard to the conceptualisation and measurement of hate crime as a way of underlining the importance of interaction between activism, scholarship, law and policy as part of a global framework for understanding and addressing targeted violence.

ONE

The adventures[2] of an accidental academic in 'policy-land': a personal reflection on bridging academia, policing and government in a hate crime context

Nathan Hall

The involvement of academia in the administration of government has been fairly common in the United States for some time. This has been progressively mirrored in recent years in England and Wales, where many policy makers in various hate crime circles both locally and nationally have, for a variety of reasons, become increasingly amenable to the notion of involving 'outsiders' in the policy-making process. As an academic with a strong interest in hate crime based at an English university, I have been fortunate enough (depending on your point of view of course) to be a part of this shift in the practitioner/policy-making ethos over a number of years. In this chapter I reflect on my personal experiences as an academic venturing into the world of hate crime policy making within the context of both policing and central government. In addition, I discuss the implications of the lessons I have learned for understanding and furthering the academic-practitioner/policy-maker relationship.

Stephen Lawrence, Sir William Macpherson and an 'accidental' academic

In order to properly discuss and explain my experiences as an academic in the world of policy making, I should probably provide some context about how I got to be in this position (there is a possibility that this might turn into something of an autobiography for a while, so I hope you'll bear with me). My journey into hate crime scholarship starts, indirectly, with the murder of Stephen Lawrence in south-east London in 1993. I should point out, however, that I was 16 years old at the time of Stephen's murder, and my only real concerns in life were about how well I would do in my GCSE examinations, what A-levels I should choose and, most importantly of all, the double anxiety of whether or not Arsenal would win the League and FA Cup finals, and whether I'd be able be to get tickets to see both games at Wembley. Ultimately, my exams went well, I got into college, Arsenal won both finals, and I was there to see them do it (those of you reading this who have any interest in football will know the current importance to an Arsenal fan of reminiscing about the past, so I hope you'll forgive my brief indulgence here). So all in all, 1993 was a pretty good year. I had no idea at the time, and nor did I for many years to come, that the tragic events of the evening of the 22 April of that year would come to shape my professional, and indeed personal, life in such a profound way.

For the record, 1993 to 1998 were quite good years too. I passed my A-levels and got a place studying psychology and criminology at university, ultimately was awarded my degree, and gained a place on a Master's programme at Portsmouth. Throughout that time, I became increasingly aware of a 'campaign for justice' by Stephen's parents, which reached a head in 1997 – midway through my undergraduate degree. Doreen and Neville Lawrence's tireless campaigning had found a receptive ear in Jack Straw, then shadow Home Secretary, who had made a commitment to the Lawrences that, should Labour be elected in the 1997 general election, then their wish for a public inquiry into their son's murder, for which nobody had been convicted at that time, would be granted.

For those of us involved in hate crime scholarship, and those involved in criminal justice policy making in the UK (and those of us who would come to flirt with both), what followed was undoubtedly our watershed moment. The murder of Stephen Lawrence, and in particular the public inquiry that published with damning conclusions and sweeping recommendations for change in 1999, are well documented elsewhere, so it is not my intention to go into detail here. I have argued previously (Hall, 2005, 2009, 2013; Hall et al, 2009) that, with the benefit of hindsight, the Stephen Lawrence Inquiry was *the* single most important event in bringing issues of hate crime to the fore in Britain. This was not just because of the Inquiry's focus on racism, victimisation and the responses to it, and not just because of the far-reaching implications it was to have across the board, but also because the Lawrence's fight with 'the system' has left a legacy that has allowed other voices to be heard where they previously would not have been. Ultimately, a deep sense of injustice relating to racism, and the unwavering commitment of Doreen and Neville Lawrence in their search for truth, has opened the door for the proper and formal recognition of other forms of targeted victimisation, and given us our academic and political focus on what we now call 'hate crime'.

In many ways, as an academic, I count myself among those voices that Stephen's legacy has allowed to be heard. In February 1999, the month that the Stephen Lawrence Inquiry was published, I was about halfway through my Master's degree and was facing the dilemma that, as a university lecturer, I now know afflicts many students every year: *what on earth would I do for my dissertation?* In among weeks of procrastinating, I had narrowed it down to 'policing' (not a significant achievement, I readily accept), but I confess that racism in relation to policing was not really screaming out to me at that time (a situation that seems ludicrous, even embarrassing, to me now). This was to change, however, following a one-off lecture at the university on the eve of the Inquiry' publication, by John Grieve, then Deputy Assistant Commissioner (DAC) of the Metropolitan Police – the man charged with the monumental task of leading the Met's response to the Lawrence Inquiry. My recollection of the hour or two of DAC Grieve's talk goes something like this:

> **DAC Grieve:** 'The Stephen Lawrence Inquiry publishes soon. It doesn't look like we're going to come out of it too well. But, we've already started making changes. We've now got Community Safety Units in every London borough, and they're responsible for investigating racist, homophobic and domestic violence incidents. We think they're doing quite a good job, but what we'd really like is someone to undertake some short-term research to see if we're right.'
>
> **Me:** *'I'll do it'* (and in my head – Policing? *Check*. Research? *Check*. Really interesting subject? *Check*. Dissertation sorted? *Check*).

Of course that's probably not an accurate account of what John said at all, but over the years that has become my abridged interpretation of the events of that day, and that's close enough for our purposes. In any event, my 'accidental' journey into hate crime scholarship had begun.

My first piece of hate crime research was therefore an evaluation of one of the Metropolitan Police's Community Safety Units (Hall, 2000), and in particular an analysis of the perceptions held by victims of racist hate crimes of the service they had received from the police. The process of conducting the research, and disseminating the findings, in hindsight revealed a lot about entering the world of policy makers.

As part of both my undergraduate and postgraduate degrees I had, of course, studied research methods in considerable depth. I had read time and again about the difficulties of researching the police, particularly in relation to things like gaining access, facilitating interviews, and generally being permitted to 'loiter' alongside those doing a difficult job where suspicion is often the norm. As an inexperienced researcher I was more than a little surprised to find that many of the obstacles I had read so much about simply were not present. Looking back, it seems obvious to me now that entering into the world of police policy and practice as an academic is a far simpler affair when those at the top have an interest in your undertaking your work, rather than perceiving you as an inconvenience that they could do without. Indeed, several years later John Grieve would recall in the foreword to my book (Hall, 2005: xiii) that:

> Some years ago, in the teeth of some ill-informed opposition, I introduced postgraduate students into the heart of the police intelligence system in the role of criminal intelligence analysts. This book epitomises what we were trying to achieve.

I doubt that I will ever really know the full extent of John's influence in the smooth running of my postgraduate research (I have asked him on a couple of occasions, but each time I was met with a knowing smile and a slight shrug of the shoulders), but his comments in my book reveal some important shifts in thinking in the police perception of, and attitude to, academics in relation to policy and practice. Clearly, there was some resistance to 'getting help' from outsiders, particularly academics and students, and the importance of open-minded practitioner-leaders cannot be understated in understanding this fundamental shift in ethos: indeed, a decade later I would conclude in my PhD research that the calibre of leadership in policing is a core issue in determining the seriousness with which hate crime is taken by police services. Combine this with what I perceived to be a general attitude within the police at that time that things could not really get any worse following MacPherson, and the door for academic involvement in policing creaked open a little wider.

A further issue that emerges from John's statement, above, relates to dissemination. While he stated that my book epitomised what he and his organisation were trying to achieve, I can say with absolute certainty that waiting six years for the findings to be made public was not what he had in mind. Of course I twist the reality slightly here. Part of the reason that postgraduate research was deemed ideal at the time was the speed at which the results could be obtained and, presumably, acted on. This of course highlights a perennial problem for the academic–practitioner relationship, namely that research necessarily takes time to provide 'answers' that practitioners need yesterday, and is usually presented at a level of detail that practitioners rarely have time to read and digest, and/or written in that curious academic language that often contains unnecessarily big words and means little to anyone but other academics.[3] The importance of this issue was starkly illustrated to me on the day I took my final bound Master's dissertation to New Scotland Yard to discuss my findings with officers from the Racial and Violent Crime Task Force (in other words, the policy makers), who worked under John Grieve's directorship. The meeting itself, which I recall lasted a couple of hours, was illustrative enough of the need for academics to be concise, to the point, and above all to provide practical 'solutions' that can be translated into some sort of useful action or policy instruction. However, the need to be anything but verbose as an academic is forever etched on my memory from my experience of leaving the Yard to head for home. I got into the lift on the twelfth floor alone, pushed the button for the ground floor, and as the doors began to close there was a shout for me to hold the lift. As the doors reopened DAC Grieve stepped in. It was the first time I had been alone with him, but he clearly knew who I was and what I had been doing. As the doors closed I distinctly remember him informing me that the lift took approximately 30 seconds to get to the ground floor, and it would be helpful if I could use that time to tell him the 'headlines' from my research. He reassured me that his team would brief him more fully following the meeting I had just had, but that day highlighted the importance of getting the point across, and was certainly a lesson in cutting out unnecessary waffle.

Part of the problem for policy makers and practitioners is that academic research in the social sciences, unlike the pure sciences, rarely provides *the* answer, or indeed *an* answer. Rather, it usually provides something of a *picture* that, like pieces of art, is usually open to a degree of interpretation. As such, academic research often produces a range of findings for the reader to consider and, in many instances, results in more questions than answers. A cynic might suggest that this is academia's way of ensuring that research continues, but the reality is that this is the nature of trying to understand complex and dynamic social situations. That said, completely unintentionally, and not at all surprisingly, my postgraduate research concluded with the need for more research to be undertaken.

Fortunately for me, the forward-thinking and research-friendly DAC Grieve maintained his belief in the importance of academic input (and it seems his faith in me as a researcher), and conveniently held off his retirement, long enough for me to apply for, and get, a position of graduate teaching assistant with a funded PhD thrown in at the University of Portsmouth. My research access with the Metropolitan Police was duly extended to allow for a considerably more detailed PhD study, which initially sought to investigate many of the questions raised by the Master's research. To deal with the time and detail associated with PhD research, a condition of access was to provide regular, and short, summaries of the findings as they emerged. The interesting thing about undertaking a PhD (or one of them at least), is that slowly but surely you become an 'expert' in your niche subject. While this might seem an obvious point to make, the net result is in my experience that the more you know, the more people will seek out your advice in the pursuit of resolving whatever issues they are currently dealing with. In my case, my 'expertise' in hate crime was about to unexpectedly, and again accidentally, expand rather rapidly.

In the summer of 2002, roughly halfway through my PhD data collection, for reasons that are unimportant here (but which I emphasise were not of my own making), I was informed that I could no longer continue my research in the London borough in which I had been working for a number of weeks, and nor could I use the data I had already collected. While I mulled over the prospect of starting that phase of the research all over again in another part of London, I took the decision to move to Portsmouth. What does that have to do with a book chapter about academia and policy making you might reasonably ask? Well, those of you that have attempted a PhD will perhaps be aware that, even with funding such as it is, it can be a pretty expensive endeavour. Consequently, I took the decision to move into shared (and therefore relatively cheap) accommodation, and it is the 'sharing' bit that is important here. My new housemate, it turned out, was a New York police officer studying in England on a Fulbright scholarship. More importantly, he was a police officer working in the office of the NYPD (City of New York Police Department) Police Commissioner.

As we were both relatively new to full-time life in Portsmouth, we frequently spent long evenings together discussing all manner of things, sometimes until one of us noticed that it was getting light outside. One such evening, the subject on our agenda was hate crime and, in particular, the different ways in which it was policed on both sides of the Atlantic. The experiences of policing hate crime that he recounted were, to my mind, fascinating, and when he suggested that I should visit New York to compare it with the evolving strategies being developed by the Met in London, I assumed that it was a suggestion that was firmly located somewhere towards the bottom of the bottle of Scotch that we occasionally indulged ourselves with. I was wrong.

In July 2003 I was granted permission by the NYPD to begin research with their hate crimes task force. My PhD had become a (even more expensive) comparative study of the policing of hate crime in London and New York City, and the construction, implementation and outcomes of the respective policing policies formed a central part of the research. Of course, all of this exposed me for the first time to the issues of international policy and knowledge transfer – knowledge, it transpired, that was (and is) in some demand.

Interestingly, the prevailing view from those I spent time with in New York was that I should, in essence, learn how they do things and to take that knowledge back to London and tell the Met how the policing of hate crime should be done. Ironically, in around 2004, members of the Association of Chief Police Officers, responsible for producing their 2005 hate crime policing manual, sought my advice on the policies implemented in New York and, following the introductions I made on their behalf, visited the NYPD before concluding that, in the post-Lawrence context, the New York way of doing things was not in fact appropriate for England and Wales (incidentally, the same conclusion that I had already drawn from my research, but perhaps I had become less convincing by then!).

In any case, as a result of my international and domestic experiences, I found myself (or perhaps more accurately, my knowledge) in demand from a host of police services and other organisations. Throughout my PhD research I had taken the decision to publish snippets in professional publications, and *Police Review* (Hall, 2002) *Police Professional* (Hall, 2006) and *Police* (Hall, 2007) for example, provided a valuable and relatively swift outlet for my work. This in turn attracted interest from practitioners working in the field from across the country, and I periodically visited and gave presentations to interested professional parties. I also contributed for a time to the police training courses held at Bramshill, and I advised on the 2005 ACPO hate crime manual. The professional links that grew out of this snowball effect gradually led to some of my undergraduate students doing research in the field with different police services, and at times it felt like history was repeating itself. Nevertheless, all this contributed in small ways to the further involvement of academia into policing.

My students also indirectly contributed to my involvement in the world of hate crime policy making in government circles – a world I had yet to experience. More accurately, it was the complaints from my students that led to this development. In October 2003 I started teaching a hate crime class at the University. At that time, the overwhelming grumble for students taking the course was that the available textbooks on hate crime were all American (a slight exaggeration, but not too far off the mark at that point) and that if I really cared about their education I would write a book that at least contained something vaguely British. Fortunately for me, Brian Willan at Willan Publishing (now subsumed by Routledge) agreed with my students and gave me a contract to write what was, to my knowledge, the first British textbook on hate crime.

I took a sabbatical from writing up my PhD to write my hate crime book (a fairly unconventional move that continues to baffle my American colleagues), which was published in 2005, and then returned to complete my PhD, which was awarded in 2009. It was, however, the publication of the book that brought about my involvement in policy making within government circles. It is perhaps indicative of the pressured world of policy making that, of the numerous practitioners that contacted me in the months and even years after the book was published with a view to somehow assisting them, hardly any had read it, but all were aware that the information that it (or I for that matter) contained may be of some value.

It is my view, based on my experiences, that one of the best ways to influence policy is by speaking at conferences and events for professionals. One of the professionals who had been made aware of my work in this area was Supt. Paul Giannasi, who has contributed Chapter Two in this volume. He had been seconded from Staffordshire Constabulary to ultimately manage the government's hate crime programme at the Ministry of Justice. I received a phone call from Paul in late 2007, in which he invited me to address ACPO's Hate Crime Conference in Birmingham in early 2008,[4] which I duly did, and examined the issues that I felt meant that hate crime should be seen as distinct from other comparable criminal activities. This has always been an important issue personally because my early PhD research had revealed what for me was a slightly worrying (but by no means overwhelming) level of antipathy and resistance to hate crime as a concept worthy of specific policy attention.

Shortly after that conference I was invited to advise on the content of the then Labour government's hate crime action plan, (HM Government, 2009) and subsequently to join what is now known as the Independent Advisory Group (IAGs are another significant legacy of Stephen Lawrence) to the Cross-Government Hate Crime Programme, which acts as a 'critical friend' scrutinising government policy and practice in relation to all manner of hate crime issues. As a part of that role, I also represent the IAG on the ACPO Hate Crime Working Group, which deals specifically with policing policy and practice at a national level. For me, these two positions represent a significant bridging between academia and policy making, particularly in relation to my recent involvement in the development of both the current Cross-Government Hate Crime Action Plan (HM Government, 2012) and the new ACPO Hate Crime Policing Manual (2014). I often wonder if this 'bridging', and therefore the experiences that I have described here, would have ever been possible without the legacy of Stephen Lawrence.

Lessons learned from the 'two worlds' of criminology and policy making

So, my personal journey into academia, and my subsequent flirting with the world of policy making at different levels and with different organisations, is a combined product of other people's tragedy, a series of 'accidents', some good fortune (although as my father often points out, one must have first got oneself into an appropriate position before one can take advantage of any good fortune that might present itself), and a reasonable amount of hard work. In reflecting on my experiences as an academic entering periodically into the world of policy making at different levels, what then are the key lessons that I can claim to have learned? In this final section I shall briefly consider some of these issues.

Determining the purpose of criminology

For me, it is important to ask questions about the *purpose* of criminology, and indeed academia more generally. I have colleagues at the university, for example, who are not what we might call 'research active', and who read, think, theorise and teach. These are all perfectly legitimate academic activities that actually have considerable responsibility attached to them. After all, the policy makers of the not too distant future may well be sitting in our classrooms and, logic would dictate, an educated and informed policy maker should be better than one who is neither.

I have always taken the view though that criminology should be able to offer something of more immediate and practical value, and I have long believed that if, as a consequence of something I have said or written, just one person's life has somehow improved (through providing or receiving a better policing response for example), even if only marginally, then I have achieved something worthwhile. But whatever our individual beliefs about the purpose of criminology, whether we intend it or not we are probably influencing policy and practice in one way or another, and as such as academics we have a duty to behave responsibly in the things that we do. Central to this is developing an understanding and appreciation of the differing working styles and cultures of academia and policy making.

Understanding the different cultures of academia and policy making

Urgency

I mentioned above that, for me, criminology should be able to offer something of more immediate value to policy makers. 'Immediate', and other similar terms, have entirely different meanings in the 'two worlds', perfectly epitomised in a conversation I had not so long ago with a colleague who had recently ended a long career in the police to take up an academic position at the university. Our conversation centred on the use of the word 'urgent' in academia (so often attached to countless emails from academics that ultimately have no real urgency at all, but I digress). In the police, he said, when something is 'urgent' it means it needs a response this very moment or, in all probability, something awful will happen. In academia, he noted with some surprise (it might have been exasperation, but it was hard to be sure) 'urgent' generally means that if you can get around to doing something at some point in the next six weeks or so then that would be good.

These different interpretations are crucial for understanding and bridging the gap between academia and policy making. Academic research and writing takes time. Often, a lot of time. And this is time that those in the other world rarely, if ever, have. Let me give you another example. In the spring of 2012 I was asked by an official in government if I would, on behalf of the IAG, put together a short internal research brief that summarised the key issues, as we saw them, in terms of the progress made by government since the election in relation to issues emanating from the Stephen Lawrence Inquiry. Fine, not a problem, I thought as we spoke on the phone. In my mind I was already thinking about methodology, interview schedules, participants, frameworks, and all the other things that go through a researcher's mind at the start of a project. If I could have it complete within two or three weeks, that would be really helpful, came the next message –

an instruction guaranteed to make any researcher a little nervous (or burst out laughing, one or the other). In the end, it took a little longer than that, and as I write this chapter the discussions about my (our) findings continue to rumble on in some circles several months later.

Ultimately, academic research within government has the potential to cause unease at times, and we mustn't forget this, but the need for speed is not at all uncommon. Research findings that are produced months, or even years, after the research starts may be hugely important in academic circles, but they are of no use to policy makers who need solutions today, tomorrow, or in some cases, yesterday. It is perhaps an inevitable clash of the two cultures but, as Le Grand (2006) points out from his experience of being an academic specialising in healthcare seconded to Downing Street, papers there are written in 24 hours rather than 24 months and they don't seem to suffer very much for being done that way. All the time spent writing academic papers, he suggests, may in fact have sharply diminishing returns. Something perhaps for academics to ponder on (but not for too long, obviously).

Responsibility

I mentioned above that, as academics, we all have a responsibility, even a duty, to the world of policy making. In comparative terms, an academic's level of responsibility is usually pretty low. If we make a mistake in a lecture, or forget to respond to an email, or are late returning our marking, or publish something that another academic disapproves of resulting in a bad review, generally nobody dies as a result. Similarly, if we critique a theory or a policy in our writing or our teaching, generally that's where our input can end if we choose. Doing something about it, whatever 'it' is, is someone else's problem (usually a practitioner). However, with regard to our engagement with policy and practice, either directly or indirectly, should our degree of responsibility as academics not increase significantly? I think it should. Critical thinking is about much more than just being critical. It is in my view incumbent on us all as academics not just to offer criticism, but also to offer up genuine alternatives that address our criticisms. In this sense I share Le Grand's (2006) view that to not do so is intellectual laziness and irresponsible.

Policy, theory and evidence

The necessary pace and nature of policy making means that on occasion this is done on the basis of 'commonsense' assumptions rather than on an evaluation of academic theory and evidence, which may simply not be available. Alternatively, such assumptions are made, and then the evidence sought to support them. A current example relates to hate on the internet, particularly in relation to hateful material posted on blogs and discussion boards concerning a particular news story. In short, we don't know for sure if there is a causal link between what 'ordinary' people read online and their subsequent beliefs and behaviours. However, common sense would suggest that *some* people *may* have their views and beliefs shaped by what they read, and that this *may* in some way influence their behaviour towards others, *perhaps* in the form of hate crime. As this seems plausible, the assumption is made within government that this is indeed a possibility (erring on the side of caution perhaps) because there is no conclusive academic evidence either way. As academics, then, I believe that it is important for us to furnish policy makers with theory and evidence (both positive and negative) relating to an issue wherever possible, and to seek to fill the gaps where both of these things are either absent or weak. Ultimately, I take the view that theoretically and empirically informed policy is likely, on balance, to be better policy.

The importance of lunch

The subheading used here is perhaps better interpreted as a metaphor for the importance of good working relationships, which of course are paramount to the effective, and above all smooth, transfer of knowledge. However, there is a considerable lesson that I have learned contained within the literal interpretation of that subheading. I know of plenty of people in my world who would disapprove of the informality of what I am about to suggest, and who would maintain that if one is to remain objective and critical then one should keep one's distance. Perhaps they have a point, and I am always careful not to compromise my integrity and credibility as an 'outsider–insider'. However, if you think about the key messages from this chapter, you may conclude that they are as follows: as an academic I have both knowledge and time (relatively speaking). A policy maker/practitioner often has little of either (and I don't mean for a second to question the intellectual ability of practitioners here, just that they don't necessarily have the particular knowledge that as academics we can impart. If they did we wouldn't need to engage at all). What undoubtedly and inevitably connects people in both worlds though is the need, at some point, to eat.

Consequently, I have found over the years that much can be achieved in terms of knowledge transfer over 'lunch'. The same can also be said for time spent on aeroplanes where, for example, Paul Giannasi and I have conducted numerous fruitful exchanges on the way to represent UK interests at some international meeting or other. In my experience then, relatively short, convenient and to the point meetings conducted in this manner frequently achieve far more than long, complicated, formal ones. Of course the latter are important and nothing would be achieved on the back of informal connections alone, but sometimes informality is appropriate and effective, and meets the needs of both worlds.

Concluding comments

In this chapter I have discussed my personal experiences in bridging the gap between academia and policy making. Of course other people's experiences may be very different indeed, but it is my hope that this reflective piece has given at least a little insight into what it means to be an academic involved in the world of hate crime policy making. Ultimately the story is rather less important than the lessons learned, and I have briefly explored some of these too. The key message is that the two worlds can indeed usefully combine, but that an understanding of the working practices and cultures on both sides is crucial. Once this is achieved, the possibilities for bridging the gap between them can become considerable, valuable and, ultimately, can begin to impact on the issues that in the end concern us all. Of course this latter point leads us to the most important message of all, namely that as academics what we say and do can and does have real life implications, whether we are yet to realise it or not. As Le Grand (2006: 322) rightly notes:

> Academics in government do have an important role to play, especially in the assessment of theory and evidence. Academics outside government also have a key role – in the long run, a more important one – in developing the relevant theories and in providing the evidence. But, wherever they are, academics have an obligation to behave responsibly. They have the power to change the world, and that power should not be exercised lightly.

References

Association of Chief Police Officers (2005) *Hate Crime: Delivering a Quality Service: Good Practice and Tactical Guidance*, London: ACPO.

Association of Chief Police Officers (2014) *Hate Crime Manual*, London: ACPO.

Hall, N. (2000) 'Meeting the Needs of Ethnic Minority Victims in London? An Assessment of a Metropolitan Police Service Community Safety Unit', Unpublished MSc thesis, University of Portsmouth.

Hall, N. (2002) 'Blind Prejudice: The Impact of Hate Crime', *Police Review*, 18 October.

Hall, N. (2005) *Hate Crime*, Cullompton: Willan Publishing.

Hall, N. (2006) 'Proactive Anti-Racism', *Police Professional*, 49: 21–4.

Hall, N. (2007) 'Policing Hatred', *Police*, March: 28–9.

Hall, N. (2009) *Policing Hate Crime in London and New York City*, Unpublished PhD Thesis, University of Portsmouth.

Hall, N. (2013) *Hate Crime* (2nd edn), Oxford: Routledge.

Hall, N., Grieve, J. and Savage, S. (eds) (2009) *Policing and the Legacy of Lawrence*, Cullompton: Willan Publishing.

HM Government (2009) *Hate Crime: The Cross-Government Action Plan*, London: Home Office.

HM Government (2012) *Challenge It, Report It, Stop It: The Government's Plan to Tackle Hate Crime*, London: Home Office.

Le Grand, J. (2006) 'Academia, Policy and Politics', *Health Economics, Policy and Law*. 1: 319–22. doi:10.1017/S1744133106004014.

TWO

Academia from a practitioner's perspective: a reflection on the changes in the relationship between academia, policing and government in a hate crime context

Paul Giannasi

Introduction

When I joined the British police in 1984, academics were on the long list of our natural 'opponents' in life. One of my early introductions was to the informal list of individuals who existed to 'undermine' our principle objectives – to 'let nice people sleep safely and to send bad people to prison'. The list was headed by lawyers who appeared twice – those who worked on criminal defence headed it, but those who prosecuted were also there. Academics came below journalists and probation officers. This was not, of course, part of any official training, which was functional, concentrating on the need to know the law and not touching on any of the 'soft stuff' like the needs of communities. As in most careers the real influence comes from experienced peers, the time-served officers who had 'been there and done it'. Our relationship with academics through the 1980s was, from our perspective at least, confrontational, with the likes of Robert Reiner and Simon Holdaway seeking to understand how the police cultures had contributed to social unrest and miscarriages of justice. This was often seen from within as an attack rather than support. Beyond these established police observers there were many others who we felt were trying to prove that we were 'Fascists', 'corrupt' or, given the ongoing national miners' strike, 'Thatcher's henchmen'.

Nearly thirty years later, my role as a police officer has changed hugely and academics, like at least some of those on the list, are seen as key allies to the police. This chapter will outline my experiences and show how academics have become far more influential in policing, which is a very different career now from how it was in the 1980s. There has been a significant cultural shift in policing and the desire to position itself as a police 'service' rather than a police 'force' for me best describes the transition. With this shift comes an openness to active partnerships with many sectors and a transparency that has begun to welcome external examination.

Police officers' core training has changed to reflect this transition, concentrating less on retention of laws and more on the needs of the individuals who require the services of the police. My son who is now a young detective in a large urban area in Northern England, is far less likely than me to know that a car manufactured after 1 April 1987 would need to have a dim-dip device fitted, but he is more likely to understand the cultural needs of a Roma victim of crime than I was. The reality is that, given the importance placed on this retention of knowledge in my training, I still recall the dim-dip regulation 25 years later but I still couldn't tell you what a dim-dip device actually is.

The murder of Stephen Lawrence

It is impossible to consider the policy areas of hate crime, community relationships or the investigation of serious crime in the UK without considering the implications of the murder of Stephen Lawrence in 1993. This is perhaps the best way to demonstrate the cultural shift in policing that has allowed the relationship between policing and academia to thrive.

When Stephen Lawrence was murdered in south-east London in 1993 it was not immediately apparent how it would fundamentally change policing in the UK and even beyond. The murder was not extensively reported in the national media and most police officers outside London would have been unaware of its implications until the public Inquiry was launched and began to gather its evidence ahead of the report in 1999.

Even as the Inquiry reported, most police officers from provincial forces stood back and watched as spectators. As a detective sergeant in a provincial police force I saw little to link the failings of 'The Met' (Metropolitan Police Service) with us. There was a common view in the provinces that the Met was a different entity and not related to our world. There was a phrase that used to sum up the distance between us and the Met and explains why the findings of the Stephen Lawrence Inquiry were initially dismissed by many as 'more Met issues'. It went

'To err is human, but to really fuck it up – you need the Metropolitan Police.'

The quote was, of course, largely unfair and the reality was probably that, given the size and challenges it faced, the Met was capable of demonstrating both the best and the worst aspects of policing. It was the force most likely to suffer from corruption, malpractice and failure but as I will indicate, it had within its ranks the leadership and expertise that would guide policing through the challenges laid bare by the Stephen Lawrence Inquiry.

1999 – the year that everything began to change

The report of the Stephen Lawrence Inquiry published in February 1999 and had a significant impact on so many areas of life in the UK. Perhaps the most significant of these was the examination of the relationship between the police and minority ethnic groups. The relationship in the 1980s had been, at least publicly, characterised by tensions that came to a head in the civil unrest in Brixton, Toxteth, Handsworth and many other cities. Most police forces responded by developing relationships with 'community leaders' who were able to report any emerging tensions and act as brokers to facilitate community activity, intended to prevent similar outbreaks of violence in the future. What the Stephen Lawrence Inquiry exposed was the risks faced by minority communities and their rights to a quality service from organisations like the police.

In Chapter One in this volume, Nathan Hall talks of the significant role played by Deputy Assistant Commissioner John Grieve in influencing the involvement of academia in police policy development. For policing, particularly those involved in hate crime and community cohesion, he was perhaps the most influential senior police officer of his generation. Many police officers have overseen significant structural and policy change, but John Grieve led a paradigm shift in the culture of policing, particularly in its response to intelligence, major investigations and perhaps, most significantly, its relationship with the communities it serves. As can be seen in Nathan's chapter, underpinning this was his relationship with academia to a level that was previously unparalleled.

On the back of the Stephen Lawrence Inquiry report, the police in London would be further tested when the 'nail bombs' were set off in Brixton, Brick Lane and Soho on 17–30 April 1999. My initial fear on hearing the news of the first attack in Brixton was that it would lead to fear and tension in the community and there was a real risk of civil disorder breaking out. This fear was not unreasonable, with relatively minor incidents starting some of the civil unrest of the 1980s and unleashing the deeper hostility that existed in the communities. To exploit and exacerbate this tension was in fact the intention of the offender David Copeland, who later told the police that his motive was to instigate a 'race war' in order to increase the support for extreme right wing politics.

Shortly after the Brixton bomb, I watched the national news and saw John Grieve standing next to Lee Jasper, a prominent black community activist, who had acted as a spokesman for the disaffected young minority community during the unrest of the 1980s. The pair gave a joint press release, standing under the iconic Brixton railway bridge. The message sought to encourage witnesses to contact the police, but most importantly gave reassurances that the police were primarily interested in protecting the community from a violent act of terrorism and to bring the offender to justice. I found this interview to be inspiring – I had heard Lee Jasper speak previously and he was, in the eyes of most police officers, one of our most vociferous critics. It seemed clear to me that such an act of unity could not be arranged hastily and remains clear evidence to me that a core part of John Grieve's approach was to build relationships with those hostile to the police as well as the friendly but often self-appointed 'community leaders', who typified provincial engagement with minority communities but who were themselves often distanced from the most disaffected parts of affected groups.

The response in Staffordshire

My police service was with Staffordshire Police, a mid-sized, Middle-England force of around 2,000 officers. When the issues highlighted in the Stephen Lawrence Inquiry began to emerge, I – like most of my peers in provincial policing – felt detached from the spotlight shining brightly on the Metropolitan Police. This sense of detachment was strengthened by our own experiences. In December 1996 I was part of a murder team that investigated the death of Delroy Nedrick, a young black man who intervened as a peacemaker in a disturbance in Stoke-on-Trent city centre. We had considered the investigation to be a success, securing several convictions of perpetrators and working to reassure family, friends and the community that the police were making every effort to bring offenders to justice.

With hindsight, the boost to our confidence was misplaced and failed to recognise the broader implications of the Stephen Lawrence Inquiry, notably the poor relationships between the police and minority communities, and the importance of building a confidence in our ability to deliver a fair and effective service.

Fortunately for us, John Grieve's reach spread well beyond the Metropolitan Police. When the Inquiry had reported, and particularly after the London nail bombs, his influence began to filter through to the rest of the country and the value of an effective relationship with academia was an integral part of his advice. My own chief constable, John Giffard, brought together a 'task-group' to learn from the lessons from the Inquiry. He established a number of sub-groups, each had a community representative as its chair and a police employee alongside in a secretariat role.

I was tasked with the secretariat role for a 'Cultures' group, which was chaired by a prominent local equality activist, Mike Wolfe, who would go on to be the first elected mayor of Stoke-on-Trent. We set about establishing a group with a clear steer to involve academics within the group. Our role was to examine prevalent culture within Staffordshire Police and to recommend activity to address any issues identified.

Negative police culture was a prominent debate during the 1980s and leading up to the Stephen Lawrence Inquiry publication, but it was considered by many to be the toughest area. Defining the prevailing culture would be challenging and measuring success would be very difficult – there was no notable statistical data to cite and my previous experiences of police change had concentrated on procedures, structures or outputs with no real concentration on or success in changing attitudes.

Mike Wolfe and myself met with, now Professors Richard Sparks and Ian Loader, who were both criminologists based at Keele University. Our early meetings were extremely positive and we soon established a mutual benefit of active collaboration between the police and the University. This was my first working interaction with academia as my previous experiences had been contained to my own undergraduate studies. In truth I entered the early meetings without great confidence. It was clear to me that, given our challenging task and the sense of the police being 'on the ropes' that we needed them more than they needed us. This did not seem to me to be a strong negotiating position but I was pleasantly shocked by the enthusiasm shown by the University, and by Ian and Richard, in particular.

What I perhaps did not understand at the time was how difficult it had been for academics to gain access to the police organisation before this time. The conflict I mentioned earlier had doubtless played its part, but the police had found it difficult to accept and trust 'outsiders'. The nature of policing has to value confidentiality and this made it inherently difficult to study from the inside. Therefore, most evaluation of police culture had come from outside the organisation, concentrating on outputs or the interaction with, and perception of the public. Given the often confrontational relationship between the Police and those subject to its enforcement activities, this provided a huge challenge to anyone intent on understanding the cultural make-up of the organisation.

Police leadership

The relationship with Keele University was integral to the work of our group, and the chief constable's insistence that we should lay our organisation open to examination was in hindsight quite a significant development in the relationship. In order to evaluate the attitudes and approach of the force executive, Richard Sparks and Ian Loader were allowed access to the top team to interview them and key people within the organisation.

Our relationship with Keele University was obviously mutually beneficial and the leadership shown by the executive team permeated down to the ground. Over the following years the degree of cooperation increased alongside the confidence built in the relationship. Notably this included long-term work by two PhD students, now Doctors Matthew Millings and Bethan Loftus. Both were granted unprecedented access to police operations and personnel and each produced significantly important pieces of work from an academic perspective. For me though, most importantly, it helped to inform police leaders and provide the information that would be invaluable in bringing around the 'paradigm shift' in policing culture, which that had been one of the most significant recommendations and challenges from the Stephen Lawrence Inquiry.

By the latter part of 1999, it was clear to me and many of my peers that these were significant events in the development of modern policing and there was a common belief among the younger and more progressive staff that the events presented opportunities that were breaking new ground for academics studying modern policing in the UK. What seemed like a common sense, mutually beneficial relationship was being held up as an exemplar of good practice within universities looking to increase their influence over the policy and the understanding and delivery of services to communities. I recall being surprised to be asked to give presentations of the collaboration to academic assemblies where it was presented as 'groundbreaking' activity and positively received by the audience.

The one frustration at this time for me was the inevitable conflict between timescales. This was a time of unprecedented demand for change in the police and while the academics from Keele demonstrated flexibility and willingness to adapt normal research methodology to meet the urgency of the situation, the long-term work carried out by Matthew Millings and Bethan Loftus will inevitably take significant time in the preparation and publication of empirical research. We had a sense of needing answers within days rather than years, but the shorter span of non-evaluated papers often allowed for earlier consideration than did the offer of financial support for, for instance, PhD research

Cross-Government Hate Crime Programme

In April 2007 I was appointed to lead a cross government hate crime programme hosted by the Office for Criminal Justice Reform and latterly the Ministry of Justice. The programme was established on the back of another piece of academic work. In 2003, Professor Gus John carried out a review of the Crown Prosecution Service and the way it responded to the issue of race. His report to the Director of Public Prosecutions, *Race for Justice*, contained the following recommendation:

Recommendation 8

> The CPS through the good offices of the Attorney General should take the lead in establishing a holistic approach, across the Criminal Justice System to the issues highlighted by this research, not least in respect of the handling of race crimes by the police, the CPS and the Courts. While most partners in the criminal justice system have been receiving training in respect of race and criminal justice, including judges and magistrates, the evidence emerging from this research would suggest that all operators in the CJS need to have their awareness raised with respect to race charge attrition, its effects on people's perceptions of the seriousness with which the CJS treats the issue of racist and religious crime and to take joint action to prevent such attrition. (John, 2003, p 36)

In 2006 the then Attorney General, Lord Goldsmith, established a task-force that reported the same year, and my programme was established to deliver the improvements called for in the *Race for Justice* reports.

Academia and the links to central policy

The relationship between academia and Westminster is much more established than had been my experience within policing. 'Embedded' academics were much more commonplace and there appeared a greater requirement for evidence and analysis than was available or even possible, given the often rapid decision making in operational policing.

Hate crime is not an area of universal consensus or support. There are academics, groups and individuals that would argue against the core premise. Some would claim that hate crime policy is a way of 'pandering to minority communities'; others that it creates a two-tier level of service. It is true to say that the term can be slightly misleading as the legislation does not require evidence of hatred for courts to impose the 'enhanced sentencing' provisions of the Criminal Justice Act 2003. Prosecutors have to prove hostility rather than hate but there has been little appetite to move away from 'hate crime' as an umbrella-term, given its historical and international use.

Despite formal and informal opposition, successive governments, agencies and parliaments have stood strong on the importance of developing effective responses to hate crime. I would argue that the provisions are not exclusive. Legislation would apply equally to majority groups as it would minorities. I believe that legislation and policy adopts a 'human rights' based approach that recognises our shared right to live our life free from targeted abuse.

The case for continued efforts to improve our responses to hate crime come from victims' advocacy groups, from inter-governmental organisations, but also from the testimony of victims' families who have suffered the tragedy of serious crime with the added burden caused by targeted hostility. My personal view is that hate crime tends to cause more harm than comparable 'random' crimes, that they have a broader impact on communities, and that they create an enhanced fear of crime. While these views were commonly accepted, it was important that they could be substantiated and for that we relied on the research of key academics. Among the most valuable was the research of Dr Paul Iganski from Lancaster University. His work to understand the findings of the British Crime Survey was invaluable to us because it was the most definitive evidence that hate crime did have a greater psychological impact on the victims.

There are many other pieces of evidence we found that backed the need for hate crime policy and improvements in service. Many came from the UK but other learning was from international academics. One such example is the work of Barbara Perry who was able to show the 'ripple effect' of hate crime, providing evidence to support our assertion that the damage of hate crime is broader than just that suffered by the victim, having an effect on family, friends and other people who belong to or care for the group subject to the hostility.

In March 2012 the Office for National Statistics published its findings from the British Crime Survey for 2011/12 (Home Office, 2012). This report is the most comprehensive study of hate crime victimisation in England and Wales and builds on the work of Paul Iganski (2008).

Defining hate crime

The core role of the Cross-Government Hate Crime Programme is to improve services by integrating all relevant departments and agencies into a single coordinated structure. One of our early tasks was to agree a common definition for hate crime. This was needed to allow effective measurement and to provide clarity to all.

In 2007 the definitions in the UK were many and varied. There was no real consensus between agencies and no formal government view. The only formalised definition was that from the Stephen Lawrence Inquiry. This was considered sound and contained key ideals that had been accepted by government and agencies, but it had limitations in that it only referred to racist crime and the lack of distinction between incidents and crimes had caused confusion in some police agencies. It is often glibly said by practitioners that: 'If you put four academics in a room and asked them to define hate crime they would emerge days later with five different definitions.'

There was and indeed is no clear expectation that a universal academic perspective could ever be found. I have stood in academic and media debates alongside academics who would argue that hate crime policy is flawed for a host of reasons, including that it 'panders to minority communities', 'promotes a two-tier service', 'is evidence of a nanny-state', 'undermines religious freedoms' and even 'is self-promoting as it alienates the majority'. We have academics who want to look at hate crime 'with a fresh pair of eyes' and from a philosophical, historical or psychological perspective and, while their debates are welcome and interesting, we had a pressing need to take a position that would allow us to develop policy and data collection methods.

One academic advising a non-government body summed it up perfectly for me, by saying: "We should not place too much emphasis on definitions. Agencies need to develop their own understanding, informed by community concerns, but their primary purpose is to allow agencies to build a policy and deliver services." Given the lack of consensus we chose to agree a definition of 'monitored hate crime' rather than seeking to define hate crime itself.

When we sought to agree the definition we identified three areas of disparity: the strands of victim groups included, the distinction between hate crimes and incidents and the appropriateness of the term itself. Academics helped us to work our way through the process and in November 2007 we got to a position where all agencies and government departments were able to agree to the definition which still stands today.

Integration of academics into the policy process

The structure for the hate crime programme was agreed prior to my arrival in 2007 and was established with a strategy board, bringing representation from all relevant Whitehall departments together with leaders from criminal justice agencies and the Judiciary. We benefited from a dedicated independent advisory group (IAG) who were in place to advise on any decisions put to ministers or executives.

The IAG was independently chaired by 'our man' Grieve. Having retired from the Metropolitan Police in 2002, John was now a professor, chair of the John Grieve Centre of London Metropolitan University and senior research fellow at Portsmouth University. The IAG is also the advisor to the Association of Chief Police Officers' (ACPO) Hate Crime Group that coordinates policy and guidance across England, Wales and Northern Ireland. The IAG is self-selecting and has been joined by other academics including Nathan Hall who also takes on the role of their representative on the ACPO Group.

The integration of external academics into the structure of policy creation is hugely valuable in that it overcomes the formality and the delays that could hinder the collaboration otherwise. It allows for immediate information sharing, but given the relatively small and collaborative circle of UK academics who concentrate on hate crime it also informs us where others are working on an area of interest. This is not solely the approach of our programme, with similar arrangements in place for the working groups looking at anti-Muslim and antisemitic hostility.

In order to build on the collaborative spirit of active academics we have hosted or supported a number of academic seminars. Bringing officials together with academics has the potential to identify and respond to gaps in our knowledge and respond to emerging issues. This is mutually beneficial in that it has the potential to identify and respond to emerging issues at an early stage, and has led to officials working with academics to support funding bids that will go onto inform our responses.

One example of an emerging issue that has been identified and presents new opportunities, is the problem of hate material shared on the internet. It highlights the challenge of conflicting views, notably the potential conflict with freedom of expression and protection from harm. The testimony of community groups has been that the internet and particularly the interactive capabilities of 'Web 2.0' has massively increased the exposure to, and damage caused by, hate on the internet. I believe that there are a couple of areas that would benefit from increased understanding: to understand the fear and tension created in affected communities, and the 'motivational encouragement' that exposure to material has on disaffected individuals with a propensity to violent offending. I appreciate that these are not easy areas to understand and quantify, but to have empirical evidence would be hugely valuable to support future discussions with international and internet industry partners.

My current work has genuinely reached the point where the integration between policy and academia has become the norm. In addition to the above examples there are many other regular interactions including student internships, academic conference speaking and lectures to criminology students. I seem to now spend more time contributing to student research than I ever did to my own studies: perhaps this is why I spent years walking the cold wet streets of Staffordshire, rather than sitting in the fireside comfort of a university study.

Conclusion

As I have outlined, I believe that my working lifetime has seen a dramatic change in the relationship between police and academia and it has provided fertile ground for beneficial collaboration. My sense is that both disciplines have the potential to benefit from this relationship but there is still further potential to embed this more broadly. I get the sense that the opportunities to collaborate are not evenly spread: some will come around through subject excellence but many require a 'stroke of luck' of being in the right place at the right time.

There is clearly going to be a place for those 'purist' academics who wish to read, interpret and teach, but for those seeking to provide more direct influence over policy delivery, I believe this integrated approach is mutually beneficial – essential to inform policy development and operational delivery but also to increase the learning of students and researchers alike.

One way of providing greater opportunity for more collaboration could be the extension of the strategic partnerships between universities and organisations like the police. The one we brokered between Staffordshire Police and Keele University provided significant opportunity for shared gain but it also allowed for advance planning to identify the long-term requirements and to overcome that inevitable conflict of timescales.

References

Home Office (2012) 'Hate Crime, Cyber Security and the Experience of Crime Among Children: Findings from the 2010/11 British Crime Survey', *Home Office Statistical Bulletin: Supplementary Volume 3 to Crime in England and Wales 2010/11*, London: Home Office.

Iganski, P. (2008) *Hate Crime and the City*, Bristol: The Policy Press.

John, G. (2003) *Race for Justice: A Review of CPS Decision Making for Possible Racial Bias at Each Stage of the Prosecution Process*, London: Crown Prosecution Service.

THREE

Reshaping hate crime policy and practice: lessons from a grassroots campaign

An interview with Sylvia Lancaster, founder of the Sophie Lancaster Foundation

Introduction

Sylvia Lancaster is the founder of the Sophie Lancaster Foundation, a campaigning charitable organisation formed in the wake of her daughter Sophie's tragic murder in 2007.[5] Sophie (20) had been walking home on the night of 10 August of that year in the town of Bacup, Lancashire, with her boyfriend Robert Maltby (21), when they fell into conversation with a group of local teenagers. After an initially amicable chat, and without any provocation, some members of that group viciously attacked Robert. As Sophie went to his aid, by trying to protect him from the blows and kicks that were raining down on him, she too was assaulted. When paramedics eventually arrived at the scene they found the victims lying side-by-side, unconscious and covered in blood. Both were in a coma and, while Robert recovered enough to be able to leave hospital about two weeks later, Sophie died as a result of the injuries she suffered (Chakraborti and Garland, 2009; Smyth, 2010).

At the trial of the assailants at Preston Crown Court it became clear that the only apparent motive for the attack was that the accused had taken exception to the 'alternative' appearance of Sophie and Robert, who had for a number of years dressed in a strikingly different style, which had led the press to describe them as 'goths' (although they did not necessarily define themselves in that way). Presciently, the presiding judge at the trial, Judge Anthony Russell QC, labelled the assault a 'hate crime', something that, as is mentioned below, Sophie's mother Sylvia felt it had been from the beginning.

In the aftermath of Sophie's murder Sylvia decided to set up an organisation, the Sophie Lancaster Foundation, in her daughter's name. Since its inception the Foundation has had two broad aims: (i) to challenge prejudice in all its forms by delivering talks and developing educational programmes and packages, aimed mainly at young people, that promote understanding and tolerance of 'difference'; and (ii) to get assaults and harassment of those who are members of 'alternative' subcultures officially recognised as 'hate crimes' by the criminal justice system. The Foundation has made significant progress with both of these aims in the years since its formation, and in this chapter, which consists of an in-depth interview with Sylvia Lancaster conducted by one of the editors in the summer of 2012, its achievements, difficulties and challenges are outlined.

The interview begins with Sylvia describing the circumstances by which she'd first heard the awful news of her daughter's murder.

SL: I'd gone out early on that Saturday morning and when I got back there was a card on the mat that had come through the letterbox, saying; 'Please ring Burnley Police Station, urgent.' I'd gone out and I had a new mobile phone that I didn't know how to work, so I'd left it at home. And when I went to pick it up I found I had 14 messages, and clicked one and it's my son Adam, and I asked, 'What are you doing?' And he went, 'Oh mum, I'm coming home, it's Sophie, she's been attacked.' And that was the first inkling I had.

Ed.:   And you felt, right from the start, that the motivation behind the attack was the way that Sophie and Rob looked?

SL: Yes, that's because of what I'd picked up through working in schools. Prior to the attack I worked in three local high schools as a Connexions Advisor. There was a group in each school that belonged to alternative subcultures. Now I'm talking punks, moshers, goths, emos, skaters as well, whatever. And it became very obvious that they felt very isolated within school, not just from their peers and the people in their class, but by teachers too, who would say: 'It's their own fault, if they didn't dress like that they wouldn't be bothered by anyone.' And I'd say, 'Hold on a minute, you're placing them – the victims – in the wrong category. It's the other sections in schools that you should be dealing with', but they just didn't see that.

I'd also done a little bit of training on hate crime and the Connexions Centre that I worked in was the third party hate crime incident reporting centre. And I remember when I was doing the training, as I was going through the criteria, I thought: 'Alternatives would fit under that nicely.' That's where my head was at, when Sophie and Rob were attacked. The first thing I said to the police was, 'Are you counting this as a hate crime?' and I was told, 'No, because it's not covered by the five strands.'[6] But in my mind I knew, straight away, it *was* a hate crime. I'd been out on the streets with Sophie and Rob, I'd heard people's comments about them, and I just knew.

Ed.: Is Bacup geographically isolated?

SL: Yes it is, definitely. But when I'd been out with Sophie and Rob, I'm not just talking about in Bacup, I'm talking about in Manchester, I'm talking about in York, where people thought it was OK to stop and take photographs of them, without asking. So yes, not just in Bacup, although Bacup is renowned for being isolated and very insular.

Ed.: And why is it so important for you to get those sort of attacks on 'alternatives', like in Sophie and Rob's case, recognised specifically as hate crimes?

SL: Oddly enough, because of the environment I was in, I'd actually decided before Sophie and Rob were ever attacked that I would do something about that.

Ed.: Through lived experience and the job that you were doing?

SL: Yes, and I'm surrounded by that culture at home, that was my home background as well. I used to be a biker when I was younger and you would see signs, 'No bikers allowed in here'. So I was always very aware of discrimination and equality. And it was odd, I'd rung Sophie on the Thursday and said to her, 'I need to speak to you.' And what I wanted to do was to see if she would come into the local youth clubs and just let young people talk to her, let them see that she wasn't the scary being that they thought she was. So it was very odd that she was attacked on the Friday.

Ed.: And when it came to the trial, the judge flagged the attack specifically as an incident of hate crime, which I know did please you.

SL: Oh definitely, personally it just felt a big thing for me, like I'd been vindicated for what I'd been saying. And also, it's about that recognition that it *is* a hate crime, and everybody knows hate crimes hurt more, and it's also the fact that those perpetrators, hopefully, would get stiffer sentences.

Ed.: And so, in the aftermath of everything that happened, how did you hit on the idea to start a foundation and do the work that you're doing?

SL: Well, it was already in my mind before Sophie died, and before we knew she was going to die, I remember saying, 'Right, that's it, I'm going to do something. I'm going to set a charity up and we'll use her name.' And my best friend, who was with me during that whole process, sat outside intensive care, and when I came out she said, 'I've thought about it', and she came up with 'Stamp Out Prejudice, Hatred and Intolerance Everywhere.'[7] So when Sophie's died, we come out of hospital and already had a strapline. What we then needed to do is put that into practice.

Then we set up a MySpace site for local bands to speak to each other. Whitby goths then got involved and they started an e-petition, because they said, 'Actually Sylvia, what you're saying is right, it *is* a hate crime, and we've had to put up with this for thirty years, so let's do something about it.'[8]

And we got 7,500 signatures and we could've got thousands more. But they then sent that to Downing Street and it was sent back saying, 'Well, we can't accept that.' So then I thought, 'I'm not having that either.' So we started going out to Manchester, and getting up on stage with John Robb, who is the lead singer of a punk band called Goldblade.

So what we did was get up on stage and talk to the audience. And when it started, you could feel the shift in people, they'd be going, 'What she's saying is right', and they started coming to this MySpace site. And then we got some money from America, they kept sending it, bless them, to the local police stations. And it turns out they thought we had to pay for medical expenses.

Ed.: What a kind thought. So was that money just from alternative subcultures in America?

SL: Goth community in particular; massive, and it meant I'd got a pot of money that really I didn't want, it was all Sophie's money that. And I thought 'What are we going to do with that now? We can't bury her until the following February. What we'll do is we'll have a gig.' So we set a gig up for 22 November, which would have been Sophie's 21st, and I decided we'd celebrate her life, we'd get her friends together. But what we did with the money was bought 500 wrist bands with the 'Stamp Out …' on. I remember thinking, 'Oh my god, that is really scary. I've put this money that's not mine into 500 wrist bands and we'll sell them.' We've just been discussing this morning about our eighty thousandth wrist band.

But I also, at this stage, went and complained to my local MP about the facilities in the court room. I also then wrote to Judge Russell and told him that I wasn't going to sit with their families. So what I started to do I think really, was send messages out, 'I'm not putting up with this, I won't have it. And you're not treating me like some sort of idiot', plus constantly on at the police about doing something about the hate crime aspect. And going out to the gigs and talking to people, and on the internet, we used social media really at that stage in the game quite brilliantly.

Ed.: So what sort of gigs were they: goth, alternative, nu–metal, punk?

SL: Punk gigs, proper punk. And Rancid were over from America, I remember getting up on stage before they came on and lecturing. Do you know people still come and say, 'I saw you at that gig and I listened to what you said.' Then Whitby goths got a bench in Whitby and that caused a bit of a stir. We stood and talked to the goths and they got behind us. So we'd got the goths coming, we'd got the punks and the network started. And we had the band, Beholder, they sent us a DVD of the song 'Never Take Us Down' and asked 'Do you fancy coming to Bloodstock and we'll have a Sophie Lancaster stage?'[9] It really started to take off in those sorts of ways.

And then the *Sun* newspaper asked me to go and speak at a fringe roadshow in Manchester. And I spoke and Cherie Blair was on the panel, Jack Straw, Michael Gove, and I proper ripped into them about the justice system.[10]

Ed.: Did you?

SL: Oh proper ripped, and Cherie Blair said something, and I said, 'Excuse me, you're not talking to me like that. You either explain yourself properly or you're wasting everybody's time.' And Michael Gove sent me a letter saying, 'David Cameron would like to speak to you, will you come down to London?'

Ed.: This was presumably while the Conservatives were still in opposition?

SL: Yes, so I went down to London, and what they asked me to do was what Helen Newlove and Brooke Kinsella are doing, but work for government.[11] And I went, 'No, no chance, that's not who I am, I don't want tying down.' Because they can say what they like, I don't owe anybody anything. So they were a bit taken aback by that. But meanwhile Illamasqua contacted us, which is a make-up company, and they thought we were a massive charity. They didn't realise it was me and Kate working at night.

And we went to Julian Kynaston[12] of Illamasqua and he's a big goth in all senses of the word. He said, 'I'd like to put your charity together with Illamasqua, your ethos is the same as ours', and that started our association will Illamasqua. We'd got Whitby goths and then we'd got the punks and the metallers, plus then in the middle of that we were talking to government to be at that stage. So we went out from Michael Gove's office and then went to speak to Jack Straw.

Ed.: How did you get on with him?

SL: Absolutely brilliantly, he was really helpful. And, obviously, he's an MP not far from where we come from, so he knew all about the case. So that was quite an interesting situation to be in, to be able to say to the Conservatives, who you know are going to be the next government, 'We're not playing your game', because you know that that's what they're trying to do. They'd rather have you inside wouldn't they than …

Ed.: … being the alternative voice outside causing a bit of trouble.

SL: Yes and I thought, 'Oh, I'm not playing your game, I don't need to.' And Julian then came on board from Illamasqua and they then started with the branding. So they then used the web photograph, which is now our brand, and that's really how it started, very piecemeal really.

Ed.: Yes, it sounds like you were getting your message out via word of mouth and through the website?

SL: Yes, we went to the gigs first, then we spoke to Michael Gove and then I got invited to speak in Lancashire. It was the first time I'd ever done it, and then Propaganda came up with *Dark Angel*.[13] So it was the first time that *Dark Angel* had ever been seen. And at that stage then, the justice board in Lancashire gave us £30,000, so that enabled us to set up an office, we got computers, phone lines in.

Ed.: So did you actually set up the websites yourselves and the MySpace and the Twitter and Facebook?

SL: And really it was the MySpace that started it all off and we didn't expect that. People would just come to the MySpace and leave messages, they would have come home from pubs, pissed or whatever, and they'd tell you about what had happened on that night, about if they'd been attacked. And sometimes it was quite horrible but that's how we started collating evidence.

Ed.: How did you formulate the aims and objectives of the campaign, when you initially started it?

SL: It was to create a lasting legacy to Sophie, that was the aim and that was what the money was for, from America. And at first I thought, 'We'll do a garden or something,' but education has always been my most important thing. I've worked in that area a long time and I know, through my own lack of education when I was younger with no support, I know what it's like to be young and have nothing and nobody. And if you can make a difference in that area, I really firmly believe that that's where it's at. I think young people, when you deal with them, they know when you mean what you're saying. They know that you believe passionately and they respond to that.

I did a pupil referral unit last week and I had them eating out of the palm of my hand by the time I'd finished, it was electric. And they were all asking, 'Can we do something?' and you think,

'That's what it's about, they're the kids that need that input.' It's the same in prisons as well.

Ed.: What has your experience of delivering sessions in prisons been like?

SL: Last time, in one of the groups, they were asking me really strange questions about the appeal and I thought, 'That's a bit odd', because I never mentioned the appeal,[14] I forget about it to be quite honest. And it turns out they were Ryan Herbert's mates.[15] And I said, 'Look I'm just being dead honest', I said, 'but now when I see people with tracky [tracksuit] bottoms on they scare me.' And it turns out this lad had gone back to his cell and he'd put his tracky bottoms away, and he said, 'I'm never going to wear them again.'

Ed.: So how have you found the difference between talking to young people in prisons, schools and then universities?

SL: It's very different because the prisoners and the pupil referral unit are very honest, searingly honest. And they'll ask you things I don't think university students would ask, so it's really quite different. But I tell you what, I'm dead honest with the prisoners and they like that. And I think that's quite profound and I think it's about safer communities as well. Those communities that they go back to, I'm sure will be safer places.

Ed.: And how easy have you found it adapting to all this public speaking and going into these places?

SL: It's an odd existence, let's put it that way. And some days it's really exciting and then other days it's not, but you've got to get that message out there, so I just go and do what I've got to do. I said to these lads last week, 'At the end of the day, I'm a working class woman from Haslingden, I'm no different than what your mum is.' Unfortunately, I've been put into a position that I really would never have chosen.

Ed.: It's a lot for somebody to take on.

SL: I find it most frustrating when people don't get what we're talking about. And you think, 'Well, we'll have to try harder then!'

Ed.: What sort of impact do you think *Dark Angel*'s had?

SL: That's been immense really and it's certainly helped with the campaigning. It's helped with the understanding, particularly for young people. You know, you can feel the atmosphere in the place go down when they've watched that. Even the lads last week in the pupil referral unit, there were four or five of them and they were tearing up. It does what it's meant to do and that's to create empathy.

Ed.: And similarly with *Black Roses* [Armitage, 2012], it's a very moving play, isn't it?[16] Did Simon Armitage approach you?

SL: Yes, Simon Armitage had approached us very, very early days, and we'd kept in touch. But the play was not what I expected.

Ed.: In what way?

SL: I think the poetry is just stunning. I don't think originally it was meant to just be my and Sophie's voices, if you will, but I think that's how they saw it and put it together. And then we sat on that for months, waiting to see how we can use it, and not the BBC. And you think, 'At the end of the day, I'm just an ordinary woman', and there I am arguing with the BBC that they're *not* going to use it, and sometimes it's all a bit overwhelming.

Ed.: Well, you're not a trained politician, are you?

SL: No, and I very often just say what I think, and people aren't used to that either, on that sort of platform, they're not. They expect you to pull your punches.

Ed.: I've just seen that the book of *Black Roses* has just come out.

SL: Yes it has, that's Simon's book. We've got the play coming up in September, at the Royal Exchange. And I'm laughing because Julie Hesmondhalgh, she wants to play me and she has been amazing.[17] You've got to use television as well, use that medium's presence because people are impressed by it.

Ed.: Who else has supported your work?

SL: Well, when I'm presenting, and if the group's small enough, I can do a one-to-one and interact with them really. And flip pictures up of the people we've got involved like Courtney Love, and Vivienne Westwood, we chat about that, and Adam Ant's on board, we chat about that.

Ed.:   Gary Numan's been involved as well, hasn't he?

SL: Yes he has, he's just come on board. We've just met Cory Taylor from Slip Knot. We've met Metallica. We do have lots of people, bless them, who every weekend are out there doing gigs for us and doing cake baking. Last weekend we were at a transgender festival in Manchester. Now they contacted us and said, 'Will you come and do a talk?', and we had a stall as well. That was an interesting one to be part of, because they saw us being there as supporting *them*.

     Also, we've started working with Pulp, who've got a chain of shops and who do parties for young people, so we are getting more and more into the mainstream. We've got the Saturdays, we've got the Hairy Bikers wearing the wristbands, people from Coronation Street, Shameless, Waterloo Road. So we've got quite a big following but we need a big band from the mainstream that will support us, and that's been quite difficult.

Ed.:   It's amazing how prevalent preconceptions are about goths being 'dangerous', because I always think of goths as being generally quite tolerant and anti-violence, rather than being the 'dark figures of evil' that some people think they are.

SL: Yes and I'll tell you what's interesting, our work in schools, where you'll find that kids don't talk badly of disabled people, or white or black people, and now they're also moving away from being so derogatory about gay people, but it's OK to say whatever they like about alternatives, and it's quite upsetting at times. In one of our recent school group sessions we put a picture of Sophie up and the children said, 'She looks like a whore, she looks like she should be in a horror movie': they used really quite strong language, but, that's part of it isn't it, challenging those preconceptions.

Ed.:   It can't be easy on a personal level though, to hear that?

SL: No, you look at them and you think, 'Where on earth does that come from?'

Ed.:   So how did you develop your school game with the various different pictures?

SL: We worked with Connexions who'd previously worked in schools on issues of race and gender. And Julian from Illamasqua put us in touch with a company called Huthwaite International, who're a massive blue chip training company and we went across to their headquarters and sat down and devised it between us. It's so professional and really tactile, and the kids love it, they like the feel of it, they like playing with the cards and the beautiful pictures. We've also been working with Leicestershire Police and they are putting the money up to have a game in every school in Leicester.

Ed.:   So, if you could sum it up, what do you think your work has achieved with the Foundation?

SL: Well, we got a message from a young lass in Wigan last week, and she wrote, 'Thank you, because I now feel safe about who I am.' And I did a talk in Lancaster recently, and there was a woman there who said, 'I've always been goth but I've pulled right back because I've been really scared. When I go home now, I'm going to dye my hair and I'm going to go out tomorrow and I'm going to be who I am.' And I went, 'Brilliant', and it's little things like that, on a personal level, giving people confidence, that we've achieved. If people on an individual basis feel better about themselves, feel that they can now be who they are with less fear, I think that's an achievement in itself. And I also know that when we go into schools we do change people's minds; not all of them, but some of them.

    Also, I think on a bigger platform we've brought the issues to the attention of people like academics and politicians, and we influenced the government's hate crime action plan [HM Government, 2012]. So I think in five years we've done an awful lot really.

Ed.:   What are your short and long term plans for the Foundation?

SL: Our short term one is to carry on, that's our biggest one of all. I also want that hate crime legislation changing, I want that wording about alternative subcultures in there. It's only about equality under law, I'm not asking for anything that other minority groups don't have, and I think that's what it should be. And if that takes another ten or twenty years, then so be it, but we'll get it in there.

Ed.:   What influence has the work of academics had on the campaign?

SL: I think your work on Sophie's and Rob's case is brilliant and was really positive for us, as it said what we were saying was right and had a proper academic basis to it, too. And I found the wider impact of Judge Russell's reference to Sophie and Rob's attack as a hate crime really interesting, as I'd just looked at it from a personal perspective and hadn't realised how big that was for academia. And I didn't realise how police forces would take that as well.

Ed.:   Yes, what's happened has really influenced things. I think it has caused police forces and criminal justice organisations to think differently, and a number of academics too, and made them think that hate crime is broader than the five recognised victim groups, and that if you're targeted because of who you are, because you're somehow 'different', that's all that counts.

SL: Absolutely, and it's simple isn't it, it's not too difficult. When I originally looked at that stuff about hate crime, that's what came to me. But I look back now and think how naïve I was, but I was so convinced in my own mind that I was right.

Ed.:   I think in some ways the hate crime debate has got far too complicated, it needs to boil down to those simple things. It's to do with human rights, the right not to be abused or harassed or attacked because of who you are; that is it.

SL: Yes, and then it's about teaching young people, and the not so young, that they've no right to bully or intimidate anybody else.

Ed.:   How do you think that academics, practitioners and campaigners can work better together? Do you think there is a gap between them and if so, how could it be bridged?

SL: I think there is a gap. I think academics come at it from a different perspective because they're not actually working on the ground. Their work's about the theoretical aspects of what's going on, on the ground, and how it fits into these theories. That's very difficult to do, and I feel that some academic work on hate crime, that would have been quite groundbreaking ten to fifteen years ago, seems quite dated now.

Ed.: Yes, I think things have changed and Sophie's case has played a big part in that. I think it's one of its key achievements, as far as the academic world's concerned, that the case has moved the debate on. Suddenly hate crime's not just about the history of marginalised communities any more, but about upholding the rights of *all* people not to be abused or targeted because of who they are.

SL: Yes, and I also think that the work of some charities is not relevant to young people as their understanding of hate crime hasn't moved on either. Young people are not daft and they know in their own minds, when you're talking to them, whether what you're saying is right or wrong. They know whether you're telling the truth, and they're very accepting, but it's got to be relevant to them, to their society and to their lives, and if it isn't you're wasting your time.

Ed.: What's been the downside of doing your work? If there's any advice you could give to anyone thinking of starting up a similar foundation or charity?

SL: I have to say I've not had a holiday or stopped for the last five years, and I am absolutely shattered. It's hard work, it's not easy, but it's also good fun, it's exciting at times. And at other times it's really sad, and you don't know which day's going to flip that switch. I was sat next to a young lad the other week, and I don't know what happened, perhaps I glanced up at the wrong time when *Dark Angel* was on, but I just burst into tears. So you can imagine, it's been a bit difficult at times.

Ed.: It must be a concern, having to fundraise all the time?

SL: Yes, all the time, and sometimes I don't sleep at nights because I'm panicking about it and that's not healthy. But at the end of the day you either believe in what you're doing and just get on with it, or don't bother really. And I'm just going to get on with it as I really believe in what I'm doing.

Conclusion

The progress that the Sophie Lancaster Foundation has made since its inception in 2007 shows what can be achieved by a small campaigning organisation through perseverance, dedication and no little ability. Through word of mouth, intelligent use of social networking sites, speaking at gigs and delivering sessions at schools, colleges and other establishments, the Foundation has developed a national and indeed international presence. It has undoubtedly helped to generate debate about the nature of prejudice and intolerance of 'difference', and what this can actually mean to those who are victimised because of it. It has also, as Sylvia Lancaster mentions above, helped to boost the confidence and empower those who feel that they cannot live their lives as they would like due to the fear of being targeted because of their 'alternative' identity.

By campaigning to get such victimisation recognised as another form of hate crime, the Foundation has challenged accepted notions of what a hate crime victim group actually is. With its roots in the civil rights campaigns of the 1960s, when it helped to highlight the commonalities of patterns and types of victimisation among a number of oppressed and disadvantaged groups, the concept of hate crime has tended to be discussed within the context of those groups' victimisations to the exclusion of those who do not fit within this framework (Chakraborti and Garland, 2012). The work of the Sophie Lancaster Foundation has challenged this understanding by arguing that the targeting of those that look 'different' also bears the hallmarks of hate crime, and thus should be considered so by the criminal justice system and academia. This has prompted hate crime academics to explore issues relating to the nature and impact of *all* types of victimisation that target an individual's identity, and to prioritise the fundamental rights of *all* sections of society to be free from harassment and abuse, regardless of them having minority status or not (see, for example, Mason-Bish, Chapter Twelve in this volume).

The Foundation has also developed strong links with a number of police forces, including those at Northamptonshire, Leicestershire and Surrey, but it is its work with Greater Manchester Police, whom it has convinced of the value of monitoring attacks on members of 'alternative' subcultures in the same way it monitors those on recognised hate crime victim groups, that marks a breakthrough in the way that the police view such victimisation. This could have profound implications for the way that the broader criminal justice system defines hate crime, and must count as one of the Foundation's biggest achievements thus far.

More broadly, the Sophie Lancaster case itself has been the catalyst for two very moving productions: the animation *Dark Angel* and the play *Black Roses*. The fact that, as Sylvia Lancaster comments above, they still have the capacity to upset her greatly, despite repeated viewings, is a reminder to the rest of us that beneath the campaigning façade lies a bereaved mother still coming to terms with the loss of her daughter in such awful circumstances. With this in mind, that Sylvia can achieve so much through the work of the Foundation is a testament to her dedication, resolve and resourcefulness. The future development of the Foundation will make for fascinating viewing.

References

Armitage, S. (2012) *Black Roses: The Killing of Sophie Lancaster*, London: Pomona.

Chakraborti, N. and Garland, J. (2009) *Hate Crime: Issues, Causes and Responses*, London: Sage.

Chakraborti, N. and Garland, J. (2012) 'Reconceptualising Hate Crime Victimization through the Lens of Vulnerability and 'Difference', *Theoretical Criminology*, 16 (4): 499–514.

HM Government (2012) *Challenge It, Report It, Stop It: The Government's Plan to Tackle Hate Crime*, London: HM Government.

Smyth, C. (2010) *Weirdo. Mosher. Freak: The Murder of Sophie Lancaster*, Reading: Pomona Books.

FOUR

Not getting away with it: linking sex work and hate crime in Merseyside

Rosie Campbell

Introduction

In the wake of concerns about high levels of unreported violent and other crime against sex workers, and a number of murders of women involved in street sex work, Merseyside Police in 2006 became the first force in the UK to treat crimes against sex workers as hate crime.[18] This chapter draws on my experiences of bridging the gap between hate crime scholarship and hate crime policy, as manager of the sex work project in Liverpool between 2005 and 2008, and as a researcher who has carried out a number of studies in the city,[19] including one that found support for the policy among police and sex workers, with a consensus that sex workers can be victims of hate crime. Sex workers are a group whose experiences of victimisation fit within a number of established definitions of hate crime but who have sat outside established hate crime groups. Locating crimes against sex workers as hate crime links some existing conceptualisations of hate with established analyses in the sex work literature of the 'othering' of sex workers and how this generates harassment and violence towards them. Sex workers' experiences of targeted victimisation generated also by 'perceived vulnerability' illustrates the complexities of hate crime, confirming the need for an inclusive conceptual hate crime framework called for by Chakraborti and Garland (2012). Such a framework would welcome other victim groups, enabling them to share in the support afforded by hate crime policies, reducing not reinforcing their marginalisation. In Merseyside the inclusion of sex workers in hate crime policing policy has seen real advantages for a group who have been relatively 'unprotected'[20] by law and policy from victimisation.

Sex worker victimisation: under-reporting, criminalisation and safety

A considerable body of research literature illustrates the levels and patterns of sex worker victimisation, showing them as more at risk of harassment and violence than the general public, with risks varying across different sectors. Offenders often display repeat and escalating offending patterns (Kinnell, 2008). As with established hate crime groups, sex worker victimisation tends to get attention when there are high profile murders (Iganksi, 2002). For sex workers this is particularly the case when serial murders occur: for example, the five women murdered by Steven Wright in Ipswich in 2006.[21] The heightened vulnerability of sex workers, particularly street based, to murder has been illustrated in a number of studies (Lowman and Fraser, 1996; Salfati et al, 2008).

Studies in the UK and globally have demonstrated that female street sex workers experience particularly high levels of work related violence committed by a range of perpetrators: for example, men who present as clients and vigilantes (Barnard, 1993; Hester and Westmarland, 2004; Kinnell, 2008; Shannon et al, 2009), with male street workers also more likely to be targeted than their off-street escorting counterparts (Scott et al, 2005). Comparing female street and off-street sex work in three UK cities, Church et al (2001) found that controlling for all variables, street work was less safe than off street: 81% of 115 women who were street workers reported ever experiencing client violence, 50% in the last six months compared to 48% (60 of 125) and 26% respectively of indoor sex workers. Being slapped, punched or kicked were the forms of violence reported most frequently by street sex workers, with 47% reporting such violence, compared to 17% for indoor workers. Among 70 street sex workers in Merseyside 79% had been attacked in the course of their work (Campbell, 2002). While studies examining the differences in prevalence between sex markets find that off-street sex work is generally safer, they do not claim there is no victimisation but illustrate varying patterns of (and factors shaping) victimisation highlighting the different organisational, situational and protective safety measures often present in sectors (Sanders and Campbell, 2007; O'Doherty, 2011).

As is well documented for other hate crime groups (Williams and Robinson, 2004; Garland and Chakraborti, 2007) for sex workers harassment and crime is under reported to police. Church et al (2001) found only 34% of sex workers who had experienced violence had reported it to the police. Only 29% of sex workers making reports into the National Ugly Mugs Scheme[22] in its first six months wanted to report formally to the police (personal communication). Reasons for underreporting include a lack of trust, and a belief the police will not treat it seriously or will treat it as an occupational hazard. Not surprisingly, sex workers are known to fear judgemental attitudes, arrest, prosecution, closure of premises and public identification (Benson, 1998; Kinnell, 2006; Boff, 2012), with some factors heightened for migrant sex workers (Mai, 2009). Some offenders are very much aware of sex worker reluctance to report and will target with a belief they will get away with crimes (Kinnell, 2008). Chakraborti and Garland's (2009) description of hate crime victim groups as historically over-policed and under-protected translates to sex workers. Central to the historically problematic relationship between sex workers and police in the UK is that the organisation in a position to protect sex workers is also responsible for enforcing the laws on prostitution, and can potentially arrest sex workers and others they work with (Campbell, 2011b). The quasi-criminalisation of sex work sets up an adversarial relationship between sex workers and the police (Lowman, 2000). Research on the regulation of sex work documents how police enforcement of laws criminalises many activities associated with sex work, perpetuates sex worker victimisation and has detrimental impacts on safety (Self, 2003; Brooks-Gordon, 2006; Hubbard, 2006; Kinnell, 2008). Criminalisation of sex work is one important factor that has contributed to sex workers' exclusion, limiting protections and creating vulnerability to violent and other crime. Indeed, Chakraborti and Garland (2012: 503) refer to a number of groups, including sex workers, whom they describe as 'typically seen as "undesirables", criminogenic or less worthy than other more "legitimate" or credible victim groups ... [and consequently] commonly excluded from view'.

Connecting sex worker victimisation, 'othering' and hate crime

Some theorists reflecting on the widening of hate crime victim groups have cautioned against overly restricting hate crime status to certain groups as it risks the creation of victim hierarchies (Chakraborti and Garland, 2009; Mason-Bish, 2010). As well as groups such as disabled people (Roulstone et al, 2011) and goths (Garland, 2010) whose experiences of hate crime are increasingly being recognised, sex workers are one group who may benefit from inclusion and the 'special protection afforded to the officially recognised minority groups' (Chakraborti and Garland, 2009: 16) and whose experiences could contribute to understanding experiences of victimisation for groups outside recognised hate crime groups. Sex workers' experiences fit various definitions of hate crime victimisation, including established ones that refer to 'othering', social hierarchies, and that define hate crimes as expressions of power and prejudice (Sheffield, 1995; Perry, 2001; Hall, 2005) 'against those without rights, privilege and prestige' (Chakraborti and Garland, 2009). Perry's (2001) emphasis on groups who experience historical social marginalisation and acts of violence and intimidation that 'put them in their place' connects directly with an substantive literature on the enduring stigmatisation, 'othering' and social marginalisation of sex workers.

This has long been identified as creating hostility and prejudice towards sex workers, leading to a denial of rights, lack of protection and victimisation (O'Neill, 1997, 2007). Roberts (1994) identified 'whore stigma' as leading to violence against sex workers and the historical tendency of the police to dismiss such violence. Theorists note female sex workers are placed on the bad woman side of madonna/whore dichotomy, positioned as breaking rules for female sexuality and constructed as a social category open to verbal, physical and sexual abuse (Pheterson, 1993). They have outlined 'rape myths' that uniquely coalesce around sex workers, fuelling sexual violence against them (Miller and Schwarz, 1995). Violence against sex workers of all genders is understood as a form of socio-political management, punishing behaviour viewed as conflicting with particular gendered or sexual normative regimes (Scott et al, 2005). Historically shifting discourses have created out-group status and 'othered' sex workers, constructing them as the source of venereal disease, pollutants and agents of social contagion in Victorian societies (Walkowitz, 1980; Spongberg, 1997); as vectors for HIV transmission (Scambler et al, 1990); as urban blight (Scoular et al, 2007) and as disposable trash via a 'discourse of disposability' (Lowman, 2000) constructed in media, public and official discourses. Kinnell (2006) has identified anti-prostitution statements from police and politicians, using the language of 'cleaning up' and 'eradication' as commonplace in the UK, reinforcing a 'rhetoric of abhorrence' condoning the victimisation of sex workers, including extreme acts of violence, via cultural disinhibition.

Sex workers share the out-group status of the 'other' central to discrimination faced by other groups who experience hate crime. The interplay between 'othering', marginalisation and criminalisation contribute to a lack of social and legal protections creating conditions in which sex worker hate victimisation can flourish.

Development and key strands of Merseyside's sex work and hate crime approach

Merseyside's approach was shaped by the socioeconomic and sex work policy context of Liverpool, where for over a decade community safety partnerships had considered the safety of sex workers (Campbell et al, 1996) with innovative initiatives on sex work project and police partnership work (Hester and Westmarland, 2004; Penfold et al, 2004). In the story of sex work and hate crime in Merseyside murder played a role in demonstrating 'clear cut examples of different forms of hate crime' (Garland, 2010: 40) that led to recognition and action (Campbell, 2011a). The police investigated a number of sex worker murders and the major incident team forged close relations with projects and built trust with sex workers. These included the tragic murders of Hanane Parry and Pauline Stephen by Mark Horner in 2003, who cut up their bodies and dumped them in bin bags in alleyways. Their murders triggered a call by Liverpool City Council for the legalisation of sex work, the commissioning of a public consultation on a managed area for street sex work, and unsuccessful lobbying of central government to support the piloting of such an area.

A new sex work project called Armistead Street was established in July 2005 (which I coordinated alongside the off-street project) within the National Health Service to provide a specialist outreach and support service for women working in street sex work and those wishing to exit prostitution in Liverpool. It provided a flexible, confidential community based service, addressing street sex workers' holistic health, safety and social welfare needs. A couple of weeks after the project was established on street outreach we saw a graffiti image of the serial murderer Peter Sutcliffe[23] with the text 'Warning: Sutcliffe Operates in this Area' (see image overleaf). The police and council treated this as hate crime graffiti, and this was the first time I was aware that a hate crime procedure could be applied to a sex work matter.

In September 2005 Anne Marie Foy, a mum, grandma and service user was murdered.[24] Armistead supported police in their investigation, developed further partnership initiatives and advocated for further change. A conviction of an offender who had raped a homeless street sex worker at knife point was secured leading to enhanced liaison between the police, sex workers and Armistead.

Graffiti image of Peter Sutcliffe, Liverpool, August 2005

In November 2006 Armistead established the first specialist independent sexual violence advisor (ISVA) for sex workers in the UK, funded by the Home Office, offering support to victims of rape and sexual assault from report to court. The area commander for Liverpool North local policing area, along with the force strategic lead on prostitution, drafted a policy memorandum that was immediately signed off on 15 December when the horrifying murders of five women in Ipswich took place (see endnote 21). This included that incidents motivated by the victims sex worker status 'should be recorded as a hate crime and follow the area strategy in dealing with such cases' (Merseyside Police, 2006). The former Chief Constable Bernard Hogan-Howe made a public video statement promoting the police force policy, as part of this he stated:

> '... Sex workers are members of the community who are vulnerable to attack....we will not tolerate violence against sex workers... Merseyside Police are determined to bring all perpetrators of hate crime to justice.'

This resulted in a range of positive outcomes. Between 2005 and 2009 there was a 400% increase in the proportion of sex workers reporting to the project Ugly Mugs Scheme making formal reports to police, while the conviction rate for crimes against sex workers in Merseyside that made it to court between 2007 and 2011 was 83%. The rate for cases involving rape and sexual offences was 75%, compared to the national 'generic' rate of 58%. As of the end of 2011, 32 victims were known to have received justice, with 25 offenders convicted, an unprecedented number in the UK.

For other areas wanting to learn from the Merseyside experience, it is important to acknowledge several key strands constituting the 'hate crime approach' (an umbrella term for a number of initiatives), all which were championed at a senior level. With changes in policing minority groups, hate crime had a wider prominence across the force so the hate crime policy itself increased the status of crimes against sex workers, signalling that reports of crime should be taken seriously and responded to professionally. Hate crime units (SIGMA units) were launched in 2007 and SIGMA north took on a coordinating role for crimes against sex workers, so there was a focused team with force-wide recognition building relations sex workers. Between 2007 and 2010 there was a close relationship between the project and the unit who led on coordinating, monitoring and investigating some crimes against sex workers. In recent years SIGMA had a less active role as officers who had championed the issue moved on, meaning that sex workers are not fully integrated into hate crime monitoring and other procedures. Wider changes to policing rape and sexual offences have seen a key role played by the specialist rape and sexual offences 'Unity' team. Since its establishment in 2010, the unit alongside the Merseyside Safeplace (Sexual Assault Referral Centre) has provided sex-worker-friendly services, reaching out to sex workers and working closely with the outreach project. The majority of sex worker victim cases that have reached court have involved sexual offences. Enhanced specialist support for victims via the dedicated ISVA working closely with the police has been a vital element for engaging victims, and the post has been recognised as a form of good practice (Blair, 2011; Crown Prosecution Service, 2012). The police proactively built trust and confidence in order to encourage reporting by appointing police sex work liaison officers and by championing a national Ugly Mugs Scheme. A proportionate policing response with limited strategic enforcement of the prostitution laws (i.e. 'public protection focused policing' (Campbell, 2011b)) made a crucial contribution to changing sex worker perceptions of the police. Sex workers began to see police as concerned about their welfare rather than just arresting them, aiding increased trust in the police necessary for reporting.

With increased interest in the Merseyside approach from other areas of the UK, and within national policy forums on sex work I was involved in via the UK Network of Sex Work Projects (UKNSWP), it was clear there was a need for policy-led research. In order to document these developments, capturing them at a moment in time when progressive work was taking place, I shifted the focus of my PhD research to explore the perspectives of sex workers, the police and service providers. An overview of some of the key themes to emerge from this research now follows.

Sex worker and police views: perceived vulnerability and targeted victimisation

Of the 40 officers interviewed, 25 (63%) were aware of the sex work and hate crime policy before being approached for interview but the large majority thought sex workers could be victims of hate crime. The detective superintendent holding the force strategic lead for sex work linked the policy to wider shifts in policing diversity and pointed to recognition of vulnerability and poor policing in the past as the key element sex workers were included: "Given their vulnerabilities they need an enhanced service ... especially the way they were treated ... After Stephen Lawrence there was a sea change in policing minority groups as victims ... this is part of that, we have to gain the confidence of victims."

The most common explanation offered for why police officers felt sex workers were victims of hate crime was that sex workers were specifically targeted because they were members of a vulnerable minority group. This is illustrated by a detective sergeant involved in establishing SIGMA North:

> 'Our approach was don't be narrow minded ... for example, there had been issues around goths as an identifiable group ... I believe it fits the criteria for the reasons that sex workers are extremely vulnerable and an identifiable group and some people will target sex workers, especially street sex workers because of their vulnerability, because of who they are and what they are doing.' (Campbell, 2014, forthcoming)

These elements – membership of a minority or identifiable group who face prejudice, targeting, vulnerability and need for an improved service – were recurrent and commonplace in the narratives of police officers.

No previous research had asked sex workers whether they think sex workers can be victims of hate crime. My research began to do that, albeit with a group of predominantly female street sex workers. While the large majority of sex workers had not been aware of the sex work and hate crime policy before interview, the reaction was positive with majority support:

'Yeah, that's right because it is a hate crime. If you're gonna throw things out the window at you shout at you or come over and punch you for nothing that's a hate crime whether it's black people, lesbians or sex workers.' (Jane,[25] 37, White British)

'Yeah it's powerful … They can't pretend anymore that these crimes don't exist, end of story, they do exist! We're classed as, what's the word? The dregs of society. There's myths about us on diseases, because of our addictions and stuff like that you know we're thought of as half a human being, that's why they treat us like that. And they think they can get away with treating the sex workers like that and they shouldn't.' (Corin, 30, Black British)

Others also made direct reference to prejudice, stigma and social outcast status. Many women offered support for the sex work and hate crime policy because it connected to their experiences of victimisation and their understanding of motivations for targeted crime against sex workers:

'I think it's good. Because the amount of stick and stones you get. And people think because you do what you do they can do what they want to you because you're lower than the low in some people's eyes.' (Fiona, 36, Dual Heritage)

The majority felt sex workers could be victims of hate crime and reported that they had experienced hate crime, describing a range of experiences of harassment and violence and often describing the presence of hate language:

'You get a lot of that. I've had beatings and they've gone "You dirty smelly, dirty bastard prostitute, junkie" and been kicked. "You're scum!" And you get a hiding. It isn't even to rob you, it was to give you a hiding because of what you did, because of what we were, what you were on.' (Bille, 40, White British)

A number of participants identified being a drug user, and also homeless status, as an additional social marker generating violence. Indeed, some felt street sex workers were particularly likely to be hate crime victims because of people's reactions to these factors[26] and additional vulnerabilities working out on the streets. In addition, responses from black British and transgender participants, who described experiencing varying types of hate crimes, raised intersectionality issues and the complexities of hate crime victimisation which have been noted by some hate crime theorists (Mason–Bish, 2010). The varied experiences of victimisation among male, female and transgender sex workers and across different sectors illustrate how hate crime victimisation is not just about identity but how this 'intersects with other aspects of their self and with other situational factors and context' (Chakraborti and Garland, 2012: 510).

A predominant theme raised by sex workers was that targeting occurred not only because of stigma and hostility but also because offenders perceived sex workers as easy targets. This was particularly the case for street sex workers because they were working in relative isolation with limited protections, and because it was assumed sex workers as a group wouldn't report to the police, or if they did they would not be taken seriously, thereby making them all the more vulnerable: "They do it because they think it's easy, they'll get away with it and they think we're scum" (Jackie, 43, White British).

'Perceived vulnerability' is used by Chakraborti and Garland (2012: 507) to describe perpetrators seeing 'their target ... as weak, defenceless, powerless, with a limited capacity to resist'. They stress that the notion of perceived vulnerability does not assume that hate crime against any particular group is inevitable or that the group are passive victims. This notion certainly helps in the context of understanding sex worker experiences of hate crime, as it was a key factor, alongside others, that sex workers identified as shaping their victimisation. The majority of sex workers were of the view that many offenders targeted sex workers specifically because of their sex worker status and in the belief that they are 'easy targets' and they (the offender) would 'get away with it'. It was the elements of hostility generated by stigma and prejudice, perceptions of vulnerability, and targeting of sex workers as a group, that sex workers described when reflecting on whether sex workers were victims of hate crime. The presence of these elements illustrates that sex workers can be victims of hate crime. Their experiences fit components found in some established definitions of hate crime and at the same time illustrate the need, proposed by Chakraborti and Garland (2012), for an inclusive, non-hierarchical, hate crime framework that includes, not only sex workers but also people with drug and alcohol problems, homeless people and other victim groups not currently recognised.

Conclusion

There have been some positive changes from initiatives in Merseyside to address crimes against sex workers, and the hate crime policy has contributed to progress. However, there are a number of ongoing challenges in sustaining this approach, including the uncertainty brought about through a climate of cuts, and the fact that the hate crime and sex work policy has not yet been fully integrated into wider hate crime policies and practices. With an ever-shifting terrain, officers in hate crime units have become less engaged and neighbourhood police have come under pressure to erode 'strategic enforcement'. There is a way to go in raising awareness among sex workers and police about the policy: senior officers champion the approach but sustaining change across all ranks on the ground is challenging (see also Chakraborti and Garland, 2009). Ongoing initiatives are needed to maintain levels of trust among street sex workers, to extend proactive community liaison work off street, to sustain quality victim support and to further embed sex workers in wider hate crime practices.

Despite these challenges I hope the sex work and hate crime policy is sustained.[27] not only because it supports changes in operational policing practices and attitudes but also because it recognises issues of prejudice, 'othering', 'perceived vulnerability' and targeting, which shape sex workers' experiences of victimisation. Naming crimes against sex workers as hate crime speaks directly to many sex workers' experiences and understanding of why people target and victimise them. It recognises a history of a problematic relationship between sex workers and the police and the need for proactive steps within policing to set that to 'rights'. The word 'rights' is vital. Approaching crimes against sex workers as hate crime locates sex worker safety in the public protection arena and recognises the rights of sex workers to safety and access to justice, complementing a wider rights-based approach to inclusion, citizenship and social justice for sex workers (O'Neill, 2007). As such it has resonated with some sex worker rights groups globally.

As a model for national policy, placing strategies to address crimes against sex workers under the hate crime banner offers a rights-based, non-stigmatising approach. It gives further support to forces in including or sustaining protection-based approaches to policing crimes against sex workers. In the spirit of the national hate crime action plan which states; 'we have been very clear with local areas that they are free to include other strands in addition to the monitored five when developing their approach to hate crime' (Home Office,

2012: 6), Liverpool is one example of a local police force area that has taken the initiative to include a group not in the monitored hate crimes strands and that has applied hate crime principles. The renewed Association of Chief Police Officers (ACPO) guidance on hate crime is likely to reinforce the message that forces locally have the discretion to include victim groups outside the monitored strands if it will achieve community safety goals (personal communication with ACPO lead on hate crime).

I have bridged a gap between scholarship on sex work and hate crime in Merseyside, service provision, local policy development and national policy advocacy, with active involvement in the UKNSWP. While negotiating this interface can be challenging, it is enriching and has benefits. It makes it possible to be directly informed by developments at the frontline, and to ground concepts in practice and lived experiences, a long established principle for action research. A research-evidenced and scholarship-aware approach to policy development encourages documentation and reflection on new and innovative practice and policy developments. Having links with, and involvement, in regional, national and international networks also enables the sharing of lessons learned and can inform national strategy and international debates. If those of us developing this approach had not been as active in national networks, the benefits and lessons from enacting hate crime policies, which include sex workers, may have taken longer to be included in national policy documents.

Wherever one sits within debates about including other groups within hate crime groups, this approach in Merseyside has contributed to achieving some very positive outcomes in terms of police–sex work community relations and criminal justice outcomes, and it has been recognised as effective practice in addressing crimes against sex workers at national level (ACPO 2011; Home Office, 2011; CPS, 2012).

References

Association of Chief Police Officers (2011) *ACPO Strategy and Supporting Operational Guidance for Policing Prostitution and Sexual Exploitation*, London: ACPO: http://tinyurl.com/nckz8ya

Barnard, M. (1993) 'Violence and Vulnerability: Conditions of Work for Streetworking Prostitutes', *Sociology of Health and Illness*, 15 (5): 683–705.

Benson, C. (1998) *Violence against Female Prostitutes*, Department of Social Sciences: Loughborough University.

Blair, E. (2011) *'I Am Not a Victim': A Preliminary Evaluation of the First Independent Sexual Violence Advisor (ISVA) Service for Men and Women Selling Sex in East London*, London: Homerton Hospital Trust.

Brooks-Gordon, B. (2006) *The Price of Sex: Prostitution, Policy and Society*, Cullompton: Willan.

Boff, A. (2012) *Silence on Violence Improving the Safety of Women: The Policing of Off-Street Sex Work and Sex Trafficking in London*, London: Greater London Assembly: http://glaconservatives.co.uk/wp-content/uploads/downloads/2012/03/Report-on-the-Safety-of-Sex-Workers-Silence-on-Violence.pdf

Campbell, R. (2002) *Working on the Street: An Evaluation of the Linx Project*, Liverpool: Liverpool Hope University.

Campbell, R. (2011a) 'A Case of Hate: Approaching Crimes against Sex Workers as Hate Crime in Merseyside', presented at *British Society of Criminology Annual Conference 2011: Economies and Insecurities of Crime and Justice*, Northumbria University, 3–6 July 2011.

Campbell, R. (2011b) 'Protection for Sex Workers: Reporting, Hate Crime and Rights', presented at *Josephine Butler Society Annual Lecture*, London, 12 October 2011.

Campbell, R. (2014, forthcoming) *Treating Crimes Against Sex Workers as Hate Crime in Merseyside*, PhD thesis, School of Applied Social sciences, University of Durham.

Campbell, R., Coleman, S. and Torkington, P. (1996) *Street Prostitution in Inner City Liverpool*, Liverpool City Council/Liverpool City Centre Challenge/Liverpool Hope University College.

Campbell, R. and Kinnell, H. (2001) '"We Shouldn't Have to Put Up with This": Street Sex Work and Violence', *Criminal Justice Matters*, No. 42, Winter 2000/2001.

Chakraborti, N. (2010) 'Future Developments for Hate Crime Thinking: Who, What and Why?", in N. Chakraborti (ed.) *Hate Crime: Concepts, Policy, Future Directions*, Cullompton: Willan, pp. 1–14.

Chakraborti, N. (2011) 'Targeting Vulnerability: A Fresh Set of Challenges for Hate Crime Scholarship and Policy', presented at *British Society of Criminology Annual Conference: Economies and Insecurities of Crime and Justice*, 3–6 July, Northumbria University.

Chakraborti, N. and Garland, J. (2012) 'Reconceptualising Hate Crime Victimization through the Lens of Vulnerability and "Difference"', *Theoretical Criminology*, 16 (4): 499–514.

Chakraborti, N. and Garland, J. (eds) (2009) *Hate Crime: Impact, Causes and Responses*, London: Sage.

Church, S., Henderson, M., Barnard, M. and Hart, G. (2001) 'Violence by Clients towards Female Prostitutes in Different Work Settings: Questionnaire Survey', *British Medical Journal*, 322: 524–5.

Crown Prosecution Service (2012) *Violence against Women and Girls Crime Report 2011-2012*, London: CPS, Equality and Diversity Unit.

Garland, J. (2010) 'The Victimisation of Goths and the Boundaries of Hate Crime', in N. Chakraborti (ed.) *Hate Crime: Concepts, Policy, Future Directions*, Cullompton: Willan, pp. 40–57.

Garland, J. and Chakraborti, N. (2007) 'Protean Times? Exploring the Relationship between Policing, Community and "Race" in Rural England', *Criminology and Criminal Justice*, 7 (4): 347–65.

Hall, N. (2005) *Hate Crime*, Cullompton: Willan Publishing.

Hester, M. and Westmarland, N. (2004) *Tackling Street Prostitution: Towards an holistic Approach*, Home Office Research Study 279, Development and Statistics Directorate.

Home Office (2012) *Challenge it, Report it, Stop it: The Government's Plan to Tackle Hate Crime*, March, London: HM Government: www.homeoffice.gov.uk/publications/crime/hate-crime-action-plan/action-plan?view=Binary

Home Office (2011) *A Review of Effective Practice in Responding to Prostitution*, London: Home Office: www.homeoffice.gov.uk/publications/crime/responding-to-prostitution.

Hubbard, P. (1999) *Sex and the City: Geographies of Prostitution in the Urban West*, London: Ashgate.

Hubbard, P. (2006) 'Out of Touch and Out of Time? The Contemporary Policing of Sex Work', in R. Campbell and M. O'Neill (eds) *Sex Work Now*, Cullompton: Willan, pp. 33–41.

Iganski, P. (2002) *The Hate Debate: Should Hate be Punished as a Crime?*, London, Profile Books.

Jeal, N. and Salisbury, C. (2007) 'Health Needs and Service Use of Parlour-Based Prostitutes Compared with Street-Based Prostitutes: A Cross-Sectional Survey', *British Journal of Obstetrics and Gynaecology*, 1 (14): 875-881.

Kinnell, H. (2006) 'Murder Made Easy', in R. Campbell and M. O'Neill (eds) (2006) *Sex Work Now*, Cullompton: Willan, pp. 212–34.

Kinnell, H. (2008) *Violence and Sex Work in Britain*, Cullompton: Willan.

Lowman, J. (2000) 'Violence and Outlaw Status of Street Prostitution in Canada', *Violence Against Women*, 6 (9): 987–1011.

Lowman, J. and Fraser, L. (1996) *Violence against Persons who Prostitute: The Experience in British Columbia*, Technical Report TR1996-14e, Ottawa, Canada: Department of Justice.

Mai, N. (2009) *Migrant Workers in the UK Sex Industry: Final Policy-Relevant Report*, Institute for the Study of European Transformations, London Metropolitan University. http://tinyurl.com/pvwtrsg.

Mason-Bish, H. (2010) 'Future Challenges for Hate Crime Policy: Lessons from the Past' in N. Chakraborti (ed.) *Hate Crime: Concepts, Policy, Future Directions*, Cullompton, Willan, pp. 58–77.

Merseyside Police (2006) *Sex Workers in Merseyside: Review of Process, Liverpool North Memorandum,* 15 December, Merseyside Police.

Miller, J. and Schwartz, M.D. (1995) 'Rape Myths and Violence against Street Prostitutes', in *Deviant Behaviour: An Interdisciplinary Journal,* 16: 1–23.

O'Doherty, T. (2011) 'Victimization in Off-Street Sex Industry Work', in *Violence Against Women,* 19: 944–63.

O'Neill, M. (1997) 'Prostitute Women Now' in G. Scambler and A. Scambler (eds) *Rethinking Prostitution,* London: Routledge, pp. 3–28.

O'Neill, M. (2007) 'Community Safety, Rights and Recognition: Towards a Coordinated Prostitution Strategy?', *Community Safety Journal,* 6 (1): 45–52.

Penfold, C., Hunter, G., Barham, L. and Campbell, R. (2004) 'Tackling Client Violence in Female Street Prostitution: Inter-Agency Working between Outreach Agencies and the Police', *Policing and Society,* 14 (4): 365–79.

Perry, B. (2001) *In the Name of Hate: Understanding Hate Crimes,* London: Routledge.

Pheterson, G. (1993) *The Prostitution Prism,* Amsterdam: Amsterdam University Press.

Roberts, N. (1994) 'The Whore, her Stigma, the Punter and his Wife', *New Internationalist,* February 1994: 8–9.

Roulstone, A., Thomas, P. and Balderstone, S. (2011) 'Between Hate and Vulnerability: Unpacking the British Criminal Justice System's Construction of Disabalist Hate Crime', *Disability and Society,* 26 (3): 351–64.

Salfati, C.G., James, A.R. and Ferguson, L. (2008) 'Prostitute Homicides: A Descriptive Study', *Journal of Interpersonal Violence,* 23 (4): 505–43.

Sanders, T. and Campbell, R. (2007) 'Designing out Vulnerability, Building in Respect: Violence, Safety and Sex Work Policy', *British Journal of Sociology,* 58 (1): 1–19.

Scott, J., Minichiello, V., Marino, R., Harvey, G.P., Jamieson, M. and Browne, J. (2005) 'Understanding the New Context of the Male Sex Work Industry', *Journal of Interpersonal Violence,* 20 (3): 320–42.

Scoular, J., Pitcher, J., Campbell, R., Hubbard, P. and O'Neill, M. (2007) 'What's Anti-Social about Sex Work? Governance, Discourse and the Changing Representation of Prostitution's Incivility', *Community Safety* (special edition 'The Prostitution Strategy: Implications for Community Safety'), 6 (1): 11–17.

Self, H. (2003) *Prostitution, Women and the Law: The Fallen Daughters of Eve*, London: Frank Cass.

Shannon, K., Kerr, T., Strathdee, S.A., Shoveller, J., Montaner, J.S. and Tyndall, M.W. (2009) 'Prevalence and Structural Correlates of Gender Based Violence among a Prospective Cohort of Female Sex Workers', *British Medical Journal*, 339: 442–5.

Sheffield, C. (1995) 'Hate Violence' in P. Rothenberg (ed.) *Race Class and Gender in the United States*, New York: St Martin's Press.

Spongberg, M. (1997) *Feminizing Venereal Disease: the body of the Prostitute in Nineteenth-Century Medical Discourse*, London: Macmillan Press.

UKNSWP (2011) *National Ugly Mugs Development Project*, Manchester: UK Network of Sex Work Projects.

Walkowitcz, C. (1980) *Prostitution and Victorian Society*, Cambridge: Cambridge University Press.

Williams, M.L. and Robinson, A.L. (2004) 'Problems and Prospects with Policing the Lesbian, Gay and Bisexual Community in Wales', *Policing & Society*, 16 (4): 213–323.

FIVE

Evidencing the case for 'hate crime'

Joanna Perry[28]

'Hate crime is a nomadic concept...' (Mason, 2005: 586)

Introduction

While international instruments and commitments to tackle racist violence are longstanding and comprehensive, 'hate crime' is a relatively new concept in the international criminal justice policy arena. It is quickly gaining ground, appearing in Ministerial Council Decisions of the Organisation for Security and Cooperation in Europe (OSCE) and research reports published by the European Union's Fundamental Rights Agencies (FRA). However there is a lack of consistency and clarity in the conceptualisation of hate crime, the terminology that is used to describe it and in how it is measured by intergovernmental organisations (IGOs). In addition, diverse social, political and historical contexts across the OSCE and EU regions, impact on terminology, data outcomes and responses in relation to hate crime at the national level, and this has significant implications for the feasibility of acquiring a clear picture of 'hate crime' as a concept with global application.

This chapter critically re-explores the case for the hate crime model as a way of understanding and responding to violence, and evaluates the role of policy makers, the academy, IGOs and non-governmental organisations (NGOs) in supporting its implementation. Questions about who should be involved in evidencing both our progress in addressing the phenomenon, and the obstacles we continue to face are considered. Finally, current work to provide guidance to OSCE member states on setting up hate crime data collection systems is described and offered as a way forward to support efforts to achieve a common approach to evidencing hate crime at the international level.

The hate crime evidence gap in international focus

Successive OSCE annual hate crime reports reveal significant gaps in data on hate crime (OSCE: 2005, 2007, 2008, 2009, 2010, 2011). The 2011 report, *Hate Crimes in the OSCE Region: Incidents and Responses,* reveals that while 50 out of 56 participating states report that they collect data, only 25 states submitted any for publication (OSCE, 2012: 6).[29] Where data is submitted, numbers range from below ten incidents[30] to 44,519 from the UK (OSCE, 2012: 23, 25). At the national level, comparable information from across the criminal justice system is rarely collected and police and prosecution systems may collect information on different types of hate crimes. NGOs submit information about several thousand incidents annually for inclusion, often including incidents that are not recorded by the authorities. In most cases, there is very little sentencing information. Taken together, these issues make meaningful international comparisons about the prevalence and nature of hate crime very difficult (OSCE, 2012: 15).

The European Union's FRA also exposes deficiencies in EU member states hate crime data collection systems. It classifies 'official data collection systems pertaining to hate crime' into three categories: 'limited data', 'good data' and 'comprehensive data', using three indicators of quality: 'range of crime types', 'number of bias motivations' and 'publication of data'. The smallest group, which includes the UK, is the 'good' group and the largest number of countries fall within the 'limited' group, the FRA's lowest category of data collection systems (FRA, 2012a).

The argument for evidencing the nature and volume of hate crime has been repeatedly made by the OSCE and FRA. The European Commission against Racism and Intolerance (ECRI) has similarly focused on the need to collect data on 'racist violence' and the UN Human Rights Council and Committee on the Elimination of Racial Discrimination (CERD) have made similar calls. For example, OSCE participating states have recognised that hate crime data collection is essential for appropriate resource allocation in support of effective policy decisions, and have committed themselves to collect, and make public reliable data and statistics including the numbers of cases reported to the police, the numbers prosecuted and the sentences imposed (OSCE, 2006, 2009). ECRI recommends that the member states of the Council of Europe, 'ensure that accurate data and statistics are collected and published on the number of racist and xenophobic offences that are reported to the police, on the number of cases that are prosecuted, on the reasons for not prosecuting and on the outcome of cases prosecuted'

(ECRI, 1996: 11). The FRA argues, 'The EU and its Member States can combat hate crime and address the related fundamental rights violations by making them ... more visible' (FRA, 2012b: 7).

These arguments have been increasingly backed by specific calls for action by international organisations to collect hate crime related data, to pass laws, to conduct training and to improve cooperation with civil society. As reported in the OSCE's 2011 hate crime report, several statements were made by CERD, the Working Group on the Universal Periodic Review, and the ECRI. For example, CERD made recommendations to improve data collection mechanisms to Georgia, Norway and Spain (CERD, 2011a: 3, 2011b: 6, 2011c). The UN Human Rights Council, in its Universal Periodic Review, encouraged Austria to establish a comprehensive system for recording and monitoring racist crimes (OHCHR, 2011:20). The ECRI issued a number of reports in its country monitoring cycle, recommending that Azerbaijan, Cyprus, Italy, Lithuania and Ukraine all improve their data collection systems (OSCE, 2011: 34). NGOs are also active in the call to improve data collection. For example, Human Rights First (HRF) has produced a ten point plan for states to improve their responses to hate crime, including clear guidance on data collection (HRF, no date).

Limited data collection systems and poor coordination across criminal justice agencies at the national level create significant obstacles to achieving a clear international picture of the nature and prevalence of this type of violence. However, a lack of consistency in conceptualising and therefore defining 'hate crime' at the international and national levels further exacerbates the problem. Recalling the significant disparity in the official picture of hate crime set out in OSCE annual reports, conceptual as well as technical improvements are needed in order to articulate how a range of violence 'fits' within the hate crime model, across very diverse political, social and economic backgrounds.

International and national constructions of 'hate crime'

The (IGOs take significantly different conceptual approaches to targeted violence, and only the OSCE and the EU's FRA actually use the term 'hate crime'. A number of UN and EU instruments set out legal duties on tackling racism and xenophobia.[31] As has been frequently commented on, 'hate crime laws' rarely mentioned the term 'hate crime' or even hate (Iganski, 2008; Hall, 2005), and this is no different at the level of international law. Specifically, Article 4 of CERD requires states to take, 'immediate measures' to criminalise, 'all acts of violence or incitement to such acts against any race or group of persons of another colour or ethnic origin'. The European Framework Decision on Racist and Xenophobic Crime aims to establish a common criminal law approach to respond to racist and xenophobic crime. In addition, the European Court of Human Rights has held that states have a positive obligation under the European Convention on Human Rights to investigate the potential racial motive of crimes (ECHR, 2007). ECRI has also called for the criminalisation of these acts in its General Policy Recommendations (ECRI, 2002).

However, the term 'hate crime' is increasingly making an appearance in IGO's monitoring reports, which reflect information submitted by governments about how this type of violence is being addressed at the policy level. As such, the concept is gaining international currency, yet a review of IGO's monitoring reports reveals an inconsistent approach in language and terminology, and the sparse data about hate crime that is available for review at the international level indicates that the concept has yet to be fully understood, defined and implemented. For example, ECRI's country reports include a section entitled 'racist violence', mainly based on official submissions from the Council of Europe Member States, which contains information about criminal offences committed with a range of, usually unspecified, racist motivations. 'Hate speech' (i.e. acts that incite hatred as opposed to violence) are addressed in a separate section. A similar approach is taken by the the Working Group on the Universal Periodic Review. The FRA does not offer a specific definition of hate crime, referring to 'data pertaining to hate crimes', which could include a wide range of information including incidents of discrimination, hate speech and hate crime, and is entirely dependent on a government's own definitions and terminology as opposed to any analytical framework applied by the FRA (FRA, 2012a; FRA, 2012b). Finally, the OSCE sets out the following definition: 'a hate crime is a criminal act committed with a bias motive', which is used in its guidance publications, and as a means to determine whether specific incidents should be included in its annual hate crime report (OSCE, 2006). A wide range of bias motivations and types of crime are reported on, and incidents of incitement to hatred or hate speech are explicitly excluded from this definition, along with acts of discrimination.

Towards a fuller international conceptualisation of hate crime: a role for academia

This quick review of current IGO approaches reveals two things: first, that the 'hate crime' concept and related terminology has yet to be fully adopted at this level; and second, that where it has been (for example, by the OSCE and the FRA), there are different underlying conceptual approaches. At this stage questions arise about the implications of introducing the hate crime concept at the intergovernmental level and how it should be defined and measured. Other areas of violence, for instance, on the grounds of religion, sexual orientation and disability are automatically conceptually connected and made equal to racist violence. Equally, the traditional criminal law focus on this type of targeted violence is broadened to a concept which spans the territory of policy and law, activism and scholarship (Iganski, 2008). 'Hate crime' both describes types of offences (e.g. assault, theft, etc.), based on a bias against or hostility towards specific characteristics (race, sexuality, religion, etc.), and their impact, and prescribes a strategy for intervention defined by enhanced punishment, victim support and community engagement (Perry, 2008). Finally, 'civil society', or activism is incorporated as a key source of information about hate crime and its impact, a source of support for victims and a wider 'victim' of hate crime itself.

'Hate crime' has been highly theorised and researched in the UK and North America, and finds its conceptual roots in the two countries' combined history of colonialism, slavery and segregation (Perry, 2003). Broadly speaking, this approach recognises that victims of hate crime come from a range of groups that share an experience of historical discrimination and a lack of access to justice, both of which are compounded by being a target of bigoted violence. It also prescribes a set of actions to address these issues and offer victims redress, with academics, activists and government each playing a key role. These features of what might be described as the 'hate crime model' elaborate on traditional descriptions of racist violence in that more than one type of bias motivation is covered and that the response to this violence goes beyond the legal sphere, and into the realm of policy actions that aim to increase reporting, victim support, practitioner training and access to justice.

The above description of hate crime shouldn't allow us to conclude that there is a full consensus on its definition. Indeed current debates in the literature about what hate crime 'is' are important, complex and on-going. For example, questions remain about which protected characteristics should be included within the hate crime rubric, with race and ethnicity at its centre and disability and gender at the edge (Jenness and Grattet, 2001; Mason-Bish, 2012). There is also debate surrounding the extent to which hate speech and acts of discrimination should be criminalised and considered hate crime (Butler, 1997).

Furthermore, there is no consensus about to what extent 'hate' is a necessary component of hate crime. Is simply choosing to target a victim 'because' of their actual or perceived membership to a particular group enough, or must the steeper threshold of 'hatred' be the only type of proven motivation that should qualify for this serious accusation. Connected to this, there is the question about the degree of hate or bias motivation, from fully to partly, that is necessary for an offence to qualify as a hate crime (Hall, 2005), and whether other concepts such as 'vulnerability' of victims as opposed to any singular identity category are more appropriate factors to determine the most targeted groups (Chakraborti and Garland, 2012).

Indeed, it may be the process of these debates and those involved, rather than their content and outcomes, which best characterises the hate crime model. The actors may take the shape of a 'triangle', with international and national policy, and law makers comprising the first point, activists and civil society the second and finally, the academy comprising the third. Activists evidence and construct the 'problem' of targeted violence, and law makers have responded by passing laws and tasking policy makers with their implementation (Jenness, 2001). Scholars provide an intellectual space to help both policy makers and activists examine the consequences of conceptualising violence through the prism of 'hate' or 'bias', and evaluate the impact and effectiveness of established policies. As such it would seem important and timely that this interactive approach is proposed as the engine for achieving a conceptual framework and related terminology that will help further define the nature and prevalence of hate crime at the international level.

This proposal gains urgency when considering that in a number political systems and contexts this triangle can become severely skewed. For example, civil society organisations may have few resources to monitor hate crime, and very limited power to influence policy makers' opinions about its prevalence and impact. The academy may not have researched the potential of recently passed laws in contexts that have only just begun to implement the hate crime approach. Thus the power to define both the concept of hate crime as well as what is measurable about individual incidents lies mainly or only with crime and criminal justice policy makers and practitioners. Without the involvement of civil society and academia, efforts to measure hate crime can be shunted into existing policy frameworks that may not provide the best fit. As a result, data from these contexts do not reflect the real prevalence and impact of hate crime, thus precluding evidenced policy making.

For example, several participating states have incorporated efforts to tackle and measure 'hate crime' within wider counter-extremism strategies, which reason that hate crime offenders are driven by a particular, and extreme, political motivation. Thus efforts to prevent and respond to these sorts of offences primarily focus on monitoring the activities of extremist political groups, as opposed to victim community engagement, for example. The impact of this approach is likely to mean fewer incidents of hate crime are reported and recorded, and less direct engagement with communities that are targets of hate crime (as opposed to those that are perceived to be at risk of extremism). As a result, this approach is also likely to miss out hate crime committed by 'ordinary racists': i.e. those offenders who are not members of extremist groups. As pointed out by the FRA, 'the almost exclusive focus on the behaviour of extremists keep "everyday" forms of prejudice and abuse ... unnoticed and unaddressed' (FRA, 2012b: 3).

Glett provides a rare analysis of the impact of importing the hate crime concept into Germany's criminal justice policy – a context which, 'has a very different historical outset, dating back to the racial and anti-Semitic hatred during the time of National Socialism' – without proper attention to identifying and conceptualising 'the actual benefits of this category for German law enforcement and crime prevention measures' (Glett, 2009: 3). Germany's hate crime data is collected within its 'politically motivated crime' data collection system, which identifies four types of motivation: 'left wing', 'right wing', 'foreign inspired' and 'other'. In addition, a monitoring definition of hate crime, comprised of criminal offences (including incitement to hatred) is used for recording purposes. In practice, the evidence suggests that in order for an offence to be recorded as a hate crime the political motivation of the offender needs to be identified (Glett, 2009: 12). Thus, a full response to hate crime is precluded. There is increased attention in Germany by academics and NGOs alike on including the victim's perception in Germany's approach to recording hate crime offences. For example, comparative reports compiled by NGOs point to significantly higher levels of hate crime, thus pointing to the importance of a collaborative approach between NGOs, academics and policy makers (Glett, 2009).

A data collection system that is more fully underpinned by what we are describing here as the 'hate crime model' is more likely to prioritise the victim's view when initially recording hate crime, and to focus efforts on measuring unreported crime. For example, the UK has implemented the following monitoring definition of hate crime: 'any criminal offence that is perceived, by the victim or any other person, to be motivated by a hostility or prejudice based on a personal characteristic' (Home Office, 2012: 6). Specific bias motivations are identified for monitoring purposes; however, this remains a wide net, which shifts the power to determine 'what happened' from the police to the victim (Perry, 2009), and is reflected in the high figures submitted by the UK for ODIHR's successive annual hate crime reports.

In an interesting development, the Czech Republic has begun to critically examine its own approach, citing the influence of academics and NGOs as a key driver. Its *Report on Extremism and Manifestations of Racism and Xenophobia on the Territory of the Czech Republic in 2011*, states, 'there has been a requirement [by academics and NGOs] to harmonize the term extremism at the level of public bodies, or to replace it by another concept. In this context there is often a talk [*sic*] about decoupling extremism from hate crimes, hate offences or hate incidents' (Ministry of the Interior of the Czech Republic, 2012: 5). The document identifies other grounds of targeted violence such as sexual orientation, disabilityand age, and accepts that these, along with racist offences that are not politically motivated, do not sit well within the extremism concept. A commitment is made to review recommendations of an academic study, conducted the previous year, which considered the merits of replacing the extremism framework with that of hate crime

Recent bitter ethnic conflict, and the legacy of Nazism, colonialism, slavery and communism each influence affected countries' understanding and conceptualisation of and approach to hate crime policy. The impact of these powerful historical and social influences on the hate crime concept is dangerously under-theorised, and insufficient attention has been paid to the connections and differences between hate crime on the one hand and often connected, yet separate concepts such as extremism and terrorism on the other.[32] It is argued that there is a gap in theory and research that needs to be addressed by the academy, in partnership with activists and policy makers. While the current academic debates are important, they are arguably over-focused on hate crime as it is defined in the UK and US, and other linguistically and legally connected contexts such as Canada and Australia, and thus they feel narrow in so far as their international focus. Efforts by Glett and others should be developed to further theorise and research 'hate crime' in more diverse legal and social contexts.

OSCE work on data collection guidance

The role of data collection and monitoring mechanisms is arguably to evidence each of aspects of the hate crime model, from a variety of sources that involve the 'triangle' of activists, policy makers and academics outline above. However, there is currently little guidance on how to achieve this. The ODIHR has the mandate to support states in their efforts to improve data collection as well as broader responses to hate crime. As indicated above, national policy makers play a powerful role in operationalising hate crime, at times at the expense of the involvement of civil society and the academy, taking decisions about which bias motivations to monitor, how to evidence reported and unreported crimes, and the police and criminal justice response. Thus the 'official' picture of bigotry is built, and precious resources for victim support and prevention are allocated.

The OSCE is developing a practical guide for policy makers who are aiming to set up or improve hate crime data collection systems. The guide was developed following good practice visits to seven countries, and the detailed input of experts from a range of OSCE participating states, IGOs and NGOs. An overarching aim is to improve the comparability of data at the international level. The guide will take a broad approach to hate crime data collection, emphasising the role of civil society in fully understanding and responding to hate crime and to evidence its prevalence, impact and the success or otherwise of prevention strategies. Broadly, five main areas of data collection will be considered: first, collecting and disaggregating data across a range of bias motivations, whether or not they are currently included in national hate crime laws; second, separating data relating to hate crime, hate speech and discrimination to improve the comparability of data at the international levels: for instance, between countries that do criminalise hate speech and discrimination (e.g. Belgium) and those that do not (e.g. the United States); third, setting up police recording systems that can take into account victim perceptions of hate crime; fourth, measuring the criminal justice response to hate crime in terms of prosecution and court decisions; and fifth, measuring the impact of hate crime on victims and the rate of unreported hate crime through national victimisation surveys and/or cooperation with NGOs.

As has been argued here, a strong conceptual framework, with clear terminology and built in partnership by academics, activists and policy makers, is necessary to support the implementation of such international tools. There are also a number of other established concepts that could support the fuller implementation of the hate crime concept at the international level, namely, 'security', the 'rule of law' and 'human rights'. These are enormous areas of scholarship and policy, to which justice cannot be done here. However, it is simply argued that attaching the hate crime model to longstanding concepts to access justice and security is necessary to fully internationalise the concept and support its implementation in a diverse range of contexts.

For example, the OSCE has connected hate crime to its own concept of security, the idea being that hate crimes can undermine community security and, if unaddressed, can escalate into broader conflict and unrest. A good example of this approach being implemented in a post conflict context is the first hate crime report published by the OSCE Mission in Bosnia-Hercegovina. From the outset, the report focuses on the importance of investigating and prosecuting hate crimes in order to, 'recognize the underlying and potentially serious risks that such crimes pose to Bosnia-Hercegovina's overall stability and future security' (OSCE, 2012 :5). The report connects incidents against returnee communities in 'former conflict hotspots', and against 'religious and sacred objects' with those associated with the 2008 Sarajevo Queer Festival, recognises the under-reported character of hate crime, and makes recommendations to the government of Bosnia-Hercegovina to improve hate crime data and responses to victims.

Conclusions: ways forward in international conceptions of hate crime

This chapter has argued that a lack of clarity in international and national policy and guidance, poor data collection mechanisms, and diverse historical, social and political contexts, combine to challenge a common conceptual understanding of the 'hate crime model' as a description of and prescription for violence. A 'triangle' of civil society, IGO and national policy makers and academia has been proposed as a model of engagement to think through these complexities and help us both understand and address key questions: what evidence should international bodies such as CERD, the FRA, ECRI and the OSCE request from governments in order to establish the prevalence and nature of hate crime and the success or otherwise of efforts to address it? What are the components of the conceptual framework that need to be in place for a shared and comprehensive approach to hate crime across diverse political, social and historical contexts? Can other international frameworks such as security, human rights and the rule of law support the implementation of the hate crime model in states that are just adopting hate crime legislation and policy such as those with a history of ethnic conflict or totalitarian ideologies? With the equal involvement of activism, scholarship, law and policy, there is great potential to make the hate crime model the global framework for understanding and addressing targeted violence in the world today.

References

Butler (1997) *Excitable Speech: A Politics of the Performative,* New York: Routledge.

CERD (Committee on the Elimination of Racial Discrimination) (2011a) 'Concluding Observations of the Committee on the Elimination of Racial Discrimination: Norway', CERD/C/NOR/CO/19-20: 6, 8 April, www2.ohchr.org/english/bodies/cerd/cerds78.htm

CERD (2011b) 'Concluding Observations of the Committee on the Elimination of Racial Discrimination: Georgia', CERD/C/GEO/CO/4-5, www2.ohchr.org/english/bodies/cerd/cerds79.htm

CERD (2011c) 'Concluding Observations of the Committee on the Elimination of Racial Discrimination: Spain', CERD/C/ESP/CO/18-20, www2.ohchr.org/english/bodies/cerd/cerds78.htm

Chakraborti, N., Garland, J. (2012) 'Reconceptualizing Hate Crime Victimization through the Lens of Vulnerability and "Difference"', *Theoretical Criminology,* 16 (4): 499–514.

ECHR (2007) Šečić v. Croatia, ECHR App. No. 40116/02.

ECRI (European Commission against Racism and Intolerance) (1996), *ECRI General Policy Recommendations No 1 on Combating Racism, Xenophobic, Antisemitism and Intolerance,* ECRI: www.coe.int/t/dghl/monitoring/ecri/default_en.asp

ECRI (2002) *General Policy Recommendation 7 on National Legislation to Combat Racism and Racial Discrimination,* ECRI: www.coe.int/t/dghl/monitoring/ecri/default_en.asp

FRA (Fundamental Rights Agency) (2012b) *Making Hate Crime Visible in the European Union: Acknowledging Victims' Rights,* http://fra.europa.eu/en/publication/2012/making-hate-crime-visible-european-union-acknowledging-victims-rights

FRA (2012a) *Fundamental Rights: Challenges and Achievements in 2011,* http://fra.europa.eu/en/publication/2012/fundamental-rights-challenges-and-achievements-2011

Glett, A. (2009) 'The German Hate Crime Concept: An Account of the Classification and Registration of Bias-Motivated Offences and the Implementation of the Hate Crime Model into Germany's Law Enforcement System', *Internet Journal of Criminology,* 1–20.

Hall (2005) *Hate Crime,* Cullompton: Willan.

Home Office (2012) *Challenge it, Report it, Stop it: The Government's Plan to Tackle Hate Crime,* London: HM Government.

Human Rights First (no date) *Ten Point Plan for Combating Hate Crime,* www.humanrightsfirst.org/our-work/fighting-discrimination/ten-point-plan/

Iganski, P. (2008) *Hate Crime and the City,* Bristol: Policy Press.

Jenness, V. (2001) 'The Hate Crime Cannon and Beyond: A Critical Assessment', *Law and Critique,* 12: 279–308.

Jenness, V. and Grattet, R. (2001) 'Examining the Boundaries of Hate Crime Law: Disabilities and the "Dilemma of Difference"', *The Journal of Criminal Law and Criminology,* 91 (3): 653–97.

Mason, G. (2005) 'Being Hated, Stranger or Familiar?' *Social and Legal Studies: An International Journal,* 14 (4): 585–605.

Mason-Bish, H. (2012) 'Conceptual Issues in the Construction of Disability Hate Crime', in A. Roulstone and H. Mason-Bish (eds) (2012) *Disability, Hate Crime and Violence,* London: Routledge.

Ministry of Interior of the Czech Republic (2012), *The Issue of Extremism in the Czech Republic in 2011,* MoI, Czech Republic: www. mvcr.cz/mvcren/file/report-on-extremism-and-manifestations-of-racism-and-xenophobia-on-the-territory-of-the-czech-republic-in-2011.aspx

OHCR (Office of the High Commission for Human Rights) (2011) *Report of the Working Group on the Universal Periodic Review:* Austria, Human Rights Council on the Working Group on the Universal Periodic Review, A/HRC/17/8, www2.ohchr.org/english/bodies/hrcouncil/17session/reports.htm

OSCE (Organisation for Security and Cooperation in Europe) (2005) *Combating Hate Crimes in the OSCE Region: An Overview of Statistics, Legislation, and National Initiatives,* Warsaw: ODIHR, www.osce.org/odihr/16405

OSCE (2006) *Ministerial Council, Decision No. 13/06, "Combating Intolerance and Discrimination and Promoting Mutual Respect and Understanding",* OSCE: www.osce.org/mc/23114

OSCE (2007) *Hate Crimes in the OSCE Region: Incidents and Responses – Annual Report 2006,* Warsaw: ODIHR, www.osce.org/odihr/26759

OSCE (2008) *Hate Crimes in the OSCE Region: Incidents and Responses – Annual Report 2007,* Warsaw: ODIHR, www.osce.org/odihr/33989

OSCE (2009) *Hate Crimes in the OSCE Region: Incidents and Responses – Annual Report 2008,* Warsaw: ODIHR, www.osce.org/odihr/40203

OSCE (2010) *Hate Crimes in the OSCE Region: Incidents and Responses – Annual Report 2009,* Warsaw: ODIHR, www.osce.org/odihr/73636

OSCE (2011) *Hate Crimes in the OSCE Region: Incidents and Responses – Annual Report 2010,* Warsaw: ODIHR, http://tandis.odihr.pl/hcr2010/

OSCE Mission in Bosnia-Hercegovina (2012) *Tackling Hate Crimes: An Analysis of Bias-motivated incidents in Bosnia and Herzegovina with Recommendations*, OSCE, www.oscebih.org/documents/osce_bih_doc_2012111310235235eng.pdf

Perry, B. (2003) 'Accounting for Hate Crime: Doing Difference', in B. Perry (ed.) *Hate and Bias Crime: A Reader*, Routledge: London.

Perry, J. (2008) 'The "Perils" of an Identity Politics Approach to the Legal Recognition of Harm', *Liverpool Law Review*, 29: 9–36.

Perry, J. (2009) 'At the Intersection: Hate Crime Policy and Practice in England and Wales', *Safer Communities*, 8 (2): 9–18.

PART TWO

Researching key issues: emerging themes and challenges

The sheer breadth of issues relevant to hate crime scholarship and policy will invariably mean that numerous issues remain unexplored or underexplored. While much good work has been done across different domains and disciplines to develop our understanding, there is much yet to learn. We still live in societies characterised by disturbingly high levels of hate, prejudice and bigotry, and using research to identify practical ways of addressing these problems and supporting victims is central to the process of overcoming the disconnect between scholarship and policy.

Part Two draws from a selection of emerging themes and challenges to explore the relationship between hate crime research and hate crime policy. It begins with Chapter Six from Marian Duggan whose analysis of collaborative engagements between criminal justice agents, community voluntary workers, public servants and lesbian, gay, bisexual and transgender communities calls for greater reflection on the part of scholars with reference to the accessibility and applicability of their recommendations for hate crime policy. Similar themes are raised in the next chapter by Chih Hoong Sin who presents a 'layers of influence' model that illustrates ways that research, policy and practice interact within the context of disablist hate crime and that has the capacity to guide prevention strategies.

The following two chapters explore issues of Islamophobic hate from different perspectives. Irene Zempi examines links between academic research, policy and practice in relation to the support offered to victims of Islamophobic hate, and advocates a more flexible needs-based approach which facilitates greater communication between statutory and voluntary service providers and community-based Muslim organisations. This leads on to James Treadwell's chapter which draws from his ethnographic research with the English Defence League (EDL) to identify ways of controlling the threat posed by this street-based protest movement to Muslim communities and to community cohesion more generally. Related themes form the basis of Chapter Ten from Stevie-Jade Hardy. Using the concept of 'everyday multiculturalism' as a lens through which to explore underlying motivations behind the expression of hate, Hardy's research highlights that young White-British people's interactions with cultural diversity are contingent on their existing fears, prejudices and frustrations. Young people are also the focus of Lucy Michael's chapter, which utilises recent survey findings from the UK to consider gaps within our understanding of the hate crimes suffered and perpetrated by student victim groups. The final word in this part of the book comes from Hannah Mason-Bish who discusses the relevance of gender to hate crime policy and research, and urges academics and practitioners to consider the complex harms caused to victims – and not just whether or not those victims belong to a particular identity group – when framing responses to hate crime.

SIX

Working with lesbian, gay, bisexual and transgender communities to shape hate crime policy

Marian Duggan

Introduction

Two decades after the watershed murder of black teenager Stephen Lawrence in 1993, expansions in UK hate crime scholarship and activism have significantly heightened awareness of, and responses to, varied forms of minority victimisation. Scholars and activists working in this area have done much to affect social, legal and political change, addressing the issue of 'hate' from both a theoretical (scholarship) and practical (activism) approach. The design and delivery of effective legislative and policy responses to hate crime also involves consultation and interaction with other 'active' stakeholders such as community representatives or laypersons who may have a personal, rather than professional or political, interest in this area.

This chapter evaluates collaborative engagements between criminal justice agents, community voluntary workers, public servants and lay citizens of lesbian, gay, bisexual and transgender (LGB&T) communities in South Yorkshire.[33] An annual average of 61 homophobic and 4 transphobic hate crimes were recorded by South Yorkshire Police (SYP) between 2008 and 2012. As a result, SYP employ several hate crime prevention and response strategies. These include having dedicated hate crime operational and lead officers, a hate crimes working group, a hate crimes multi-agency group (involving public authorities as well as statutory agencies), independent advisory groups, involvement with hate crime scrutiny panels, operating third party reporting centres, co-ordinating Safer Neighbourhood teams (and within these the community engagement officers), and facilitating wider educational and awareness campaigns to shape hate crime policy across all strands. The chapter draws on the author's involvement in, and reflective participant observation of, a South Yorkshire LGB&T independent advisory group and a hate crimes scrutiny panel over a period of between one and three years. These reflections are supplemented with an interview undertaken with Sarah,[34] a detective inspector at SYP and SYP hate crime strategy lead, which provides a statutory perspective on the observed avenues of interaction.

The analysis illustrates how historical criticisms about the treatment of LGB&T communities by the criminal justice system has affected new and inclusive working relationships under a shared aim of reducing hate crime. It demonstrates the necessity for knowledge exchange and transfer, particularly with regards to marginalised or less visible groups, or 'minorities within minorities'. The role scholarship can play in directing how these latter groups are identified, contacted and represented is of particular note in the analysis. Building on this, the chapter concludes with recommendations for enhancing engagement between all invested stakeholders, not just those charged with enacting policy, to ensure that community representation is as holistic, inclusive and accessible as possible.

Recognising and responding to LGB&T hate crime

In 2003, s.146 of the Criminal Justice Act established enhanced sentences for crimes motivated by sexual orientation hostility following demands from scholars and activists working in this area. A decade later, the Legal Aid, Sentencing and Punishment of Offenders Act 2012 amended s.146 to include offences motivated by hostility towards gender identity as a result of similar pressures by stakeholders involved in enhancing the profile of transgender communities.[35] Previously, while the police could record, investigate and collect evidence about transphobic offences, no statutory legislation existed on which to *prosecute* such an offence, so it was left to judicial discretion on the weight of the supporting evidence (Crown Prosecution Service, 2007).

Once subject to enhanced criminalisation themselves, members of LGB&T communities are now encouraged to achieve justice through the use of 'hate crime' legislation, effectively transitioning from persecution to protection within a lifetime (see Weeks, 2012). A key factor in this development has been coordinated activism by LGB&T groups, coupled with the production of research highlighting enhanced levels of victimisation fuelled by homophobia and transphobia (Comstock, 1991; Herek, 1992; Herek and Berrill, 1992; Dick, 2008). Collaborative involvement between LGB&T stakeholders has been necessary to get these issues on the political, social and legal agenda, but the conflation of very different identities and types of victimisation under the umbrella term of 'homophobic hate crime' means that some identities take precedence over others. Furthermore, assimilating sexual orientation with gender identity rather than seeing these as two separate areas can exacerbate some of the misconceptions that lead to transphobic victimisation (Norton and Herek, 2012). Therefore, the recognition of transphobia as a separate form of victimisation demonstrates a significant shift in legal, social and political approaches to sexual and gender minorities.

However, barriers to engagement with the criminal justice system (CJS) – if engagement is what is desired – remain for LGB&T communities which, if left unaddressed, render such progress tokenistic. Continued discrepancies between official and unofficial reports of homophobic and transphobic incidents indicate that victims remain unable or unwilling to seek redress through the CJS. One of the largest UK studies into hate crime towards LGB&T people indicated that up to 75% of victims chose not to report their victimisation to the police (Dick, 2008), while Kelley (2009) suggested that many victims of homophobia would prefer to report to agencies *other* than the police. Studies have cited reluctance as being based on fears of being taken seriously or not being believed by officers; that little or nothing will be done; of being 'outed' during the investigation or trial process; of encountering further victimisation; and fearing further reprisals (Mason and Palmer, 1996; Quiery, 2002; Jarman and Tennant, 2003; Dick, 2008). Without addressing these issues, the efficacy of hate crime legislation and policy to reflect the needs and wants of LGB&T communities remains questionable.

McManus and Rivers (2001) suggested that in order for hate crime policy to be effective, strategies needed to take a collaborative approach, such as carefully forging partnerships, recognising diversity of identities, consulting with LGB&T laypersons and carefully auditing hate crime victimisation. Implementing these objectives may be hindered by issues of LGB&T visibility and accessibility, which has been demonstrated as varying widely across the UK. Social factors affecting LGB&T communities in rural or conservative areas (often reported as being less accepting of difference) may be less relevant for those in urban or liberal areas, some of which are notable for their large and visible sexual 'minority' populations (i.e. London, Manchester or Brighton) (Jarman and Tennant, 2003; Duggan 2012). Even within these more populated areas, organisations or events labelled 'LGB&T' may be more focused on (or representative of) the 'L and G' and rarely the 'B or T'. This is also a criticism with scholarship, where the dominant focus is on mainstreaming information on the more visible aspects of LGB&T identities with lesser visible forms often annexed off as part of the nuanced area of 'queer theory' or similar.

Furthermore, within any homogenised label, minorities within minorities will exist, causing some aspects of the group to be more visible than others. Within this LGB&T grouping, overlooking the diversity of ethnic, age, ability, class, etc. identities further marginalises minorities within minorities who are ultimately rendered less visible within the 'community' (Formby, 2012). Social and support organisations may also be divided along gendered, classed, raced, generational, etc. lines, with little interaction taking place between members. As Weeks (1996) suggests, ideologically based 'communities of identity' form out of resistance to oppression and solidarity of experience, thus they may be less visible even within their own 'label'. Therefore, when assessing statutory engagement with 'LGB&T communities' or representatives thereof, McGhee (2003: 349) recommends considering the form in which such 'active citizenship' takes in a practical sense, the implications of this, and who exactly is (and is not) being represented. With this in mind, the analyses of the various forms of stakeholder engagement that follow are assessed in light of recognising and responding to issues of representation, visibility and voice.

Collaborative approaches to reducing hate crime

The reflective participant observation on which this chapter is based relates to Sheffield, South Yorkshire. With a population of 1.34 million people, South Yorkshire comprises four Metropolitan Boroughs: Barnsley, Doncaster, Rotherham and Sheffield. In terms of minority representation, the county has a lower than average minority ethnic population (5%, comprising mainly of Somali, Pakistani and Irish Travelling communities) but a higher than average number of people who are registered disabled (South Yorkshire Police, n.d.). Statistics for 2011/12 indicate that 496 hate crimes were recorded in South Yorkshire (4.9 per 1,000 crimes), which was less than half of the national average (11 per 1,000 crimes for England & Wales). Of these, racially motivated crimes accounted for 89.3%, vastly outnumbering sexual orientation (7.1%), disablist (1.8%), religious (1.2%) and transgender (0.6%) (Home Office, 2012).

LGB&T 'communities' exist in social and political guises, converging around events or interests and which may or may not be static or fixed in relation to space or geography (Weeks, 1996; Formby, 2012). Sheffield is the fourth largest city in England, yet the LGB&T population is less noticeable than comparable cities such as Manchester or Brighton, thus identifying LGB&T 'communities' may be hindered through less discernible spaces or social/commercial venues. There are fewer dedicated LGB&T social venues or spaces in South Yorkshire as a whole, rendering what Bell and Valentine (1995) call lesbian and gay 'geographies' less overt. This means that statutory interaction with the community needs to be more proactive, although opportunities are increasing as a result of grass roots activism. The annual gay Pride event is now a key method of contact, the first having been held in Sheffield in 2008 with Barnsley, Doncaster and Rotherham duly following suit. Plans are underway to furnish police vehicles, ambulances and fire engines in South Yorkshire with Pride's rainbow flag sticker to promote inclusion and acceptance.[36] After decades of persecution, this partnership, consultation and liaison approach is characteristic of the New Labour-inspired shift from policing of, to policing with, minority communities and one which is aimed at protection rather than persecution (McGhee, 2003).

A core form of community engagement is the South Yorkshire LGB&T Independent Advisory Group (IAG), which operates alongside the Black and Minority Ethnic IAG. Members comprise of representatives from the police force, police authorities[37] and general public. Described as a 'critical friend', the IAG:

> ensures the policies, procedures and practices of the Force meet the strategic aims of the Equality Diversity and Human Rights (EDHR) strategy and provide a safeguard against the service disadvantaging any section of the community through lack of understanding, ignorance or mistaken beliefs. (South Yorkshire Police Authority, n.d.)

Recruitment to the IAG was undertaken by the Police Authority, an organisation that has been replaced by the establishment of police and crime commissioners. As a result of this change, the future of the IAG is uncertain at this point. However, in the event that it continues in its current guise, application for membership is somewhat dependent on knowledge of the various recruitment strategies (usually advertised through email lists or via community organisations) and volunteers' own willingness to put themselves forward for selection. Inclusion, therefore, is dependent on knowledge of these initiatives and the ability to be involved in them. This reliance on 'active citizenship' is not without its drawbacks; as McGhee (2003) indicates, questions remain regarding how representative these IAG members are of the diversity of identities and needs within their particular communities.

SYP's consultations with IAG members led to the development of targeted publicity materials aimed at the strategic priorities of responding to and reducing hate crime in the county. One suggestion, to produce hate crime reporting leaflets, led to lengthy debates around defining hate crime, illustrating Gerstenfeld's (2011) notion that hate crime is a popular, if little understood, area of interest. Indeed, many of the discussions which continue to plague academics about what a hate crime is and who should be included (see Jacobs and Potter, 1998) arose in the leaflet planning stages. In the end, the more pressing issue was focused on, as Sarah (detective inspector and SYP hate crimes lead) indicated:

> 'What we're trying to do is move on from discussing whether it's a hate crime and towards getting it reported. So after much debate we decided that the message was: just report it and let [the police] worry about whether it's a hate crime or not.'

For SYP, the ACPO-endorsed perspective of the victim or any other person is enough. Training is given about diversity issues but, rather than responding according to identity categorisations, each case is treated on its individual merits. Officers are trained to address people's *needs* as opposed to presupposing these based on their *identities*. This focus on need mirrors a shift in hate crime theorising that seeks to address victimisation on the basis of vulnerability and 'difference' (Chakraborti and Garland, 2012). For people who are identified under the 'LGB&T' label, this 'needs' approach may prove more appropriate for encouraging engagement with the criminal justice system. The approach also means that prior to the recent legislative developments, statutory discrepancies between sexual orientation and gender identity hostility had less of an impact on police inquiries and evidence collection as all recognised hate strands were treated equally in the investigative stage.

The hate crime reporting leaflets produced by SYP were coupled with hate crime prevention posters addressing the general public. Sarah commented on the purposeful use of impactive language in the posters to attract wider attention (i.e. *'It's being homophobic that's queer'*):

> 'The posters are also important to get people to realise that it's not acceptable and some of the responsibility for tackling hate crime lies with the general public and society. It's not

just about the individual offending; take race: look how long it's taken us to come as far as we have there. We need to start that same journey with the other groups. LGB&T verbal abuse is accepted in a way that racial abuse isn't any more and that's what [society] needs to work towards changing.' (Sarah, SYP hate crimes lead)

These posters signal a shift from targeting victims (to report victimisation) to targeting potential perpetrators (to refrain from victimising), reflecting a core aim driving the theorising of violence: to reduce it. Ghettoising messages (i.e. confining it to the community being persecuted) may indicate that prevention initiatives have no bearing on the wider population when in fact it is members of the mainstream who need to be interacted with to recognise the role they can play in preventing or helping to reduce the victimisation of minority groups.

Accountability in responding to victimisation

Community engagement and interaction is not limited to the police service; the establishment of monthly hate crime scrutiny panels was designed with the Crown Prosecution Service (CPS) in mind as well as the police. The panels are organised by Stop Hate UK and comprising of representatives from the organisation, the police and the general public. Panel members review and comment on decisions taken by the CPS in randomly selected hate crime cases, highlighting any commendations or concerns with the overall process. The Panels provide a useful supportive function addressing good practice and areas for improvement for those involved, from call handlers through to sentencers. This may boost criminal justice agents' confidence in light of uncertainty around hate crime protocol:

> The HCSP for CPS South Yorkshire and Humberside continues to help us identify strengths and weaknesses in the way we handle hate crime cases … Panel members have also brought us closer to our diverse communities by sharing their experiences of working with us and challenging misconceptions. (CPS, 2010: 4)

The panels provide an opportunity for lay members of the public to see the full workings of the CJS in relation to hate crime. This enhances transparency, accountability and responsiveness in relation to hate crime policy and procedure while also fulfilling the police's requirement for community engagement. However, as with the IAGs, the diversity and representativeness of the Panel is determined by those who are aware of their existence and who choose to volunteer. The diversity of cases assessed is also dependent on a variety of hate crimes being reported and investigated, thus some forms of hate crime disproportionately feature more regularly than others and some types hardly feature at all.

Panel members ensure that the needs and wants of the victim remain paramount despite recognising the importance of enhancing reporting, investigation and prosecution rates. Members have commended CPS policies relating to strategic decisions not to pursue cases with weak evidence which otherwise may cause distress or dismay to unsuccessful victims or not pursuing cases withdrawn by the victim (CPS, 2010). This latter point links to research indicating that people may wish to avoid the 'victim' label as a result of the negative connotations of this with passivity and powerlessness, yet this reluctance 'has implications for the work of police, housing, and support services in responding to homophobic abuse' as victims may be less likely to seek recourse to justice through the available criminal justice system (Dunn, 2012: 21). As Sarah noted above, the police need the crimes to be reported in order to begin the investigation process. Victims may report crimes yet not recognise them as being motivated by hate. Indeed, in several of the cases reviewed by the author as part of a Panel it was the call handler who flagged the incident as hate related. Most usually, this was due to some indication of the identity of the victim, the language used, the location of the incident, etc. Therefore, this could cause potential auditing discrepancies when evaluating the effectiveness of strategies aimed at increasing hate crime reporting by *victims* when it is *staff members* who are identifying the hostile motivation and increasing the numbers of 'reported hate crimes'.

In other cases, it was apparent that multiple hostility factors, most commonly religious and racial, were being conflated or not equally recognised. Hate crime theorising has moved towards addressing this issue of *intersectionality* (the presence of multiple identity factors) in incidents of victimisation, yet there is still much work to be done with regards to scholarly and statutory interventions to address expressions of hostility *across* hate crime strands. In some cases, multiple factors may exacerbate hostility or render a person especially vulnerable to victimisation within their own community. Multiple hostility factors *can* be noted and investigated by SYP, whereon it is up to the CPS to pursue the most viable case. However, this is redundant if minorities *within* communities (i.e. LGB&T persons of minority faiths) find it more difficult to report victimisation as a result of these intersectional (multiple) identity factors and fears about community responses.

Conclusion: enhancing interaction

This chapter's analysis of engaging with LGB&T communities to shape hate crime policy has provided a reflective assessment and account of the current strengths being demonstrated by stakeholders in this area and identified avenues for future development. The author's observations as a participant in a variety of LGB&T organisations and events have provided a valuable insight for her own work, and useful feedback to others involved in policy design, development and delivery. Greater links between scholarship and practice are possible yet reliant on some changes or considerations about the available resources, abilities and access to information affecting others working in similar fields or to shared objectives.

Most pressing among these areas for development is the recognition of *who* is and is not being represented in efforts to engage with 'minority communities' and how issues of intersectionality can be affecting hate crime victimisation within minority communities. This may be on a more obvious level (such as accounting for gendered experiences of LGB&T victimisation) or less visible by comparison (such as inter- and intra-group victimisation). In practical terms, there are opportunities for statutory agents to engage with this issue by way of the Panels (comprising of representatives of different minority communities) and the two IAGs (the other being focused on black and minority ethnic [BME] issues), which currently have minimal interaction with one another. During the review of the policing hate crime strategy, South Yorkshire Police brought the BME and LGB&T groups together to comment on policies and procedures. Part of this discussion highlighted the above intersectionality issue, as well as the presence of hostility across minority strands: i.e. some faiths being perceived by LGB&T members as homophobic. Should the IAGs remain operational in light of the establishment of police and crime commissioners, further interactions have been suggested by the author as a way of combining knowledge about the nature and impact of different forms of victimisation across hate crime strands.

A key barrier to a more robust working relationship *between* stakeholders may be the accessibility of academic output allowing for theory to inform or shape practice. Although current discussions concerning the move to open access resourcing of academic literature seeks to partly address this issue, the approach, purpose and style of much scholarship was highlighted as a potential limitation by Sarah. She cited the 'Hidden in Plain Sight' report (Equality and Human Rights Commission, 2011) as being of more use to practitioners like herself, largely due to its applied and directive instructions that could then be translated into policy aims or strategic objectives; an area she felt academia still had some way to go in terms of practical use:

> 'From my point of view, although we have some reports, they don't tend to be academic – they're more practical reports such as those from voluntary organisations, although there may be academic research informing them ... Academia should drive what's happening. It's about progression, so there needs to be a stronger relationship and engagement between [scholars and practitioners].' (Sarah, SYP hate crimes lead)

Academic insight is therefore useful, yet is often harder to physically access, requires more time to read and may ultimately be less solution-orientated than desired by practitioners. It is clear that hate crime cannot be effectively addressed by those working in the criminal justice sector alone, not least as they are often tasked with focusing more on offenders rather than victims. Much of the hate crime scholarship available is concerned with the victim's experiences of crime and the criminal justice system, thus areas for academic development in terms of research on perpetration may benefit from more practical and collaborative engagement.

Taking Sarah's point of academia being in the driving seat when it comes to progressing knowledge about hate crime prevention, it might be the case that academics need to focus more reflectively on what *we* can do to aid theory-driven practice. In other words, perhaps we need to reflect on accessibility or applicability of our recommendations. Scholarship offering insights into minority groups and victims' needs has aided developments such as targeted community interventions or culturally sensitive approaches by statutory agents, yet could go much further. How policy is being implemented in practice and where future gaps may be arising are important lines of inquiry, but how best these can be addressed with respect to different working practices might be the more useful aspect of knowledge transfer.

References

Bell, D. and Valentine, G. (1995) 'Introduction: Orientations' in D. Bell, and G. Valentine (eds) *Mapping Desire: Geographies of Sexualities,* London: Routledge.

Chakraborti, N. and Garland, J. (2012) 'Reconceptualising Hate Crime Victimization Through the Lens of Vulnerability and "Difference"', *Theoretical Criminology,* 16 (4): 499–514.

Comstock, G. (1991) *Violence Against Lesbians and Gay Men,* New York: Columbia University Press.

Crown Prosecution Service (CPS) (2007) *Policy for Prosecuting Cases of Homophobic and Transphobic Hate Crime* (Online), www.cps.gov.uk/ publications/docs/htc_policy.pdf

Crown Prosecution Service (CPS) (2010) *South Yorkshire and Humberside Hate Crime Scrutiny Panel Annual Report 2009–2010,* www.cps.gov.uk/ yorkshire_humberside/assets/uploads/files/aaS%20Yorks%20and%20 Humberside%20HCSP%20Annual%20Report%202009-10.pdf

Dick, S. (2008) *Homophobic Hate Crime: The Gay British Crime Survey,* London: Stonewall.

Duggan, M. (2012) *Queering Conflict: Examining Lesbian and Gay Experiences of Homophobia in Northern Ireland,* Farnham: Ashgate.

Dunn, P. (2012) 'Men as Victims: Victim Identities, Gay Identities, and Masculinities', *Journal of Interpersonal Violence,* 27 (17): 3442–67.

Gerstenfeld, P. (2011) *Hate Crimes: Causes, Controls and Controversies,* 2nd edn, London: Sage.

Herek, G. (1992) 'The Social Context of Hate Crimes: Notes on Cultural Heterosexism' in G. Herek and K. Berrill (eds) *Hate Crimes: Confronting Violence Against Lesbians and Gay Men,* London: Sage.

Herek, G. and Berrill, K. (eds) (1992) *Hate Crimes: Confronting Violence Against Lesbians and Gay Men,* London: Sage.

Home Office (2012) *Hate Crimes, England and Wales 2011/12 Tables* (Online) www.homeoffice.gov.uk/publications/science-research-statistics/research-statistics/crime-research/hate-crimes-1112-tabs

Equality and Human Rights Commission (2011) *Hidden in Plain Sight: Inquiry into Disability-Related Harassment* (online) available at: www.equalityhumanrights.com/uploaded_files/disabilityfi/ehrc_ hidden_in_ plain_sight_3.pdf

Formby, E. (2012) *Connected Lesbian, Gay, Bisexual and Trans Communities? A Scoping Study to Explore Understandings and Experiences of 'Community' Among LGBT People,* Swindon: Arts and Humanities Research Council.

Jacobs, J. and Potter, K. (1998) *Hate Crimes: Criminal Law and Identity Politic,* New York: Open University Press.

Jarman, N. and Tennant, A. (2003) *An Acceptable Prejudice? Homophobic Violence and Harassment in Northern Ireland*, Belfast: Institute for Conflict Research.

Kelley, P. (2009) *Filling in the Blanks: LGBT Hate Crime in London*, London: Galop.

Mason, G. and Palmer, A. (1996) *Queer Bashing: A National Survey of Hate Crimes Against Lesbians and Gay Men*, London: Stonewall.

McGhee, D. (2003) 'Joined-up Government, "Community Safety" and Lesbian, Gay, Bisexual and Transgender "Active Citizens"', *Critical Social Policy*, 23 (3): 345–74.

McManus, J. and Rivers, I. (2001) *Without Prejudice*, London: Nacro.

Norton, A. and Herek, G. (2012) 'Heterosexuals' Attitudes Toward Transgender People: Findings from a National Probability Sample of U.S. Adults', *Sex Roles*, 1–16.

Quiery, M. (2002) *A Mighty Silence: A Report on the Needs of Lesbians and Bisexual Women in Northern Ireland*, Ballymena: LASI.

South Yorkshire Police (n.d.) *South Yorkshire Local Policing Plan 2012/13*, www.southyorks.police.uk/sites/default/files/LPP%202012%20-%20 13_july_10_version.pdf

South Yorkshire Police Authority (n.d.) *Background to Independent Advisory Groups in South Yorkshire* (online), https://www.southyorks. gov.uk/SYJSHome/PoliceHome/IndependentAdvisoryGroup.aspx.

Weeks, J. (1996) 'The Idea of a Sexual Community', *Soundings*, 2: 71–84.

Weeks, J. (2012) *Sex, Politics and Society* (3rd edn), London: Pearson.

SEVEN

Using a 'layers of influence' model to understand the interaction of research, policy and practice in relation to disablist hate crime

Chih Hoong Sin

Introduction

The BBC's Panorama television special, *Undercover Care: The Abused Exposed*, was first broadcast on 12 May 2011. This uncovered a regime of shocking abuse by care staff against residents of Winterbourne View, a private hospital near Bristol, England, providing healthcare and support for adults with learning disabilities, complex needs and challenging behaviour, including those liable to be detained under the Mental Health Act (1983). During five weeks spent filming undercover, Panorama's reporter captured footage of some of the hospital's patients being repeatedly pinned down, slapped, dragged into showers while fully clothed, taunted and teased. Methods of restraint and punishment were often dangerous and illegal. The programme decided to film secretly after being approached by a former senior nurse at the hospital who was deeply concerned about the behaviour of some of the support workers caring for patients.

In the immediate aftermath, politicians, the Care Quality Commission, professionals, and all segments of society were quick to express disgust and shock. The developments that unfolded exemplify how the influence of recent research may be detected, but also point simultaneously to areas where research has yet to have much impact on policy and practice.

In this chapter, what happened at Winterbourne View and the responses thereafter are used to frame a wider reflection on the impact that research has had on policy and practice in the area of disablist hate crime. By virtue of the sheer breadth of issues raised by this scandal, the discussion that follows is necessarily selective and is intended to highlight specific instances where research is perceived to have made an impact, and others where the evidence base has yet to make perceptible inroads into policy and practice. While the Winterbourne View case involved, specifically, people with learning disabilities and autism, the issues raised here go beyond the confines of impairment specificity.

A 'layers of influence model'

In order to conceptualise how we interpret what happened at Winterbourne View, and its wider relevance for understanding disablist hate crime, the analysis that follows draws on a 'layers of influence' model. 'Layers of influence' was proposed by Göran Dahlgren and Margaret Whitehead in 1991 as a 'social model of health' for understanding the determinants of health.

Dahlgren and Whitehead (1991) described a social ecological theory to health whereby they attempted to map the relationship between the individual, their environment and disease (Figure 1). This model has been extremely influential in conditioning the way we think about different types of interventions; recognising that to achieve certain outcomes for a particular group, we cannot simply target interventions at that group.

Figure 1: A 'layers of influence' model in relation to disablist hate crime

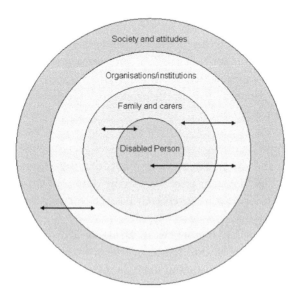

This 'social model of health' lends itself well to a 'social model of disability' approach in understanding disablist hate crime. In the sections below, the model will be used to explain disablist hate crime as the result of complex interactions within and across the different layers of influence. Both structure and agency are acknowledged in this model, and are understood as the interdependency of various levels of social aggregate within which any individual is positioned. Positionality is not fixed, and is always contingent and contextual. This model may be a powerful heuristic device not only to think through interventions but also in clarifying the impact of, and gaps, in evidence.

The model in action

The disabled person

In the centre of the model is the disabled person with his or her set of characteristics. For far too long the academic and popular discourse around disablist hate crime has revolved around the characteristics of disabled people themselves: in particular, those that render disabled people 'vulnerable'. A number of implications flow from this. First, the hate crime scholarship has, until very recently, demonstrated an obsession with understanding what types of hate crime happen to what types of disabled people; the prevalence and experience of such crime; how disabled victims respond and seek help, etc. There is the danger that policy makers and practitioners may come to think that we can tackle disablist hate crime by finding out more about disabled people and what makes them 'at risk'. It is perceptible that commentators felt that the residents in Winterbourne View experienced such appalling treatment *because* of their vulnerability; that their vulnerability stemmed from their having learning disability and/or autism; and that their vulnerability is a fixed condition.

Unfortunately, appeals to a sense of social justice on identities constructed around representations of vulnerability can often be met with sympathy but little real commitment to change. Endemic low aspirations for such groups can lead to fatalistic acceptance that disabled people cannot expect anything different because they are inherently vulnerable. The best that may be done for them is to 'protect'. This does not challenge fundamentally the structures that reproduce vulnerability and the contexts in which disabled people experience hate crime. This approach will never prevent hate crimes from happening, and only serves to locate disabled people in a way that enables them to be managed.

While the disablist hate crime scholarship has moved to critique the representation of vulnerability (e.g. Sin et al, 2009; Roulstone and Sadique, 2012), the response from all segments of society to the Winterbourne View scandal demonstrate that disabled people can still be perceived as 'vulnerable' and in need of care. Cases such as Winterbourne View can actually serve to reinforce an entrenched 'charity model' of disability where disabled people are depicted as victims of circumstance and deserving of pity.

It is telling that the residents within Winterbourne View Hospital have been represented solely as 'vulnerable' and 'disabled'. Detailed analysis of the composition of residents yields interesting and surprising findings. The age profile of residents was notably younger than the inpatient learning disability and mental health populations, while the gender balance was more even in comparison to the typical profile of inpatient learning disability and mental health populations that tend to have a higher proportion of men. How these characteristics may have influenced or contributed to what happened is unknown. Yet, we know from the wider evidence base that younger disabled people, and disabled women, are known to experience disproportionately high levels of victimisation even in comparison with disabled people in general (Petersilia, 2000; Mencap, 2007; Sin et al, 2009). Sin et al (2009) posited that this may be due to the combination of different identities that compound power imbalance.

Yet, the homogenising effect of the 'vulnerability' narrative casts the residents as 'disabled and vulnerable' before they are 'man/woman', 'old/young', etc. This effect is so complete that we overlooked the fact that only 27% of residents had 'severe to moderate' learning disability, while 65% had 'mild to borderline' learning disability and, surprisingly, 8% had no learning disability at all (NHS South of England, 2012: 23).

Despite emerging evidence (Cunningham and Drury, 2002; Shamash and Hodgkins, 2007; Barclay and Mulligan, 2009), there is still a dearth of research looking at the intersectionality of identities when it comes to disablist hate crime. 'Hate crimes' do not always fall neatly under one category and it is crucial that relevant agencies acknowledge the multiple identities and multiple needs of the victim. Certainly, policy and practice has been almost completely untouched by considerations of intersectionality (see Balderston and Roebuck, 2010, for an exception).

Family, friends and carers

The next circle in the 'layers of influence' model represents immediate networks such as family, friends and/or carers. Issues such as the size, quality and composition of these various networks are of importance, as are issues relating to the attitudes and behaviours of these people.

In the Winterbourne View case, carers were perpetrators of violence towards the residents. The wider evidence base suggests that 'victimisation by caregivers and peers' may be more common in comparison to those who live in the community (Petersilia, 2001: 664; Sobsey, 2006). The evidence identifies coercion and punishment as enactment of unequal power relationships through which a caregiver gains control over the victim's behaviour. However, to understand the scandal in terms of 'rogue' carers is to over-simplify what happened. The judge and a number of defendants in the Winterbourne View case acknowledged that the structurally unequal positions of the different players were amplified by a number of other factors. The recognition of the structural conditions around the perpetration of violence towards disabled people is not meant to absolve the perpetrators' responsibility and accountability. Instead, it cautions against looking for obvious 'villains'. A Home Office report, for example, stated that people that perpetuate hate crimes against people with learning disabilities are primarily of working age and are 'adults leading everyday lives' (Home Office, 2007: 3).

As Iganski et al (2011) observed, there has been little applied research on the question of why particular people offend in particular circumstances, while many others who live in the same environments and experience the same circumstances do not offend. There is a real gap in the research evidence base, while policy and practice have suffered from the paucity of relevant findings.

In the Winterbourne View case, a common thread through the response from family members was that they had an implicit trust in the professionals charged with the care of their sons or daughters. Not only were professionals trusted, but their accounts were privileged over those of their own kin. For example, even though Wendy Fianders' daughter told her mother about the restraints that she was subjected to and the fact that she had fingers broken, she chose to believe the answers from professionals in response to her queries as 'you believe the professionals over and above your own child' (BBC, 2012). Wendy's daughter has autism and displays challenging behaviours.

The discrediting of disabled people, even by those nearest and dearest to them, is despairingly common. By being 'disabled', a number of assumptions are made about individual's 'competencies' and 'capabilities' (Sin and Fong, 2007; Sin, 2009). Research shows that disabled people often have their accounts or credibility doubted not only by family members, friends and carers, but also by statutory agency staff including the police (Sin et al, 2009; Sheikh et al, 2011). While the 'nothing about us without us' clarion call from the disability rights lobby has been ringing out loud and clear for a number of years, and policy and legislative developments have increasingly embraced the meaningful involvement of disabled people, there is still a very significant implementation gap (Ferrie et al 2008).

Organisations and agencies

The next 'layer' in the model represents the different organisations, agencies and institutions that disabled people may come into contact with either in their everyday lives or when experiencing hate crime. These include, for example, disabled people's organisations, the police, housing associations, health and social care organisations, and others.

The Winterbourne View case exemplifies how services for disabled people can still be underpinned by an assumption that disabled people are dependent and in need of 'care' (Barnes, 1990). Services have evolved to sustain this perceived dependency (Prime Minister's Strategy Unit, 2005). The majority of residential placements in the UK, for example, involves adults; with the largest group being people with learning disabilities (Department of Health, 2007). Despite improvements, people with learning disabilities are still more likely than others to live in institutional settings.

The continuing inappropriate housing and disproportionate institutionalisation of people with learning disabilities mean that they are often socially marginalised and isolated. Infringements of their human rights are thus less likely to be observed or addressed (Joint Committee on Human Rights, 2008). This was exactly what happened at Winterbourne View.

Inflexible and inappropriate service provision affects other disabled people, and not just those with learning disabilities. According to the Voluntary Organisations Disability Group (VODG), an umbrella group of third sector providers of social care for disabled adults, there are around 500 disabled people every year whom they deal with, affected by funding wrangles between local authorities which cause disabled people to get stuck in unnecessary residential care settings (VODG, 2010). Even more widely, the evidence base points to the 'aggregation of disabled people', referring to the situation where disabled people, by virtue of being poorer in comparison with non-disabled people, are accommodated in difficult-to-let areas. This geographical concentration increases their visibility and can attract negative attention (Williams, 1995). Despite the existence of compelling evidence in this area, and policy initiatives aimed at improving the inclusion of disabled people, practice 'on the ground' has not kept pace with the rhetoric of inclusion.

Wider society and attitudes

Last but not least, the outermost circle in the 'layers of influence' model indicates the importance of wider society and attitudes. While the focus in the reporting of the Winterbourne View case centred largely on 'vulnerable individuals', on 'rogue' care home staff, and on the failings of an individual hospital, we must not be blind to how wider attitudes towards disability and disabled people have conspired to sustain the structures that reproduce violence.

A survey conducted by the charity Turning Point in 2010 found that a third of Britons questioned think that people with learning disabilities cannot live independently nor do jobs, while almost a quarter imagined they would be living in care homes. Nearly one in ten (8%) expected them to be cared for in a secure hospital out of town (cited in Samuel, 2010). It is unsurprising, therefore, to find that people with learning disabilities are disproportionately more likely to be in out of area placements (NHS Information Centre, 2008), even though this has been recognised as bad practice and against government policy (Department of Health, 2006) that aims to 'focus on those with complex needs and shift care closer to home'. Despite numerous policy drives, and with the weight of evidence behind them, the impact on practice has been painfully slow.

Tellingly, Winterbourne View was not the first time such scandals have hit the headlines. After all, the former Healthcare Commission and the Commission for Social Care Inspection investigated the abuse of people with learning disabilities in Cornwall Partnership NHS Trust in 2006, and in Sutton and Merton Primary Care Trust in 2007 (Joint Committee on Human Rights, 2008). Yet, these investigations and their recommendations did not prevent the Winterbourne View scandal from happening. Such an outmoded model of care persists, in all likelihood fuelled by wider societal perception of disabled people combined with the structural positions occupied by disabled people. Negative attitudes towards the capacity of disabled people to make decisions for themselves about their own lives sustain paternalistic approaches towards their 'care'. These permeate most segments of society, and have pernicious

– often implicit and unexamined – impact on the way we think what is 'good enough' or 'good for' disabled people, resulting in them being excluded. Once 'out of sight', they fall 'out of mind'.

Pejorative attitudes towards the capacity of disabled people to contribute sustain endemic low aspirations and fatalistic acceptance that disabled people should not expect to live fulfilling lives. The Conservative MP Philip Davies sparked anger in 2011 by claiming that disabled people 'by definition, cannot be as productive in their work as somebody who has not got a disability', and therefore should be willing to receive lower pay in order to secure employment (Stratton, 2011). Yet this neglects the fact that many disabled people already receive less pay for doing the same job as their non-disabled counterparts, and yet still suffer from lower levels of employment (Sheikh et al, 2011).

This pernicious de-valuing of disabled people indicates a disdain for their equality as human beings. This lends itself easily to the de-valuation of the residents in Winterbourne View hospital whom the staff had stopped seeing as complete people. This lends itself to the ease with which Fiona Pilkington's repeated and desperate pleas for help fell on deaf ears as the police and the council dismissed her experience and those of her disabled daughter Francecca Hardwick as nothing 'other than low level nuisance behaviour', and not priorities for action (Leicestershire and Rutland Safeguarding Adults Board, 2008). This lends itself to the countless instances when we look away as a disabled person is subjected to verbal abuse and ridicule in the streets or on public transport.

While we would like to think that the success of the London Paralympic Games marked a watershed moment, a report by Hardest Hit (2012), a coalition of 90 disabled people's organisations, alluded to the polarised public perceptions of disabled people. The talents and achievements of Britain's Paralympians were lauded on a scale never before seen in this country.

Yet this is only part of the story. The Disability Hate Crime Network still shows daily postings of reports on attacks against disabled people. The British Social Attitudes Survey, published in September 2012, showed a hardening of public attitudes towards the recipients of welfare (see also Rigg, 2007). How are we to make sense of these contradictory views? It seems that for certain sections of the public a deserving/undeserving dichotomy has formed, in which a relatively small number of successful disabled athletes are viewed with respect, while the majority of less privileged disabled people are treated with disdain. The more positive 'superhuman' representations of disabled people (like the Paralympians) can be problematic in promoting the idea that all disabled people can overcome barriers if they put their minds to it, and if they do not it is because they have not tried hard enough (see Barnes, 1992).

As the glitz and the glamour of the Paralympics fade away to leave the harsh economic reality that preceded them, perhaps we have to accept that on the whole, people's attitudes towards disabled people have not moved on quite as far we would like to think they have. Media coverage of disabled people between 2004/05 and 2010/11 has become more negative, while articles on disability benefit fraud have become more prevalent (Briant et al 2011). Unsurprisingly, primary research conducted with members of the public found that around 70% of respondents thought that claimants of disability-related benefits are fraudulent even though figures from the Department for Work and Pensions show that only around 0.5% of claimants are fraudulent (DWP, 2011).

Despite the wealth of research on public attitudes towards disability and disabled people, as well as the evidence on the impact of media representations on wider attitudes towards disability and disabled people, there has been little or no discernible impact on policy and practice. This is particularly stark given the exhortations from disabled people's organisations about the need for the government and the press to combat the increasingly negative representation of disabled people, compounded by the welfare reforms.

Conclusion

The above discussion has attempted to cover a huge and complex terrain through selective exemplification of the ways in which research, policy and practice interact, through the lens of a 'layers of influence' model. By using the case of the Winterbourne View scandal as a starting point, this chapter has made reflections on the wider evidence base, policy and practice around disablist hate crime more generally. It further acknowledges issues that are impairment-specific as well as those that have relevance for disabled people more generally.

It is easier to point out where research has had little or no impact on policy and practice, and much more difficult to claim with any degree of certainty that research has had impact. What is clear, however, is that disablist hate crime has moved up the agenda in recent years. A number of key developments have either been influenced by research or have acknowledged specific pieces of research. For example, the Cross-Government Hate Crime Action Plan states explicitly that the evidence pointing to severe under-reporting of disablist (and other) hate crimes have contributed to a specific focus in the plan to encourage reporting (Home Office, 2012: 7–8). Similarly, the Crown Prosecution Service (CPS) issued additional guidance around prosecuting cases of disablist hate crime in recognition of the evidence base around the need to avoid assuming 'vulnerability' uncritically when dealing with disablist hate crime (CPS, 2010).

Certainly the CPS's response to the Winterbourne View case has been encouraging in its recognition that the care home case *is* disablist hate crime, and by asking the judge to treat the offences as disablist hate crime which would increase the level of sentences. This marks a significant shift from the tendency in the past to treat care home abuse as a 'care failing issue' rather than a criminal justice issue (see Perry, 2004; Sin et al, 2009).

On the other hand, the heightened profile of disablist hate crime cannot simply be attributed to research alone. High profile media coverage of key incidents (particularly those with tragic outcomes), such as the intense coverage of the tragic deaths of Fiona Pilkington and Francecca Hardwick, have contributed significantly to raising awareness, spurring public outrage and consequent actions. The Panorama Winterbourne View programme, for example, has encouraged others to speak out about concerns of private hospitals, with the Care Quality Commission reporting that more than 4,300 whistleblowers have come forward in the past 20 months to complain about the treatment of elderly and disabled people in care, partly as a result of the programme. Disability organisations have also reported a surge in inquiries. Beverley Dawkins, the national manager for profound and multiple learning disabilities for Mencap, for example, stated that this was not because 'there are more and more awful things happening, but [because] awareness has been heightened ... People know who to contact and to do it as soon as possible when they become concerned' (quoted by Cafe, 2012).

While research may have contributed directly or, more often, indirectly, to broad directions of travel in policy and practice, there is less evidence that the nuances in the evidence base are being picked up. For example, while there are strong indications that research has contributed towards the growing recognition of the need to encourage better reporting, actions taken to support reporting have been rather crude and do not seem to reflect important inflections in the evidence relating to the reporting of disablist hate crime. As Sin (2012: 148) argued:

The willingness of the criminal justice system to replicate initiatives, perhaps drawn from the experience of other forms of hate crime, can be based upon unproven assumptions as to the cause of under-reporting of disablist hate crime. For example, the reasons for under-reporting homophobic hate crimes are quite different from those for disablist hate crimes.

Research is perhaps most directly influential on policy and practice when it is being considered within the confines of hate crime and criminal justice. Yet, to understand hate crime holistically and to be able to put in place sensible interventions, we cannot simply look at disablist hate crime as a criminal justice issue. The layers of influence model points very clearly to the fact that the determinants of hate crime are positioned at various degrees of 'closeness' to disabled people and to the direct incidence and experience of the hate crime itself.

Besides helping us understand the different factors contributing towards disablist hate crime, the model further suggests what needs to be done at the various layers to prevent hate crime from happening. Simply looking at how research on disablist hate crime itself has or has not had an impact on policy and practice may lead us simply to address the symptoms of the problem, and not the causes. Greater priority should be given to the prevention of hate crime. To do so, we need to draw together the evidence across the various layers within the model. In the Winterbourne View case, for instance, instead of thinking of disabled victims of hate crime as being inherently vulnerable, which merely contributes to actions that remove them from harm, we can more fruitfully ask ourselves the following question: how do our attitudes towards disability and disabled people influence the way we design and commission services that isolate disabled people, thereby compounding the risks to them? The layers of influence model shifts our narrow focus away from the disabled person towards a recognition that we all have a role to play in preventing disablist hate crime. Disablist hate crime is not a minority issue.

References

Balderston, S. and Roebuck, E. (2010) *Empowering People to Tackle Hate Crime: Trans Women and Disabled People Working Together With Victim Services in North East England*, Manchester: Equality and Human Rights Commission, Gay Advice Darlington and Durham, Victim Support (Northeast Region) and Vision Sense.

Barclay, H. and Mulligan, D. (2009) 'Tackling Violence against Women – Lessons for Efforts to Tackle Other Forms of Targeted Violence', *Safer Communities*, 8 (4): 43–50.

Barnes, C. (1990) *Cabbage Syndrome: The Social Construction of Dependence*, Lewes: Falmer.

Barnes, C. (1992) *Disabling Imagery and the Media*, Halifax: The British Council of Organisations of Disabled People and Ryburn Publishing Ltd.

BBC (2012) 'Winterbourne View: Care Workers Jailed for Abuse', www.bbc.co.uk/news/uk-england-bristol-20092894.

Briant, M., Watson, N. and Philo, G. (2011) *Bad News for Disabled People: How the Newspapers are Reporting Disability*, London: Strathclyde Centre for Disability Research and Glasgow Media Group for Inclusion London.

Cafe, R. (2012) 'Winterbourne View: Abuse Footage Shocked Nation', *BBC News Bristol*, 26 October, www.bbc.co.uk/news/uk-england-bristol-20084254.

Crown Prosecution Service (CPS) (2010) *Disability Hate Crime – Guidance on the Distinction between Vulnerability and Hostility in the Context of Crimes Committed Against Disabled People*, London: CPS.

Cunningham, S. and Drury, S. (2002) *Access All Areas: A Guide for Community Safety Partnerships on Working More Effectively with Disabled People*, London: Nacro.

Dahlgren, G. and Whitehead, M. (1991) *Policies and Strategies to Promote Social Equity in Health*, Stockholm: Institute for Future Studies.

Department for Work and Pensions (2011) *Fraud and Error in the Benefits System: Preliminary 2010/11 Estimates*, Leeds: DWP.

Department of Health (2006) *Our Health, Our Care, Our Say*, London: Department of Health.

Department of Health (2007) *Services for People With Learning Disability and Challenging Behaviour or Mental Health Needs*, London: Department of Health.

Ferrie, J., Lerpiniere, J., Paterson, K., Pearson, C., Stalker, K. and Watson, N. (2008) *An In-depth Examination of the Implementation of the Disability Equality Duty in England*, London: Office for Disability Issues.

Hardest Hit (2012) *The Tipping Point: The Human and Economic Costs of Cutting Disabled People's Support*, London: Hardest Hit.

Home Office (2007) *Learning Disability Hate Crime: Good Practice Guidance for Crime and Disorder Reduction*, London: Home Office.

Home Office (2012) *Challenge It, Report It, Stop It: The Government's Plan to Tackle Hate Crime*, London: HM Government.

Iganski, P., Smith, D., Dixon, L., Kielinger, V., Mason, G., McDevitt, J., Perry, B., Stelman, A., Bargen, J., Lagou, S. and Pfeffer, R. (2011) *Rehabilitation of Hate Crime Offenders,* Manchester: Equality and Human Rights Commission.

Joint Committee on Human Rights (2008) *A Life Like Any Other? Human Rights of Adults with Learning Disabilities*, London: House of Lords, House of Commons Joint Committee on Human Right; HL paper 40-I HC 73-I session 2007–08.

Leicestershire and Rutland Safeguarding Adults Board (2008) *Executive Summary of Serious Case Review in Relation to A and B*, Leicester: Leicestershire and Rutland Safeguarding Adults Board.

Mencap (2007) *Bullying Wrecks Lives: the Experiences of Children and Young People with a Learning Disability*, London: Mencap.

NHS Information Centre (2008) *Community Care Statistics 2008. Supported Residents (Adults), England*, London: The NHS Information Centre for Health and Social Care.

NHS South of England (2012) *Report of the NHS Review of Commissioning of Care and Treatment at Winterbourne View*, Bristol: NHS South of England.

Perry, J. (2004) 'Is Justice Taking a Beating?', *Community Care*, 1 April: 44–5.

Petersilia, J.R. (2000) 'Invisible Victims: Violence Against Persons With Developmental Disabilities', *Human Rights*, 27 (1): 9–12.

Petersilia, J.R. (2001) 'Crime Victims with Developmental Disabilities: a Review Essay', *Criminal Justice and Behavior*, 28 (6): 655–94.

Prime Minister's Strategy Unit (2005) *Improving the Life Chances of Disabled People*, London: The Cabinet Office.

Rigg, J. (2007) 'Disabling Attitudes? Public Perspectives on Disabled People', in *British Social Attitudes. The 23rd Report*, London: Sage.

Roulstone, A. and Sadique, K. (2012) 'Vulnerable to Misinterpretation: Disabled People, "Vulnerability", Hate crime and the Fight for Legal Recognition', in A. Roulstone and H. Mason-Bish (eds) *Disability, Hate Crime and Violence,* London: Routledge, pp. 25–39.

Samuel, M. (2010) 'Survey Reveals Prejudice against Learning Disabilities. People with Learning Disabilities Still Face Widespread Prejudice and Ignorance among the General Population, a Turning Point Survey Reveals Today', *Community Care*, 14 July, www.communitycare.co.uk/Articles/14/07/2010/114900/Survey-reveals-prejudice-against-learning-disabilities.htm.

Shamash, M. and Hodgkins, S.L. (2007) *Disability Hate Crime Report*, London: Disability Information Training Opportunity.

Sheikh, S., Sin, C.H., Pralat, R. and Sarwar, S. (2011) *All In This Together? The Impact of Spending Cuts on Deaf and Disabled Londoners,* London: OPM for Inclusion London.

Sin, C.H. (2009) 'Medicalising Disability? Regulation and Practice around Fitness Assessment of Disabled Students and Professionals in Nursing, Social Work and Teaching Professions in Great Britain', *Disability and Rehabilitation,* 31 (18): 1520–8.

Sin, C.H. (2012) 'Making Disablist Hate Crime Visible: Addressing the Challenges of Improving Reporting', in A. Roulstone and H. Mason-Bish (eds) *Disability, Hate Crime and Violence,* London: Routledge, pp. 147–65.

Sin, C.H. and Fong, J. (2007) 'Are Caring Professions Restricting Employment of Disabled People?', *Journal of Integrated Care,* 15 (6): 44–8.

Sin, C.H., Hedges, A., Cook, C., Mguni, N. and Comber, N. (2009) *Disabled People's Experiences Of Targeted Violence And Hostility,* London: OPM for EHRC.

Sobsey, D. (2006) 'Special Cases, Not Double Standards, Please', *CRIN Newsletter,* 19: 30–3.

Stratton, A. (2011) 'Tory MP Philip Davies: Disabled People Could Work for Less Pay', *The Guardian,* 17 June, www.guardian.co.uk/society/2011/jun/17/tory-philip-davies-disabled-people-work

Voluntary Organisations Disability Group (2010) *Not In My Back Yard. Ordinary Residence, Discrimination and Disabled People. Three Years On,* London: VODG.

Williams, C. (1995) *Invisible Victims,* London: Jessica Kingsley.

EIGHT

Responding to the needs of victims of Islamophobia

Irene Zempi

Introduction

Support for victims of crime is a fundamental part of a civilised justice system. However, in the current climate of austerity – with the police, courts, prisons, probation and support services facing significant financial cuts – the criminal justice system in the UK falls short of meeting the different and changing needs of communities across the country. As I write this chapter, the police service face a 20% cut in their budget. Undoubtedly, this reality challenges the capacity of police forces to tackle crime, and raises concerns about the quality of service offered to victims of crime. Broadly speaking, victims often need emotional and practical support to recover from the consequences of crime and support services should aim to achieve this outcome. Criminal justice practitioners – particularly those based in diverse communities – must have sufficient knowledge and understanding of the specific needs of their clients (Ahmed, 2009). This a contributing factor to offering a more responsive service, which is accessed by the so-called 'hard-to-reach' or 'hidden' communities. Crime, even when seemingly 'low level', can have a devastating impact on victims, particularly where a person is deliberately or persistently targeted. This should be taken into consideration when support is provided to victims of hate crime, where they are targeted on their actual or perceived disability, race, religion, gender identity or sexual orientation.

Against this background, Muslims emerge as the largest faith group experiencing hate crimes (Ahmed, 2012). In a post-9/11 climate, there is an increase in violent attacks targeting Muslims, those perceived to be Muslims, and mosques in the West. In the British context, for example, there has been a rise in violent assaults – some fatal – on British and other Muslims living in the UK, in verbal and physical attacks towards Muslim women who wear headscarves (*hijab*) and face veils (*niqab*), and in the alarming growth in the number of mosques, cemeteries,

Islamic centres and Muslim properties that have been the targets of criminal damage, such as graffiti and arson attacks (Engage, 2010). The establishment of, and subsequent demonstrations by, the English Defence League have contributed to this reality of a rising anti-Islamic, anti-Muslim hostility. Similarly, the British National Party has launched a highly explicit Islamophobic campaign on the basis of resisting the 'Islamification of the UK'. At the time of writing, a new far-right political party called 'True Brits', which consists of former members of the British National Party, has formed within the UK alongside other disparate movements. In Europe, support for far-right political parties and street-based movements is also on the increase (Bartlett et altler, 2011), while Islamophobia is becoming increasingly 'institutionalised'. Correspondingly, Switzerland has prohibited future construction of minarets on their soil while France, Belgium and Italy have criminalised the Muslim veil through legislation that bans the wearing of the face veil in public places. Opposition to the face veiling, and indeed Islam at large, has prompted calls to implement similar legislation in Spain, the Netherlands, Scandinavia, Germany, Canada and Australia.

With these points in mind, this chapter outlines the link between academic research, policy and practice in relation to offering support to individuals who have suffered Islamophobic hate crime/incidents, whether through verbal abuse or physical injury. First, I examine relevant theory in order to identify the specific religious and cultural needs of victims of Islamophobia. Secondly, I assess contemporary policy and practice by looking at the effectiveness of criminal justice responses to this victimisation within the UK. Statutory criminal justice agents, such as the police and Victim Support, in parallel with faith-sensitive voluntary organisations, such as the Measuring Anti-Muslim Attacks programme and the Muslim Youth Helpline, provide support to victims of Islamophobia. However, there are often barriers to the effective delivery of conventional support services, including a lack of understanding and awareness of victims' distinct cultural norms and religious practices. Thirdly, I consider what more we can do to alleviate the impact that this victimisation can have on victims in terms of offering intelligent support to them, and to this end 'getting it right' for victims of Islamophobia. Within the discussions that follow I make the case for a more flexible and effective approach to engaging with victims of Islamophobia; one that facilitates greater communication between statutory and voluntary service providers and community-based Muslim organisations such as mosques, Islamic schools and Islamic community centres.

Islamophobia and its impact on victims

Islamophobia has been described by Chakraborti and Zempi (2012: 271) as 'A fear or hatred of Islam that translates into ideological and material forms of cultural racism against obvious markers of "Muslimness"'. Within this framework, Islamophobia can be interpreted through the lens of cultural racism whereby Islamic religion, tradition and culture are seen as a 'threat' to 'national identity', while 'visible' Muslims are viewed as 'culturally dangerous' and threatening the 'British/Western way of life'. In this context, Islam and Muslims find themselves under siege. Muslim men have emerged as the new 'folk devils' of popular and media imagination, being portrayed as the embodiment of extremism and terrorism, while Muslim women have emerged as a sign of gender subjugation in Islam, being perceived as resisting integration by wearing a headscarf or worse still the face veil. Such stereotypes provide fertile ground for expressions of Islamophobia in the public sphere. Following this line of argument, Islamophobia manifests itself as an expression of anti-Islamic, anti-Muslim hostility towards individuals identified as Muslims on the basis of their 'visible' Islamic identity. Expressions of Islamophobia include verbal abuse and harassment, threats and intimidation, physical assault and violence (including sexual violence), property damage, graffiti, offensive mail and literature, and offensive online and internet abuse.

The research evidence suggests that since 9/11 Muslims have been particularly vulnerable to harassment, intimidation and violence when displaying visible signs of their faith. McGhee (2005) observes that there was a four-fold increase in the number of racist attacks reported by British Muslims and other Asian, ostensibly 'Muslim-looking', groups in the UK during the months immediately after 9/11. This heightened sense of vulnerability since 9/11 has also been reported in Garland and Chakraborti's (2004) studies of racism in rural England. In the three weeks following the 7/7 bombings, police figures showed a six-fold increase in the number of religiously motivated offences reported in London, the vast majority of which were directed against Muslim households and places of worship, while in the same three-week period over 1,200 suspected Islamophobic incidents were recorded by police force across the UK (BBC, 2005). As of 2012, police figures indicated that anti-Muslim hate crimes had reached record levels. Equally, in the period between the events of 9/11 and 2010 successive Crown Prosecution Service (CPS) racist incident monitoring reports show Muslims to have accounted for more than half of all incidents of religiously aggravated offences at 54%, while up to 60% of mosques,

Islamic centres and Muslim organisations suffered at least one attack (Ahmed, 2012). In 2011, over half of British Muslims reported having experienced at least one incident of Islamophobic abuse, harassment or intimidation in public (Ahmed, 2012).

Muslim women in veil have been particularly vulnerable to manifestations of Islamophobia in the public sphere on the basis that they are easily identifiable as Muslim. From this premise, 'visibly' Muslim women may be targeted because they are seen as more visually 'threatening' than Muslim men, particularly when they wear the full veil (Chakraborti and Zempi, 2012). At the same time, popular perceptions of veiled Muslim women as submissive, oppressed or subjugated render them 'easy subjects' against whom to enact Islamophobic attacks (Chakraborti and Zempi, 2012). Githens-Mazer and Lambert (2010), whose research included interviews with victims, perpetrators and witnesses of anti-Muslim hate crimes in London, found that veiled Muslim women have become widespread targets for verbal and physical abuse, including being spat on and having their veils torn from them. This line of argument highlights the vulnerability of veiled Muslim women to Islamophobic attacks in the public sphere.

Similar to any crime, Islamophobic victimisation carries a human cost: it can have a devastating and long-term impact on victims, particularly those who are the most vulnerable such as women, disabled and elderly Muslims. The emotional effects of this victimisation might include fear (particularly of repeat attacks), anger, post-traumatic stress, depression, anxiety as well as physical symptoms, including panic attacks. In some cases the impact of Islamophobic victimisation is so severe that it can cause victims to change the way that they live their lives because the emotional trauma makes them afraid to leave their house. Tarlo (2007) reveals the reluctance of both *hijab* and *niqab* wearers to visit areas in London where they will be in a sartorial minority. Moreover, some Muslims are driven to adopt Western names and pretend not to be Muslims at all, while others emphasise their Asian-ness in order to draw boundaries between themselves and other 'visible' Muslims (Afshar, 2008).

For those subjected to more violent attacks, the impact can be life-changing injury or bereavement. In July 2009, Marwa al-Sherbini, a 32-year-old Egyptian pharmacist, who was three months pregnant at the time, was stabbed to death in a German courtroom while preparing to give evidence against a German man of Russian descent, who had tried to remove her Muslim headscarf and had called her an 'Islamist', 'terrorist' and 'whore' in a public park in Dresden, Germany (BBC, 2009). In May 2010, a Muslim woman was attacked by a robber who stole thousands of pounds worth of valuables before wrapping her in a carpet, setting fire to her and then saying: 'This is your Eid present, you Muslim' (MailOnline, 2010). It was during Friday prayers at the end of Ramadan[38] when this incident occurred in the victim's house in London. Islamophobic victimisation is unique in the consciousness of the wider Muslim community through reference to the notion of *ummah* (the worldwide community of Muslim believers). Whether Islamophobic attacks are targeted at people or buildings, Islamophobic victimisation is commonly perceived by the victim to be an attack on Islam and Muslims as a whole (see also Chakraborti and Zempi, 2013).

At the same time though, victims of Islamophobia are not a homogenous group. Experiences and effects of manifestations of Islamophobia are likely to be shaped by a range of characteristics of the victim such as age, gender, class, education, ethnicity, sexuality, geographical location and socioeconomic status. However, little focus has been given to the intersectionality across victims' multiplicity of identities, or even to multiple disadvantage. This line of argument indicates the complex needs of some victims of Islamophobia, such as individuals who are disabled, or those who do not speak English, and those suffering from domestic or sexual violence. Also, refugees and asylum seekers are faced with specific barriers, including a lack of awareness of the existence of support services and language difficulties. When these multiple factors are combined with each other, it becomes clear that victims experience a range of intersectional issues and this should be taken into account when needs are assessed and support is provided. Certainly, the experience of receiving support should minimise the suffering of victims and not inadvertently add to it. In what follows, I review the range of services available before analysing the strengths and weaknesses of these services in terms of their capacity to address the distinct religious and cultural needs of victims of Islamophobia.

Contemporary support services

At the time of writing, Victim Support is the primary provider of victim and witness support services in England and Wales.[39] Victims have access to face-to-face and over-the-telephone emotional and practical support provided by Victim Support through the police automatically referring victims to these services, unless they choose not to be referred. In essence, Victim Support services are designed to offer support to all those referred by the police rather than specialising in support for those in greatest need, and of course, not all victims are willing to contact the police themselves. This 'one size fits all approach' is potentially flawed for victims of Islamophobia on the basis that it does not take into consideration distinctive faith and cultural needs. Based on my qualitative research in relation to the targeted victimisation of veiled Muslim women in public, victims were less likely to access the police and as a result Victim Support services because of both religious and cultural factors (Zempi, forthcoming).[40] For example, victims reported that they found it difficult to engage with male police officers and support workers, while others stated that they found it challenging to visit an organisation such as the police or Victim Support. At the same time, some victims did not have any knowledge of Victim Support and its services.

In addition to conventional support services such as Victim Support, both the Ministry of Justice and the Home Office provide funds to other voluntary organisations that offer support to victims of crime. In the context of Islamophobia, support services include the Measuring Anti-Muslim Attacks (MAMA) programme and the Muslim Youth Helpline (MYH). Launched in 2012, the MAMA programme is a non-profit organisation which is co-ordinated and implemented by an interfaith organisation, Faith Matters. It offers services to Muslims in England, to individuals perceived to be Muslims (e.g. Sikhs) and who have suffered attacks, and to Muslims who have been attacked by other Muslims because they are perceived to be from a minority group within Muslim communities (MAMA, 2012). The scheme operates as an alternative reporting system on the basis that if victims want the attack logged and passed onto the police (but they are not willing to contact the police themselves) MAMA will do this on their behalf. There are various ways that victims can report to the MAMA programme including via a freephone number, sms, Facebook, twitter, e-mail and online. As such, the MAMA programme contributes to supplementing official statistics through a variety of reporting mechanisms, including the use of social networking sites.

One of the strengths of the scheme is that it contributes to bridging the gap between official data and the true extent of the problem of Islamophobia through mapping, measuring and analysing data on cases received. Although the vast majority of incidents to date have been examples of hostility and violence targeted towards Muslims and people perceived to be Muslims,[41] a quarter of cases involved dissemination of anti-Muslim literature, while over ten % of cases involved an attack on mosques and other Muslim related physical sites (MAMA, 2012). Correspondingly, the scheme uses 'crowdmapping' software to compile results of attacks – whether physical, verbal, written or online – into a database which is then distributed to police forces across the UK.[42]

Launched in 2004, the Muslim Youth Helpline (MYH) provides support services to Muslim youth nationally via the telephone, email, internet, online web chat and through the post. Its services include a free and confidential helpline service run by young, male and female, Muslim volunteers, and an online support service called 'muslimyouth. net' (MYH, 2012). In addition to these services, the Muslim Youth Helpline has an advocacy department which supports vulnerable young British Muslims, who might be unable to obtain legal advice from their own resources (MYH, 2012). A core characteristic of the Muslim Youth Helpline is that it operates under the ethos of being youth led. Its services are based on the premise that peer support by Muslim volunteers is the most effective way of empathising with the challenges that young British Muslims face in a post-9/11 climate.

Analyses of the cases received by the MYH (2012) illustrate the marginalisation endured by young British Muslims. Issues such as the defamation of the Muslim identity by its relation to extremism and terrorism, a lack of awareness of existing services available (thereby suggesting that many Muslim youth do not benefit from current policies), and a sense of deep mistrust and fear of non-Muslim institutions are among the key characteristics of the marginalisation of Muslim youth. Based on the cased received so far, victims reported that they were increasingly reluctant to access mainstream support services for fear of being discriminated against and misunderstood (MYH, 2012). Certainly, if young British Muslims are reluctant to access support from conventional service providers for fear of being misunderstood, the results are likely to be experiences of further isolation and marginalisation. Accordingly, mainstream support services are struggling to identify, contact and ultimately, serve 'hard-to-reach' minority Muslim youth (MYH, 2012). This is especially true at a time when budget cuts are putting pressure on all parts of the criminal justice system, challenging its capacity to deliver high quality services for victims of all types of crime, let alone for victims of Islamophobia.

Effectiveness of contemporary practices

The current public spending reductions in criminal justice and elsewhere, in parallel with significant changes to crime policy (such as the introduction of elected police and crime commissioners in England and Wales) increase our need for a thorough understanding of Islamophobia – in line with any type of crime – through robust, consistent data collection and analysis. Both the MAMA programme and the Muslim Youth Helpline provide Muslim faith and culturally sensitive support services to victims of Islamophobia, while attempting to identify the nature and extent of British Islamophobia through the collection, analysis and mapping of anti-Muslim attacks in the country. Clearly, data collection and information gathering are pivotal to 'intelligence-led policing' – currently seen as one of the most positive contributions that policing can make to crime prevention and reduction. However, conventional support services such as Victim Support are designed to offer support to victims of crime referred by the police. Ultimately, this approach masks the true extent of the problem of Islamophobia on the basis that both police figures and Victim Support records ignore the experiences of victims who have not reported this victimisation.

While policy agendas have been heavy with initiatives designed to encourage victims of hate crime to contact the police, remarkably little attention has been directed to understanding the obstacles that stand in the way of victims of Islamophobia from coming forward and reporting this victimisation. Indeed, reporting an incident to the police sets in motion a range of other processes over which the victim has little or no control (Dignan, 2004). These processes may inflict additional costs and further hardship on the victim; a consequence that is understood as 'secondary victimisation' (Dignan, 2004). This is especially true for victims with multiple needs, who have to try to understand and negotiate a complex criminal justice system, which they may never have dealt with before. In my research, victims – that is, veiled Muslim women who have been verbally or physically attacked in public places – cited the frequency of Islamophobic victimisation, the fear of criminal justice procedures and the belief that they would not be taken seriously by the police as the main reasons for their hesitance (Zempi, forthcoming).

Unfortunately, this level of non-reporting translates into hundreds of cases that did not reach any formal complaints bodies. Equally worryingly, this finding indicates that victims did not receive the level of emotional and practical support that they needed. This potentially exacerbates both their vulnerabilities and their invisibility to front-line law enforcers and criminal justice practitioners. This is in line with academic research which highlights the invisibility of hate crimes due to victims' negative perceptions of service providers, fear of reprisals, previous discriminatory experiences, language, religious and cultural barriers, and a historical mistrust of the police (Chakraborti and Garland, 2004; Dignan, 2004; Williams and Robinson, 2004; Sharp and

Atherton, 2007; Paterson et al, 2008; Mythen et al, 2009; Christmann and Wong, 2010; Githens-Mazer and Lambert, 2010).

At the same time though, change should also come from the Muslim community itself. A contributing factor to the invisibility of this victimisation is the fact that British Muslim communities remain ill-equipped to deal with the current challenges faced by Muslims. Islamophobic victimisation – in line with other sensitive issues such domestic violence, sexual abuse, forced marriages, drugs and alcohol addiction – is not discussed openly within the Muslim community, which can only serve to increase victims' alienation and vulnerability. The reasons for which both schemes, the MAMA programme and the Muslim Youth Helpline, were initially established are likely to remain undiminished: the lack of faith and culturally sensitive support services available to Muslims by conventional support services in parallel with the culture of taboo, shame, silence and condemnation that surround sensitive issues within the Muslim community that together prevent victims from seeking help (MYH, 2012). In order to break the silence, it is imperative to break the cycle of non-reporting. This necessitates an 'intelligence-led' service provided by statutory and voluntary service providers in synergy with community-based Muslim organisations such as mosques, Islamic schools and Islamic community centres.

Is there a silver lining?

Governments have a moral and legal responsibility to ensure that first class support – such as counselling services and practical advice – is provided to help victims recover from the consequences of crime. However, services are not available all over the country while standards are not consistently high (Ministry of Justice, 2012). In the current climate, the criminal justice system falls short of meeting the needs of victims of Islamophobia on the basis that religious and cultural needs are not consistently recognised. It is important that statutory support services such as Victim Support – whereby support is mainly offered to those victims who have already contacted the police and agreed to receive support – take steps to improve their outreach work with 'hard-to-reach' communities whose members are less likely to contact the police. In this context, victim support services should be provided to victims of Islamophobia through an effective and efficient referral system, based on joint working between the police, Victim Support, the MAMA programme, the Muslim Youth Helpline, and local Muslim organisations such as mosques, Islamic schools and Islamic community centres.

In addition to supporting victims of Islamophobia through culturally aware and faith-sensitive counselling and practical assistance, it is important that support services drive social change in order to remove the conditions in which vulnerable Muslims are forced to endure their experiences of Islamophobic victimisation in silence. Taking into consideration that trust and confidence in the criminal justice system promote social integration and contribute to the successful application of the model of community cohesion, the need to dismantle barriers between criminal justice agencies and victims of Islamophobia becomes apparent. In a climate of growing Islamophobia, the vulnerability of 'visible' Muslims cannot be ignored. Reforms must be made to provide 'at risk' victims with a more accessible and effective mechanism of reporting and, of receiving support, tailored to victims' needs. Accordingly, religious and cultural sensitivity is crucial in offering high-quality support. Service providers need to be trained to deliver a service that is both faith- and culturally sensitive. An alternative to this would be to appoint staff members who have some knowledge and understanding of Islam to be able to identify with the background from which victims present themselves.

It is also important to provide adequate language services for recent immigrants who do not speak English, as a language barrier can make the provision of services much more difficult. At the same time, it is important that both policy makers and criminal justice practitioners understand the diversity within the Muslim population which covers ethnicity, nationality and theology but most importantly, gender. Services need to be flexible to meet the needs of (un)veiled Muslim women and these differ considerably from those of Muslim men who have suffered Islamophobic victimisation. For example, access to female staff members is an important need for some Muslim women who will not otherwise access services. Similarly, the option of home visits by female police officers and support workers should be made available to veiled Muslim women who have been victims of Islamophobia.

While it is important that support service providers working with victims of Islamophobia recognise both the principles of the religion and the specific cultural backgrounds of those with whom they are working, it is also crucial that sensitivity does not stop there. Support service providers should develop the capacity and flexibility within their programmes to allow repeat victims to return to the organisation for additional and continued support. In order to achieve this, it is essential to empower professionals to exercise their judgement in assessing needs while there should be a working assumption that victims of Islamophobia may well require significant support. In cases where victims' needs are not fully recognised, the lack of appropriate support can add to the injury inflicted on the victim. Accordingly, a lack of adequate support services can be a source of distress, disappointment and frustration for those who experience it. It can also make victims feel isolated, which can worsen the distress caused by the crime itself. In some cases it can lead victims to drop out of a case while it is being prosecuted. Clearly, the way in which victims are treated has an impact on the likelihood of crimes being reported in the future.

Pragmatically though, in an ongoing climate of austerity criminal justice agencies and support services are faced with the immense challenge of providing the same quality of service, even as they face significant cuts to their budgets. A lack of resources makes it difficult to meet victims' needs, particularly in relation to vulnerable and marginalised individuals who have a range of complex needs, which compounds the problem further. However, the key to meeting the needs of victims of Islamophobia lies in understanding their distinct cultural and religious needs rather than financial investment. In other words, the silver lining to improving victim support services does not necessarily require more money, but instead requires more work in the area of recognising victims' needs, an approach which can be cost-effective. Ultimately, recognising, understanding and meeting victims' distinct needs is critical to the overall success of the criminal justice system.

References

Ahmed, S. (2009) *Seen and Not Heard: Voices of Young British Muslims*, Markfield: Policy Research Centre.

Ahmed, N.M. (2012) *Race and Reform: Islam and Muslims in the British Media. A Submission to the Leveson Inquiry*, London: Unitas Communications.

Afshar, H. (2008) 'Can I See your Hair? Choice, Agency and Attitudes: The Dilemma of Faith and Feminism for Muslim Women who Cover', *Ethnic & Racial Studies,* 31 (2): 411–27.

Bartlett, J., Birdwell, J. and Littler, M. (2011) *The New Face of Digital Populism*, London: Demos.

BBC (2005) 'Hate Crimes Soar after Bombings', http://news.bbc.co.uk/1/hi/england/london/4740015.stm.

BBC (2009) 'German Courtroom Killer Gets Life', http://news.bbc.co.uk/1/hi/world/europe/8354963.stm.

Chakraborti, N. and Garland, J. (eds) (2004) *Rural Racism,* Cullompton: Willan.

Chakraborti, N. and Zempi, I. (2012) 'The Veil under Attack: Gendered Dimensions of Islamophobic Victimisation', *International Review of Victimology*, 18 (3): 269–84.

Chakraborti, N. and Zempi, I. (2013) 'Criminalising Oppression or Reinforcing Oppression? The Implications of Veil Ban Laws for Muslim Women in the West', *Northern Ireland Legal Quarterly*, 64 (1): 63–74.

Christmann, K. and Wong, K. (2010) 'Hate Crime Victims and Hate Crime Reporting: Some Impertinent Questions' in N. Chakraborti (ed.) *Hate Crime: Concepts, Policy, Future Directions*, Abingdon: Willan Publishing, 194–208.

Dignan, J. (2004) *Understanding Victims and Restorative Justice*, Maidenhead: Open University Press.

Engage (2010) *All Party Parliamentary Group on Islamophobia*, London: Engage.

Garland, J. and Chakraborti, N. (2004) 'Racist Victimisation, Community Safety and the Rural: Issues and Challenges', *British Journal of Community Justice*, 2 (3): 21–32.

Githens-Mazer, J. and Lambert, R. (2010) *Islamophobia and Anti-Muslim Hate Crime: A London Case Study*, London: European Muslim Research Centre.

Measuring Anti-Muslim Attacks (MAMA) (2012) *Making Your Voice Heard,* http://tellmamauk.org/main.

MailOnline (2010) 'This Is Your Eid Present', www.dailymail.co.uk/news/article-1273838/This-Eid-present-What-attacker-told-Muslim-woman-wrapped-carpet-set-alight.html.

McGhee, D. (2005) *Intolerant Britain? Hate, Citizenship and Difference*, Maidenhead: Open University Press.

Ministry of Justice (2012) *Getting It Right for Victims and Witnesses*, London: Ministry of Justice.

Muslim Youth Helpline (2012) *Research and Training*, www.myh.org.uk/information.

Mythen, G., Walklate, S. and Khan, F. (2009) "I'm a Muslim, but I'm Not a Terrorist': Victimisation, Risky Identities and the Performance of Safety', *British Journal of Criminology*, 49 (6): 736–54.

Open Society Institute (OSI) (2005) *Muslims in the UK: Policies for Engaged Citizens*, London: OSI.

Paterson, S., Kielinger, V. and Fletcher, H. (2008) *Women's Experiences of Homophobia and Transphobia – Survey Report*, London: Metropolitan Police Service.

Sharp, D. and Atherton, S. (2007) 'To Serve and Protect? The Experiences of Policing in the Community of Young People from Black and Other Ethnic Minority Groups', *British Journal of Criminology*, 47 (5): 746–63.

Tarlo, E. (2007) 'Hijab in London: Metamorphosis, Resonance and Effects', *Journal of Material Culture*, 12 (2): 131–56.

Victim Support (2012) 'We are Victim Support', www.victimsupport.org/.

Williams, M. and Robinson, A. (2004) 'Problems and Prospects with Policing the Lesbian, Gay and Bisexual Community in Wales', *Policing & Society*, 14 (3): 213–32.

Zempi, I. (forthcoming) *Unveiling Islamophobia in Leicester: The Victimisation of Muslim Women in Veil.*

NINE

Controlling the new far right on the streets: policing the English Defence League in policy and praxis

James Treadwell

Introduction

In the UK since 2009 the face of the far right has become synonymous with that of the English Defence League (EDL), a street-based protest movement that have been regularly embroiled in disorderly protests in English cities and whose rapid growth is largely unprecedented in recent times (Garland and Treadwell, 2010; see also Allen, 2011). While academic accounts have now started to recognise the potential threat to public order that are the hallmarks of this new social movement there has yet been little discussion from criminology or the policing literature that sets out the broader challenge to policing that this group presents. Initially dismissed in the mainstream media or condemned as simply a 'racist' far-right organisation, there has been little empirical engagement with those in the organisation (Copsey, 2010; Garland and Treadwell, 2010; 2012; Treadwell and Garland 2011). Instead, the academic literature on the EDL is has been predominantly based on secondary and survey material (Githens-Mazer and Lambert, 2010; Allen, 2011; Bartlett and Littler, 2011). Yet in the wake of the 2011 Norway terrorist attacks that claimed a total of 77 lives, the recognition of the threat that the new counter-jihad movement presents (of which the EDL is a beacon organisation), is steadily growing (Hope Not Hate, 2012).

Elsewhere, the author has been involved in mapping out the contours of the EDL, using as method both covert and overt participant observation of the group as well as interviewing those inside it, facilitating better understanding of the attitudes and values of its supporters (see Garland and Treadwell, 2010, 2012; Treadwell and Garland, 2011). This research has typically entailed periods of involvement as a participant at EDL demonstrations that were subject to a heavy police presence and surveillance, while on other occasions a form of more distanced observation of the policing of the EDL was utilised. This has involved observations of, and interviews with, police officers, active members of the EDL and also extensive research fieldwork (see Treadwell and Garland, 2011; Garland and Treadwell, 2012). On occasion, as a covert EDL member, it has involved having to evade swinging police batons, and being section 60 detained, threatened with arrest, contained and held for long periods on cold car parks and train stations, and witnessing this happen to others. It has also allowed insight into the very real threat to public order, and to the police attempting to maintain that order, that the EDL presents. Therefore, the research that produced these observations on policing is not simply the product of ivory towers, but of the streets, and it is an authentic form of 'streetwise' criminology, and derives theoretical benefit from that ethnographic methodological proximity to the topic under discussion (Denfeld, 1974).

To date, the policing of the EDL has involved responding to its physical presence, and to this end two distinct styles of policing have been apparent since its inception. In the first instance, the policing of the EDL's street protests was heavy-handed and largely prohibitive, seeking to robustly contain its activities. This policing strategy was largely reactive, as the challenge of keeping the peace between the EDL and counter protest groups, such as Unite Against Fascism (UAF), saw the police making high numbers of arrests of EDL supporters and counter protesters, with violent disorder extremely common (see Lowles, 2011). More recently that style of policing has given way to, and contrasted with, a much more neutral, non-confrontational approach, premised largely on preventing any real contact between rival protester groups and a less confrontational public order maintenance strategy. This latter approach has also seemingly coincided with a fall in the number of arrests at EDL demonstrations, and has generally been hailed by the authorities themselves as a success.

In many ways this shift in the style of policing employed when policing the EDL has mirrored theoretical and academic arguments concerning police public order strategy. Where the policing of public order is concerned, there has been a shift from what could be termed orthodox crowd psychology (Le Bon, 1895) and confrontational public order policing (wed in practice to policing strategies that respond to the violence of a minority in crowds by aggressively clamping down on all members) to a more revisionist social-psychologically informed policing (Waddington and King, 2005) developed principally out of the work and theories of psychologist Stephen Reicher (1984, 1987, 1996).

In his seminal study of the 1980 riot in St. Paul's, Bristol, Reicher provided the authoritative outline of his distinctively 'social psychological' approach to crowd psychology, in which he draws on social psychology in order to explain the common behaviours and sentiments of crowd participants in terms of the process by which members of a diverse social group become familiar with the core attitudinal and behavioural norms associated with group membership. The St Paul's riot was a confrontation triggered by a police drugs raid which resulted in an angry, mixed-race crowd attacking the police. According to Reicher, participants in the riot almost universally perceived themselves as belonging to the common social category of the community of 'St. Paul's'. The definitive shared characteristics of members of this category were that they unanimously considered themselves exploited and impoverished by the government and financial institutions and perceived themselves the victims of regular police discrimination. They felt they also suffered constant degradation due to their dependency on statutory welfare; they were resentful of local retailers whose goods were unaffordable to the community, and they felt that they had collectively lost the ability to exert any command over community matters (Reicher, 1984, 1987).

Reicher avers that it was this shared definition of participants that determined (as well as impose limitations on) the conduct of the crowd during the riot. Thus, in keeping with the above self-definition and perception, crowd members targeted their aggression towards representatives and/or symbols of those institutions deemed responsible for their exploitation and humiliation; for example, police personnel and vehicles, expensive retail outlets and banks were targets, as were social security offices. However, symbols as distinct to the community (or rioters') identity were not. More recently, in a range of contexts Reichers' arguments have been incorporated into understandings of football hooliganism (Stott and Reicher, 1998; Reicher, Stott, Cronin and Addang, 2004; Stott and Pearson, 2007). This work has similarly argued that aggressive policing which treats crowd members as potentially hostile may actually give rise to public disorder. For example, Stott and Pearson (2007) have argued, in the context of football, that less tolerant policing strategies may essentially be counter-productive as they create a unified perception of police maltreatment in what was in the first instance a diverse crowd, shifting even those who are initially opposed to violence into conflict and identification with the minority of crowd members set on confrontation. Again, drawing on empirical evidence gathered when travelling with supporters of the England football team (a group perhaps not that demographically different to EDL supporters) they argue that tough policing strategies can contribute to an escalation in the level and scope of collective conflict, and create the very problem that they seek to elevate. This point has been re-enforced by academic calls for public order policing that promotes a 'Corporate Social Responsibility' (CSR) model of public order policing with a greater emphasis on negotiated consensual 'order maintenance that strikes a balance between order, security and safety on one hand and the absolute right under the Human Rights Act 1998 on the other' (Gravelle and Rodgers, 2011: 5).

Policing the EDL

In the context of Europe post-Breivik and Utøya, there is a renewed recognition of the danger of the emerging counter-jihad and anti-Islamic protest movement in Europe (Hope Not Hate, 2012). In part this stems from the growth of anti-Muslim sentiments in the wake of 9/11, and bombings in London and Madrid (Allen, 2010). The rise of the new English anti-Islamic movements have been rapid and while these groups themselves deny they are negative generally toward Islam and Muslims, themes of difference and protectionism are clearly to the fore of their concerns:

> ... the English Defence League do not 'fear' Islam, we do not have a 'phobia' about Islam, we just realise the very serious threat it poses ... Muslims can have their faith, that is their right, but when that faith infringes on our hard fought freedoms, our democracy, our right to freedom of speech and expression then we will counter it at every opportunity because it is a threat to our way of life, our customs, our rule of law.[43]

From its own perspective, the EDL is opposing what it sees as the very real and legitimate threat posed by (militant[44]) Islam to 'our way of life, our customs, our [*sic*] rule of law'. Yet it is certain that there is very real violence at the centre of some members' activities, even if that stands in contradiction to the managed impression created by the organisation's leadership (Githens-Mazer and Lambert, 2010; Treadwell and Garland, 2011). While most hate crime is not the preserve of such groups, that does not mean that they are not serious, or that their potential in terms of inflaming wider public disorder should be forgotten (Garland and Chakraborti, 2009).

What is certain is that the counter-jihad movement has grown substantially and can now regularly amass significant numbers to march in towns and cities across England. Aside from the 3,000–4,000 active supporters it has mobilised to march on individual demonstrations, it is extremely difficult to know exactly how big or how well supported the EDL really is. In terms of more passive support, the EDL likely has a much larger mass of supporters that may not appear in the real physical world of demonstrations, but support the organisation virtually using social networks (Bartlett and Litter, 2011).

This is arguably the first problem of policing the EDL, as while just what constitutes the EDL is not clear, then neither can be the best response in terms of policing. The policing task is in reality a two-fold problem, and in actuality is very different, reflecting the different faces of the organisation. On one hand, the EDL and its supporters are a physical presence, often containing a high number of football risk supporters (a euphemism for those involved or suspected of involvement in domestic football violence) who descend on volatile locations (comprising of large Asian and Islamic local populations) in substantial numbers in a provocative attempt to engender a hostile reaction.

This was in evidence for example in the organisation's early forays into Birmingham in 2009, when the presence of the EDL quickly provoked street fights between the marchers and groups of Asian youths on the street. However, in the few days following the disorder, EDL internet forums capitalised on the fact that the police appeals to the public, to name those involved featuring CCTV images of suspects, revealed that the majority of suspects the police were seeking were Asian males, accused of assaulting whites in the city centre. This allowed the EDL to circulate the story that the police had appeased 'radical Islamists' and that white people legitimately protesting against extremism had been the victims of Muslim violence facilitated in part by police 'political correctness'.

Of course, such 'politically correct' policing does not really exist because, as has been highlighted elsewhere, a visit from the EDL to any town in the UK largely makes it likely that any ethnic minority and particularly young Asian male on the streets will similarly face restrictive policing. In the context of the first EDL demonstration in Leicester in October 2010, for example, it was suggested that:

> Young Muslim men congregating in or around the city centre were dealt with robustly and with significant force …

> The movement of people of Asian appearance was restricted throughout the day. The Clock Tower area, which is a major shopping area, had become a contested area between EDL and UAF supporters. Police formed a loose cordon here, allowing shoppers to pass through, but restricting access to anyone they deemed to be a supporter of Unite Against Fascism. Legal observers reported to us that, in practice, this resulted in some black and Asian people being moved on or denied access to certain areas (even if they were there merely to shop) while white people were unimpeded. (Netpol, 2012: 3–7)

This raises the issue that just in deciding to protest in an area with a minority ethnic population, the EDL can potentially inflame local tensions between minority groups and the police, as well as creating a climate of general anxiety and fear (Lowles, 2011). To the EDL, the 'inequity' of policing has become a recurrent theme and the group often make capital out of claims that the British police 'turn on their own people to appease the Muslim populations', who in turn repay Britain with 'terror plots and threats of death and murder' or that 'EDL patriots loyal to Britain are arrested and imprisoned while those Islamists who preach hatred against Britain and bleed the country's benefit system dry are free to walk the streets'.

Such sentiments, however confused, are more acceptable than the continual references to 'pakis' made on social networking sites used by some EDL members which highlight the real racism that belies the publically managed 'non-racist' image portrayed by the leadership, and could constitute criminal offences (even though they are rarely detected, prosecuted or treated as such). The difficulty in policing the internet is not confined to the case of hate crime and is encountered in a range of settings, including more traditional criminal offences (Treadwell, 2012). Yet there is perhaps an imperative to take online hate speech involving the new far right more seriously than has been the case previously, especially given the way in which it can sustain and underpin the attitudes and justifications that ultimately can give rise to much more extreme forms of violence, as so clearly shown in the case of Anders Breivik in Norway. Yet in contrast to how the EDL are policed on the street, there is little to suggest there is any real imperative to police this online hate involving EDL supporters.

To date, then, the main perceived challenge for the police has been in the physical policing of EDL demonstrations. Just the threat of an appearance by the organisation can have a significant impact on police services, and in an age of austerity, the prospect of costs of £500,000–plus for policing an EDL march, gives the group a degree of power. Of course, the longer-term effect of a protest can create concern and tension among targeted local communities that continue long after the demonstration itself has passed, and managing this issue also requires further police resources. In the aftermath of an EDL march, fears of attack by EDL groups and individuals may grow among Muslim communities. That stated, the main fear for the police and local authorities is controlling the EDL (and any rival or counter protests) on the day. This is a massively costly operation in itself: for example, the first national EDL march in Leicester reputedly cost Leicester City Council some £137,000, while the direct policing costs were some £850,000 (Garland and Treadwell, 2012). In addition, local businesses often report a decline in takings of between 40–70%. In total, policing the EDL and its activities has cost millions of pounds, and even with that spending, there is no guarantee that events will pass peacefully. It therefore seems imperative for praxis to develop sophisticated and cost-effective ways of policing the EDL.

How can the EDL best be policed?

After over four years of monitoring countless EDL protests, two distinct patterns have emerged in the methods employed to police English Defence League demonstrations, and the way that the two separate national EDL demonstrations in Leicester were policed (held 15 months apart) exemplifies both of these strands. The first of these events, held in the city in October 2010, revealed a police strategy of robust containment of the EDL, while the second, in February 2012, showed a different police tactic: one of less aggressive policing, featuring dialogue and accommodation of the organisation's wish to march in the city centre.

On the occasion of the first of these demonstrations, in 2010, the EDL had planned to march through some sensitive areas of the city of Leicester but, as this was prohibited by order of the Home Secretary due to the very real threat to public order, the EDL instead held a static rally in the city centre, in Humberstone Gate East. On the morning of the demonstration the EDL were permitted to assemble at several of the city centre pubs which were designated as muster points by Leicestershire Constabulary. As the ban on processions prevented them from then marching from the pubs to their rally point, EDL supporters were then transferred there in buses. It was during this transfer that serious disorder occurred. Pub windows were smashed, and on arrival at Humberstone Gate East several busloads of EDL supporters attempted to break out of the designated protest area. There was a serious confrontation with police, who deployed riot shields and batons, along with dogs and horses, during fierce clashes. Flares, smoke grenades, bottles and other missiles were thrown; one police officer was seriously injured (Netpol, 2012).

However, a significant number of EDL supporters did not manage to make it to the pubs that morning; several large groups of EDL supporters travelling on the motorway network to the city were deliberately delayed by police while another large group, numbering several hundred, had congregated in nearby Market Harborough. These separate groups eventually arrived directly at the demonstration site, provoking further disorder as their frustration at being deliberately delayed spilled over. Later, at the culmination of the static protests, EDL supporters broke through police lines and made a concerted attempt to reach the nearby Muslim area of Highfields and St Matthews, attacking a fast food outlet where a number of young Muslim people were gathered (Netpol, 2012). They were contained by police before reaching those areas, where hundreds of local people had gathered to protect their communities and Mosques from a widely anticipated EDL attack. Although small groups of EDL members fought running battles in side streets, and EDL members and local Muslim youths briefly managed to assault each other, fortunately there were no serious injuries reported and the situation did not escalate into more serious disorder, though this may have been as much to do with luck as policing design. The police made 17 arrests during the day and a number more in its aftermath.

While the EDL organisationally may claim not to support or approve of violent action, clearly the same cannot be said for individual members (Treadwell and Garland, 2011), and it is well known that disorder can arise from far-right provocation, as riots in Northern English milltowns in 2001 showed (Cantle, 2001). On a number of occasions from 2009–11, groups of EDL protestors have been responsible for breaking through police lines at a number of rallies in towns and cities across the country, throwing projectiles at the police and counter protestors, and engaging in street fights. In that way it is understandable that a heavy handed and pro-actively aggressive approach to policing the EDL characterised the early style of policing them.

However, this more retaliatory and forceful style of policing has largely declined at recent demonstrations, where the authorities have instead employed a contrasting approach witnessed at EDL demonstrations in Newcastle, Preston and during the second national

Leicester demonstration in February 2012, when the police sought dialogue and agreement with the EDL and offered a much more neutral and softer approach to policing (Lowles, 2012). Indeed, and in contrast to the previous demonstration in Leicester described earlier, on this occasion the EDL was allowed to march. Their designated route, though, had been clearly thought out by police, for while it did take the EDL through the city centre it mainly consisted of a series of side streets and the city's ring road, well away from potential flashpoints such as mosques or Islamic centres. The EDL's opponents, the UAF, were also kept hundreds of yards from any points along the march's route. Tellingly, and in contrast to the violent events surrounding the October 2010 demonstration, there was very little trouble at all and no arrests on this occasion.

The absence of large scale disorder in this context is being taken as evidence of the success of this 'non-confrontational' accommodation strategy, which bears some of the hallmarks of the ideas contained in Reicher's work discussed above. However, for critics such as anti-fascist organisations like the UAF, the policing agenda smacks more of 'appeasement' and comes from a failure to recognise the extremist nature of the EDL, as evidenced by:

> The official police and Home Office position is being driven by the National Domestic Extremism Team and the National Public Order Intelligence Unit, both of which are answerable to Detective Chief Superintendent Adrian Tudway, the National Coordinator for Domestic Extremism. In late November [he] announced that while the EDL was a threat to community cohesion the street gang was certainly not an extreme-right organisation. (Lowles, 2011, n.p.)

Of course, the extent to which the EDL is seen as a threat or not varies in academic and policy circles, with different viewpoints on the nature and character of the organisation and how it is best policed. For example, Detective Superintendent John Larkin, head of the West Midlands Counter Terrorism Unit, has suggested that protests by the EDL act as a catalyst in promoting an increase in the type of extremism in Muslim communities that they publically proclaim to resist (Fentiman, 2010). This again adds an interesting additional dynamic to the consideration of how to respond to the group. Indeed the renewed debate about the style and function of policing public protest demonstrations (particularly in the light of the death of innocent bystander Ian Tomlinson at the 2009 G20 protests in London, as well as the clashes between students and the police at the demonstrations in the same city in 2010) has been further complicated by the 'professionalisation of protests' and the appearance of more diverse groups campaigning on a range of social issues (Gravelle and Rogers, 2011: 5–6).

Conclusion

From findings gathered while observing and participating in EDL demonstrations it is evident that the policing of the group's marches has evolved from a hard line public order approach to a more managed, less confrontational negotiated accommodation of protest, mirroring a 'shift in perspective' that has occurred more broadly in public order policing in England (Waddington and King, 2005). Now, rather than the prohibition and banning of EDL demonstrations, the more recent approach has been regarded by some as 'appeasement', allowing the group to demonstrate but keeping them away from rival protesters and potential 'flashpoints' (Waddington et al, 1989).

However, while arrests at EDL demonstrations have declined over the past two years, there are potential problems with this less authoritarian and more consensual style of policing. A 2012 EDL demonstration in Walsall turned violent despite relatively low key policing and culminated with missiles, including bricks, wood, bottles and litter bins being thrown at the police. Film footage posted on the internet showed a police officer lucky to avoid serious injury when he was struck by a large piece of wood thrown by an EDL supporter.

EDL supporters claimed that this violence only arose as a result of a lack of police response to a bottle provocatively thrown into their midst by counter demonstrators. The reality though was that it showed all too well that even when public order policing begins in a relatively hands off manner, it does not guarantee that violence will not follow. Lowles suggests that while an EDL demonstration in Peterborough was notionally peaceful and free from arrests and policed in a non-confrontational manner, it culminated with a group of 50 EDL supporters fighting a pitched battle with local Muslim youths and anti-fascists in a nearby park with some 200 people involved for at least five minutes before the police arrived to restore order (Lowles, 2012).

Yet, as with Reicher's original studies, what is common among EDL supporters is a palpable sense of grievance and frustration, a feeling of being alienated from government and financial institutions and a perception that it is they themselves that are the victims of regular police discrimination and some degree of statutory political, social, cultural and economic marginalisation (Garland and Treadwell, 2012). Much of the EDL's support appears to stem from communities that are situated where a large Asian and Islamic population is found near to such white working class communities (for example, in Birmingham and Luton). It is often in these areas where poor, socially excluded communities live in close proximity to one another that there can often be very little interaction between these groups, and where mutual suspicion and hostility can develop (Cantle, 2001). Ultimately, no form of policing can contribute towards alleviating these deeply-embedded socio-cultural factors.

The practices of policing the EDL cannot easily be separated from broader considerations of perception. In adopting a more managed and conciliatory public order strategy, there is the danger that some sections of the public simply come to see the police as apologists for the EDL, or worse still, as sympathetic to the movement's cause. This is important as while the EDL formed as a reaction to the activities of Islamic extremists, it is clear that a large segment of its rank and file membership is motivated by opposition to *all* Muslims and Islam as a religion (Garland and Treadwell, 2010; Allen, 2011;). Campaigns against mosques and shops selling halal meat are hardly targeted protests against Islamic extremism, but instead Islam generically. Just as these protest 'performances' can reinforce the perceived senses of injustice and being ignored by the mainstream among EDL members (Jackson, 2010), they also clearly have the potential to create an environment in which extremist views can be openly aired, as has been evidenced in previous ethnographic work (Garland and Treadwell, 2010; Treadwell and Garland 2011). On these occasions, minority communities, already concerned at broader policing practices, often feel further isolated from the agency that is responsible for protecting them. If the police are perceived as being sympathetic to the EDL, then this isolation will only increase.

It may be best to view the EDL as a carefully managed organisation which, while not explicitly endorsing violence or hate, creates and promotes the political discourse, identity-based grievance and contextual setting in which individuals, who are willing to cross the line from legitimate protest into illegal activity, can be found. This may in part explain why the EDL's so-called 'peaceful demonstrations' are often accompanied by an unacceptable level of violence, and overt criminality. The problem then may be that while recently policing has moved to a more negotiated approach, it may seem like a surrender rather than a compromise in the eyes of the groups targeted by the EDL, and in particular Muslim and minority ethnic communities who find the organisation threatening. The activities of the EDL may give comfort and encouragement to racists up and down the country, and growing reports of people identifying themselves with the EDL when carrying out racist attacks are likely to only exacerbate this problem further (Githens-Mazer and Lambert, 2010; Treadwell and Garland, 2011).

The challenge for the police is to find something of a middle way; a means of working with the EDL but not allowing the perception that they are dictating the terms of their policing. This requires a policing approach that is both gradual and not premised on initial confrontational or forceful public order policing, but nevertheless places restrictions and limitations on the activities of the group. Such an approach also needs to remember the social impact of a visit from the EDL and work to reassure people, including minority communities, that the police are impartial and partisan peacekeepers. Of course, such claims are easily made, but translated into praxis, such policing is difficult to recognise.

References

Allen, C. (2010) *Islamophobia*, London: Ashgate.

Allen, C. (2011) 'Opposing Islamification or Promoting Islamophobia? Understanding the English Defence League', *Patterns of Prejudice,* 45 (4): 279–94

Bartlett, J. and Littler, M. (2011) *Inside the EDL: Populist Politics in a Digital Age*, London: DEMOS.

Cantle, T. (2001) *The Cantle Report – Community Cohesion: a Report of the Independent Review Team*, London: Home Office.

Copsey, N. (2010) *The English Defence League: Challenging Our Country and Our Values of Social Inclusion, Fairness and Equality* London: Faith Matters.

Denfeld, D. (1974) *Street-wise Criminology*, Massachusetts: Schenkman.

Fentiman, P. (2010) 'EDL Fuel Islamic Extremism Claim Police', *Independent*, 19 November, www.independent.co.uk/news/uk/home-news/edl-fuel-islamic-extremism-claim-police-2138387.html.

Garland, J. and Chakraborti, N. (2009) *Hate Crime: Impact, Causes, and Consequences*, London: Sage

Garland, J. and Treadwell, J. (2010) 'No Surrender to the Taliban!' Football Hooliganism, Islamophobia and the Rise of the English Defence League', *Papers from the British Criminology Conference*, 10 (1): 19–35.

Garland, J. and Treadwell, J. (2012) 'The New Politics of Hate? An Assessment of the Appeal of the English Defence League Among Disadvantaged White Working Class Communities in England', *Journal of Hate Studies*, 10 (1): 99–122.

Githens-Mazer, J. and Lambert, R. (2010) *Islamophobia and Anti-Muslim Hate Crime: A London Case Study*, Exeter: European Muslim Research Centre, University of Exeter.

Gravelle, J. and Rodgers, C. (2011) 'Engaging Protesters: A Smarter way for Policing Demonstrations', *The Police Journal*, 84 (1): 5–12.

Hope not Hate (2012) *The 'Counter-Jihad' Movement: The Global Trend Feeding Anti-Muslim Hatred*, London: Hope not Hate.

Jackson, P. (2010) *The EDL: Britain's New Far Right Social Movement*, RNM Publications, University of Northampton.

Le Bon, G. (1895) *The Crowd: A Study of the Popular Mind*, London: T. Fisher Unwin.

Lowles, N. (2011) 'Policing the EDL', *Searchlight*, 428: 6–7.

Netpol (2012) *Report on the Policing of the English Defence League and Counter Protests in Leicester on 4th February 2012*, www.scribd.com/doc/96993341/Report-on-the-Policing-of-the-EDL-and-Counter-Protests-in-Leicester2012.

Reicher, S. (1984) 'The St. Paul's Riot: an Explanation of Crowd Action in Terms of a Social Identity Model', *European Journal of Social Psychology*, 14: 1–21.

Reicher, S. (1987) 'Crowd Behaviour as Social Action', in J.C. Turner, M.A. Hogg, P.J. Oakes, S.D. Reicher and M.S. Wetherall (eds) *Rediscovering the Social Group: A Self Categorization Theory*, Oxford: Blackwell.

Reicher, S. (1996) '"The Battle of Westminster": Developing the Social Identity Model of Crowd Behaviour in Order to Explain the Initiation and Development of Collective Conflict', *European Journal of Social Psychology*, 26: 115–34.

Reicher, S., Stott, C., Cronin, P. and Addang, O. (2004) 'An Integrated Approach to Crowd Psychology and Public Order Policing', *Policing: An International Journal of Police Strategies and Management*, 27: 558–72.

Stott, C. and Pearson, G. (2007) *Football 'hooliganism', policing and the war on the English Disease*, London: Pennant Books.

Stott, C. and Reicher, S. (1998) 'How Conflict Escalates: The Intergroup Dynamics of Collective Football Crowd "Violence"', *Sociology*, 32: 353–77.

Treadwell, J. (2012) 'From the Car Boot to Booting it Up? eBay, Online Counterfeit Crime and the Transformation of the Criminal Marketplace', *Criminology and Criminal Justice: An international Journal*, 12 (2): 175–191.

Treadwell, J. and Garland, J. (2011) 'Masculinity, Marginalisation and Violence: A Case Study of the English Defence League', *British Journal of Criminology*, 51 (4): 621–34.

Waddington, D., Jones, K. and Critcher, C. (1989) *Flashpoints: Studies in Public Disorder*, London: Routledge.

Waddington, D. and King, M. (2005) 'The Disorderly Crowd: From Classical Psychological Reductionism to Socio-Contextual Theory – The Impact on Public Order Policing Strategies', *The Howard Journal of Criminal Justice*, 44 (5): 490–503.

TEN

Developing themes on young people, everyday multiculturalism and hate crime

Stevie-Jade Hardy

Introduction

One of the lasting implications from decades of public and political debate on the meaning, application and impact of a multicultural population is the assumption that the younger generation have fully embraced the 'multicultural ideology'. To Berry (2006: 728), multicultural ideology is 'the general and fundamental view that cultural diversity is good for a society and for its individual members'. Since the disturbances in Bradford, Burnley, Leeds and Oldham in 2001, involving young people from different ethnic and religious backgrounds, there has been a growing concern that such a view is naïve and underplays the lived reality of a multicultural society. One cannot fully understand how young people come to understand and engage with ethnic and religious difference and diversity without exploring how they actually interact with their surroundings on a daily basis. It is through this methodology that research, policy and practice can achieve a more 'real' approach to understanding and dealing with social and community cohesion. As Navak (2003: 178) explains, when it comes to exploring the barriers to social cohesion and cross-cultural relationships, we 'need to engage more closely with lived experience and the changing cultural and material geographies of young lives'.

Although using the notion of 'everyday multiculturalism' has come to feature more readily in academic research (as seen in Colombo and Semi, 2007; Wise, 2007; Harris, 2009), it has yet to be adopted as a lens in which to assess the underlying motivations of hate crime perpetration. It could be argued that racist and religiously motivated hate incidents and crimes are 'motivated by intolerance between communities in close proximity to each other' (Valentine, 2008: 328). By engaging with young people and therefore learning the ways in which they negotiate and interpret ethnic and religious diversity, we can begin to build a theoretical explanation, rooted in empirical data, of hate crime motivation and causation. The importance of addressing the challenges and complexities of everyday multiculturalism cannot be overstated, as Banks (2004: 291) suggests:

> Although it is essential that all students acquire basic skills in literacy, basic skills are necessary but not sufficient in our diverse and troubled world ... the world's greatest problems do not result from people being unable to read and write. They result from people in the world – from different cultures, races, religions, and nations – being unable to get along and to work together to solve the world's intractable problems.

Focusing predominantly on a study conducted in the city of Leicester but also drawing on research conducted further afield, this chapter highlights the importance of recognising the everyday nature and reality of multiculturalism. By using Leicester, a city known for its multicultural population as the backdrop to this chapter, we begin to examine the lived reality of young people in a diverse society. What became apparent from participant interviews and surveys is that young people's experiences and interactions with cultural diversity are dependant on their existing fears, prejudices and also frustrations with individual circumstances. Using the concept of everyday multiculturalism to frame young people's opinions and experiences of hate crime illustrates that those who express negative and hostile views about Leicester's multicultural population are most likely to admit to being involved in racist and religiously motivated hate crime. This chapter concludes by outlining several themes that could be developed in order to tackle existing barriers between different communities, and consequently target the underlying motivations for hate crime perpetration. It is through identifying and analysing young people's beliefs, assumptions and fears when it comes to accepting or rejecting multiculturalism and the practical influence this has on engaging with difference and diversity, that the first and most significant step towards developing effective prevention and intervention programmes can be undertaken.

Conducting a study in a 'multicultural utopia'

The study this chapter predominantly focuses on was a product of my experiences working with the Youth Offending Service. I worked for a project that used detached youth workers, deployed within a given area known to have a problem with antisocial behaviour, to identify the causes of offending and design and deliver a range of activities and workshops to engage young people at risk of, or already engaged in, antisocial behaviour. The areas in which I was working in were observed as being predominantly inhabited by White-British people and characterised by socioeconomic disadvantage. Over the course of a year what became ever more concerning was the openness and willingness of young people to express racist and religiously motivated prejudice, and recall stories in which they had committed hate incidents and crimes. This was particularly alarming because this was happening in Leicester, a city which has been praised nationally and internationally for its success in achieving what ostensibly appears to be an integrated, socially cohesive, multiculturalism (Clayton, 2009).

Before discussing the study in depth it is worth providing a brief synopsis on the demographics of Leicester. The city has been described as being 'super-diverse' (Vertovec, 2007: 1025) as after the Second World War Leicester experienced some of the largest waves of migration from the Africa and Asian subcontinents to Britain (Willmott, 2003), and more recently, the city has become home for significant Polish, Somali, Iraqi and Zimbabwean communities, to name but a few (Leicester County Council and Leicester Partnership, 2007; Leicester City Council, 2008). It is the city's long history of apparently trouble-free immigration and integration that has facilitated the assumption that Leicester's inhabitants have fully embraced the 'multicultural ideology' (Berry, 2006). However, as Clayton (2006: 16) argues, Leicester should not be naively labelled as a multicultural utopia, as the street-based, lived reality within such a diverse city can be very different. In the most recent Census statistics Leicester officially became the first plural city (Simpson and Finney, 2007) due to White-British people forming less than half (45%) of the population (Office of National Statistics, 2012). This characteristic was an important influence on the study, as Pettigrew (2012) comments, what appears to be neglected within the field of multiculturalism and social cohesion and the field of 'race' more widely, is the White-British narrative. It was this gap in knowledge, coupled with my primary experience with young, White-British people in Leicester, that formed the basis of the study this chapter is based on.

In order to conduct a study that uses the concept of 'everyday multiculturalism' as a lens through which to explore the underlying motivations of hate crime perpetration, it was essential that the research methodology could capture the daily challenges, complexities and barriers for young, White-British people living in Leicester. For this reason an ethnographic strategy was developed to enable regular weekly contact for six months with a core group of young, White-British people in an area situated on the border of the city. One of the consequences of employing such an intense methodological approach was that only 15 young people from a specific socio-cultural demographic were included in this initial round of data collection. For this reason a survey was developed and rolled out in four separate schools (in both the city and wider county of Leicestershire), each characterised by different socioeconomic conditions and contexts. The survey was designed to collect opinions on British current affairs, multiculturalism and community cohesion in Leicester, and it was these everyday negotiations and interactions of living in a multicultural city that could then be used as backdrop to their experiences of being involved in racist and religiously motivated hate incidents and crimes. In total, 425 surveys were returned, including those completed by the subgroup, and of this sample of White-British young people, 47% (201) were female and 53% (224) were male, ranging between the ages of 14 and 19 years of age. The next section outlines the findings from both the subgroup interviews and survey, and discusses these within the context of everyday multiculturalism, and the impact this had on racist and religiously motivated prejudice and hate crime perpetration.

Young people, multiculturalism and prejudice

One of the key features this research was keen to explore was whether young people, who had grown up in the 'super-diverse' city of Leicester, had fully normalised their ethnically and religiously diverse surroundings. When asked whether England's multiculturalism was a positive attribute, 75% (309) of the survey sample answered 'Yes', compared to 20% (83) answering 'No', and 5% (19) 'Sometimes'. Some of those who answered 'Yes' could be described as adhering to the 'multicultural ideology', providing textbook answers that in a multicultural society 'people can understand different people's cultures', 'people learn how to become friends with people from different ethnic backgrounds' and that 'everyone is different and it makes it more interesting'. Conversely, of those that answered 'No', some of their explanations tended to be based on the belief that England's multicultural population was detrimental to what they perceive to be *their* opportunities, culture and national identity. Some examples stated that 'England should be England' and that immigrants 'take our jobs', 'take over the country' and 'try to bring Sharia law into the UK'. Although it is not possible to draw substantial conclusions from comparing such a large school sample (410) to that of 15 surveys provided by the subgroup, it is still worth mentioning that every member of that latter answered that England's multicultural society was *not* a positive attribute; all of the subgroup's explanations mirrored, although in a more overt and extreme manner, the same fears, concerns and prejudices as those detailed above.

The results from the first question seem to suggest that three quarters of young, White-British people in Leicester are accepting and understanding of ethnic and religious diversity and difference. However as Clayton (2006: 16) warned, regarding Leicester as a 'multicultural utopia' is perhaps naïve, as the everyday interactions can be to the contrary. In order to try to focus on the context-specific experiences within the survey, participants were asked whether they thought people from different ethnic and religious backgrounds got on well together in their city. 37% (150) answered 'Yes', 40% (160) said 'No' and 23% (95) stated 'Sometimes'. Of those who answered 'Yes', a substantial proportion echoed the positive message of the previous question that because they had been 'brought up to get along' and that 'Leicester has such a mix and we are always exposed to each other', it had 'become the norm to live among different ethnicities so there is less discrimination'. However, with the majority of the survey sample answering that they felt people from different ethnic and religious backgrounds *do not* or only sometimes get on well together, there appears to be a stark difference between understanding the multicultural philosophy and the everyday experience of living within it. What became evident was that the reasons given to explain answering 'No' could be generally sub-divided into the categories of fear, speculation and geographical division. For example, a selection of participants felt that 'In schools they [people from different ethnic groups] get on but where everyone lives it is quite divided', 'Everyone sticks to their own race', that there was 'Too much clash between cultures' so that people 'don't feel it necessary to integrate in society', and finally that 'There are a lot of assaults and stabbings between the ethnic groups'. Providing the Leicester-specific context enabled the participants to draw on their own, personal experiences of whether people from different ethnic and religious backgrounds got along on an everyday level, conveying an at time troubling perspective of urban multiculturalism.

One of the issues with exclusively using survey data is that although you can begin to tentatively analyse and categorise the negative views towards multiculturalism and social cohesion, you are unable to gain the socioeconomic or cultural context in which that young person is from. Employing an ethnographic strategy was key to undertaking a much deeper exploration and understanding of language use, norms, values as well as opinions and experiences of ethnic and religious diversity. With the subgroup I was able to take a much more active role in getting to know the group members and gain their trust. This is essential for being able to identify individual demographics and group characteristics that could be important indicators for not only the prejudices they express but also the hate crimes they commit. I was able to determine that all of the participants came from a low socioeconomic background, were between the ages of 14 and 19 years old, and would define themselves as being either 'White British' or 'White English'. Interestingly, and often identified within similar studies, all but one of the young people within the group were born within the area they still lived, and had multiple extended family members living in close proximity. Particularly noticeable was the strength of the bond felt by the group members with each other and their immediate environment, as they knew each other's families, as well as their neighbours, community members and local business owners. This sense of inclusion and belonging, felt by members of the subgroup towards their surroundings, community and most importantly friendship group, was in stark contrast to the exclusion they felt from education and employment.

Of the nine who were in full-time education, one attended a specific behavioural school and three had been expelled at some point, collectively explaining that they 'rarely' attended school. The impact that school, or more aptly, a lack of qualifications, had on how the group felt about themselves and their future aspirations was very apparent. Regularly the six males who were not in education, employment or training (NEET) would express great frustration with wider societal issues and economic conditions, with one individual explaining 'There's just no jobs … I do all those things … yeah the courses, I've been on all of them and I've not even had a job interview.' It was through taking considerable time and effort to listen to and engage with the group within the context of their surroundings and social and economic circumstances that I noticed that they began openly to express experiences with people from different ethnicities or faiths, and more generally their opinions of living in a multicultural city. What became apparent was that rather than being able to assess *how* the group members interacted and negotiated with difference and diversity, it was more apt to ascertain why they *did not*. Participants would openly admit to travelling rarely outside of their 'local' familiar area to the city centre or surrounding areas, inhabited by large minority ethnic communities for fear of being 'stabbed up', or even 'blown up'. If one was to engage the group in why they felt so opposed to living in a multicultural city, they would explain how they now 'can't get a job 'cuz they [referring to individuals they perceive to be 'Asian'] take them all', that 'even the schools around here are just full of them', and they 'eat weird food', 'smell', 'don't wash' and 'don't speak English'. Overall, the group's overwhelming hostility and rejection of Leicester's multiculturalism appeared to be exacerbated by their strong need for inclusion and belonging within their immediate locale, a finding only identifiable through an ethnographic strategy of everyday multiculturalism. This near rejection of ethnic and religious diversity must be recognised against the backdrop of young people grappling with perceiving themselves to be failures while possessing the basic need to belong.

Everyday multiculturalism and hate crime

As mentioned, 'everyday multiculturalism' has yet to be used as a framework in which to assess the underlying motivations and causations of hate crime perpetration. One of the starting points in using this concept as a lens in which to explore racist and religiously motivated hate crime was to gauge what exposure young, White-British people had had to racist and religiously motivated prejudice. As mentioned above, although it is not possible to draw realistic conclusions from comparing the survey responses from both the school and subgroup sample, the latter will be singled out to demonstrate further characteristics of the group members. Of the student sample 86% (340) answered that at some point in their life they had heard prejudiced and derogatory views towards ethnic and religious minorities, compared to 100% (15) of the subgroup sample. Interestingly, when both groups were asked about the frequency in which they heard racist and religiously motivated prejudices, 29% (91) of the student sample said 'regularly' and 12% 'daily', compared to 93% (14) of the subgroup answering 'daily'. It is difficult to say conclusively that the ethnographic strategy led to the subgroup members feeling much more comfortable in expressing their everyday experiences and opinions on ethnic and religious diversity or that their exposure was much higher anyway. Regardless of this, 41% (133) of the total White-British sample answered that they regularly heard racist and religiously motivated prejudice, a figure that mirrors the number of those who believed that people from different ethnic and religious backgrounds did not get along together in Leicester. The survey finished by asking respondents if they themselves had committed racist and religiously motivated hate crime. When asked if they had ever verbally or physically abused someone because of their ethnicity or religion, 21% (80) of the school sample answered 'Yes', compared to 93% (14) of the subgroup. I happened to be present when the subgroup sample were filling in their surveys and from these observations I believe the ethnographic strategy made a considerable difference to how comfortable they felt in being honest and open about their involvement in hate crime.

This study raises the question of whether the exposure to racist and religiously motivated prejudice undermines how young people come to engage with multiculturalism, or whether the lived reality of ethnic and religious diversity perpetuates fear, speculation and intolerance of the 'Other'. Maybe a more realistic conclusion is that the two cannot be separated, and in fact it is the cyclic process of these experiences which comes to influence how young people feel about their multicultural city. The results from the survey demonstrate that although the majority of young people are aware of the positive attributes of multiculturalism, the understanding of the ideology is very different to their context-specific experiences of ethnic and religious diversity in Leicester. This was especially true within the subgroup, who were keen to share their feelings of being marginalised from education and employment and that this was a result of ethnic and religious minority communities in 'their' city. Pivotal to being able to gain this insight into a group of young people who were lacking a strong sense of identity, worth and belonging, was engaging with them on a platform in which they felt comfortable and empowered. It through the framework of 'everyday multiculturalism' that I was able not only to learn the ways in which young people negotiate and interpret ethnic and religious diversity but also gain invaluable, empirical data on hate crime motivation and causation.

Developing themes to address fear, ignorance and frustration

Although the study detailed above was conducted in the city of Leicester and therefore was to some extent context specific, it is still believed that there are issues identified that represent more general everyday experiences of multiculturalism. Accounting for the 'everyday' enables a closer inspection of the ordinary relationships and social spaces in which young people throughout the country experience their lived reality. It is through analysing young people's beliefs on ethnicity, religion and multiculturalism more generally, and how they engage with diversity and difference, that tailored prevention and intervention programmes can be developed. As mentioned previously, of those survey respondents who thought England's multicultural status was negative and that people from different ethnicities did not get along, the explanations offered could be categorised as demonstrating fear, speculation and ignorance. Pagani and Robustelli (2010: 252), who conducted a similar study in Italy of young people's opinions of multiculturalism, subdivided fear into three more specific influences; fear for their own safety and for their welfare, fear of loss of identity, and fear of losing other people's affection. As the majority of negative and hostile views in both the Leicester-specific study and Pagani and Robustelli's were motivated by both ignorance and fear, it is clear that the development of a tailored programme or initiative to address such issues is of great importance.

What becomes increasingly evident in studies conducted further afield on young people and their attitudes and experiences of everyday multiculturalism is that young people are lacking a platform in which they can openly express and debate the concept of belonging, difference and cultural barriers (McLeod and Yates, 2003; Harris, 2009). Pagani and Robustelli (2010: 252) argue that prejudice and racism, which are underpinned by ignorance, is the 'most obvious, matter-of-fact, easiest to identify and to combat of all the basic motivations', and that the most effective way of counteracting these stereotypes, misconceptions and fears is through providing knowledge within an educational environment. In 2000, the delivery of citizenship education was made compulsory within the school curriculum in England due to the growing fear that society's social mortar was being undermined by a lack of cohesion, shared values and civic ties (Pettigrew, 2012). The addition of citizenship was just one aspect of a wider shift to develop educational policy and guidance that embraced the discourse of equality and diversity in schools. However, written policy on teaching 'citizenship' and recognising discrimination does not go far enough. More and more educators are expressing concern with how and where to develop effective lessons on such issues as multiculturalism, racism, prejudice, difference and diversity, when constrained by the normal school curriculum (Johnson, 2003; Pagani and Robustelli, 2010). As Pagani and Robustelli (2008) note, due to these areas not generally being embedded in the everyday teaching curriculum, when multiculturalism, equality and diversity are touched on in the classroom, they tend to be taught in a vague, incompetent and naive manner (as cited in Pagani and Robustelli, 2010: 256).

Oddly, it appears that young people's involvement within research into this area is one of the few ways in which they can actively engage in a two-way dialogue on the challenges and complexities of everyday multiculturalism. As Clayton (2009) found when asking young, White-British people in Leicester about their experiences and interactions with ethnic and religious diversity, the focus groups provided the participants with a 'rare space' where they could openly discuss their beliefs without the fear of repercussion or ridicule. Within the study I conducted in Leicester, I found that the key to accessing such open and honest opinions from young people was breaking down the barriers that usually occur through power imbalances between the researcher and participants. The subgroup members often commented that this was the first time that they had been asked about living in a multicultural city and their experiences with people from different ethnic and religious backgrounds, and felt more valued for it. In addition, when they were asked about from whom they were most likely to hear racist and religiously motivated prejudice, 100% (15) of the group said their 'Friends', 87% (13) 'Family' and the 20% (3) who also ticked 'Other,' wrote 'Everyone'. It is clear that the subgroup members in particular were immersed in a climate of prejudice and lacked a social space in which they could engage in a more open, informative and educational debate. Interestingly, Pettigrew (2012) also found that the students within her study had little to no understanding of history, which Cole (2004) suggests is fundamental to tackling contemporary expressions of racism. Pettigrew (2012) revealed that few of the students could recall a lesson in which they had been actively involved in a discussion about racism. It was for this reason that these participants wished that they could have specifically tailored lessons where they could explore the issue of racism and identity, and 'where you could just talk about language and stuff' (Pettigrew, 2012).

Research within this field further demonstrates that young people are often given no language with which they can discuss and debate the topics of race, faith and multiculturalism which does not reduce them to being perceived as intolerant, offensive or perpetrators of hate crime (McLeod and Yates, 2003). Importantly, it must be recognised that young people are most likely to occupy the types of everyday geographical spaces to encounter and engage with ethnic and religious diversity, such as schools, city centres and other public locations. They are equally likely to use everyday language to negotiate and interpret these events (Harris, 2009). We are often too keen to interpret young people's experiences and opinions through an adult–centric lens, using the formal labels and concepts of multiculturalism, citizenship and social cohesion with which young people rarely identify. Various studies demonstrate that young people struggle to express their experience of multiculturalism in these terms (Schech and Haggis, 2000; Harris, 2009). Equally important for researchers and educators is to realise that when engaging young people in a discussion on the challenges and complexities of multiculturalism, and their experiences of interacting with ethnic and religious diversity, their opinions and beliefs are very subjective and relative. The concern is that if the underlying tensions and misconceptions are not addressed, then these prejudices are able to manifest, evolve and ultimately provide the motivation for committing hate crimes.

Conclusion

The study this chapter is based on was my first step to addressing the paucity of knowledge in the field of young people, the White–British narrative and multiculturalism. One of the most important aspects of this research was the appropriateness and effectiveness of employing an ethnographic strategy that was then supported by surveys. It was this methodology that enabled me to explore the concept of 'everyday multiculturalism' and capture the daily challenges, complexities and barriers for young, White–British people living in Leicester. In terms of embracing the idea of multiculturalism, the majority of these people within this study are accepting and understanding. It is when these findings are juxtaposed with how the sample perceived ethnic and religious cohesion within their own city, that the idea of Leicester being a 'multicultural utopia' is threatened. Of those who expressed negativity towards the city's ethnic and religious diversity, their reasons for such views were motivated by fear, prejudices and also frustrations with their individual circumstance. The concept of 'everyday multiculturalism' was developed further in order to act as a lens in which to explore the underlying motivations of hate crime perpetration. It was found that those who expressed trepidation towards Leicester's multiculturalism are also most likely to admit to being involved in racist and religiously motivated hate crime. Further empirical research into identifying and analysing young people's beliefs, frustrations and fears of multiculturalism and the practical influence this has on engaging with diversity is needed in order to effectively develop educational programmes aimed at preventing these underlying motivations of hate crime.

One of the issues with enabling a platform in which young people can freely and openly discuss their attitudes towards multiculturalism, is that academics and practitioners are coming from a standpoint where prejudiced, racist and faithist views are deemed incorrect and therefore condemned out of hand. This can be seen from Allport's view that 'Ethnic prejudice is an antipathy based on a faulty and inflexible generalization' (Allport, 1954: 10) and as Worchel (1988: 449 cited in Brown, 2010) states, prejudice is 'an unjustified negative attitude toward an individual based solely on that individual's membership in a group'. These definitions imply that the prejudice that certain individuals or groups hold is in some way false or lacking an evidential basis, in the sense that their beliefs and generalisations are unfounded. Such definitions are assuming that individuals and groups have not had a way in which to establish or find 'correctness' or 'justification' in their opinions. From spending considerable time with the subgroup in Leicester, it could be argued that their truth and justification is provided by being surrounded by friends, family and a wider community whom all believe and verbalize 'stereotypical', 'biased' views about minority ethnic and religious groups, which is then reinforced when seeing those individuals in positions of employment, living in better housing or being markedly more wealthy. It is both the perceived normality of these entrenched views for certain young people and the reluctance of researchers and educators to engage in a meaningful two-way dialogue, whether this be due to the perceived sensitivity of such topics or curriculum constraints, which creates considerable barriers to addressing the challenges and complexities that young people face in everyday life. It is when these fears, perceived prejudices and inward frustrations are not dealt with that they are likely to undermine the everyday interaction of young people with ethnic and religious diversity, and that increases the likelihood of young people condone and even commit hate crimes.

References

Allport, G. (1954) *The Nature of Prejudice*, Cambridge, MA: Perseus Books.

Banks, J.A. (2004) 'Teaching for Social Justice, Diversity, and Citizenship in a Global World', *The Educational Forum*, 68 (4): 289–98.

Berry, J.W. (2006) 'Mutual Attitudes among Immigrants and Ethnocultural Groups in Canada', *International Journal of Intercultural Relations*, 30 (6): 719–34.

Brown, R. (2010) *Prejudice: Its Social Psychology*, Chichester: Wiley.

Clayton, J. (2006) *Multiculturalism in Question: A Study of Inter-ethnic Relations in the City of Leicester*, PhD Thesis. Durham: Durham University.

Clayton, J. (2009) 'Thinking Spatially: Towards an Everyday Understanding of Inter-ethnic Relations', *Social and Cultural Geography*, 10 (4): 481-99.

Cole, M.A. (2004) '"Brutal and Stinking" and "Difficult to Handle": the Historical and Contemporary Manifestations of Racialisation, Institutional Racism, and Schooling in Britain', *Race, Ethnicity and Education,* 7 (1): 35–56.

Colombo, E. and Semi, G. (2007) *Multiculturalismo quotidiano. Le pratiche della differenza,* Milano: Franco Angeli.

Harris, A. (2009) 'Shifting the Boundaries of Cultural Spaces: Young People and Everyday Multiculturalism', *Social Identities,* 15 (2): 187–205.

Johnson, L.S. (2003) 'The Diversity Imperative: Building a Culturally Responsive School Ethos' *Intercultural Education,* 14 (1): 17–30.

Leicester City Council (2008) *The Diversity of Leicester: A Demographic Profile,* www.lrsport.org/core/core_picker/download.asp?id=1955.

Leicester County Council and Leicester Partnership (2007) *Evidence to the Commission on Integration and Cohesion,* Leicester: Community Cohesion Project.

McLeod, J. and Yates, L. (2003) 'Who is Us? Students Negotiating Discourses of Racisms and National Identification in Australia', *Race, Ethnicity and Education,* 6 (1): 29–49.

Nayak, A. (2003) *Race, Place and Globalization: Youth Cultures in a Changing World,* Oxford: Berg Publishers.

Office of National Statistics (2012) Ethnicity and National Identity in England and Wales 2011 Office for National Statistics; London.

Pagani, C. and Robustelli, F. (2010) 'Young People, Multiculturalism, and Educational Interventions for the Development of Empathy', *International Social Science Journal,* 61 (200-201): 247–61.

Pettigrew, A. (2012) 'Confronting the Limits of Antiracist and Multicultural Education: White Students' Reflections on Identity and Difference in a Multiethnic Secondary School', *Sociological Research Online,* 17 (3), www.socresonline.org.uk/17/3/3.html.

Schech, S. and Haggis, J. (2000) 'Migrancy, Whiteness and the Settler Self in Contemporary Australia' in J. Docker, and G. Fisher (eds) *Race, Colour and Identity in Australia and New Zealand,* Sydney: University of NSW Press, pp. 231–9.

Simpson, L. and Finney, N. (2007) *'Minority White Cities?',* Cathie Marsh Centre for Census and Survey Research.

Valentine, G. (2008) 'Living with Difference: Reflections on Geographies of Encounter', *Progress in Human Geography,* 32 (3): 323-337.

Vertovec, S. (2007) 'Super-diversity and its Implications', *Ethnic and Racial Studies,* 30 (6): 1024–54.

Willmott, R. (2003) 'The Power of Community Action: Creating the Momentum to Sustain Just and Peaceful Communities', *Local Environment*, 8 (3): 337–43.

Wise, A. (2007) 'Multiculturalism from Below: Transversal Crossings and Working Class Cosmopolitans' in A. Wise, and S. Velayutham (eds) *Everyday Multiculturalism Conference Proceedings*, Sydney: Macquarie University, pp. 2–23.

ELEVEN

Hate crimes against students: recent developments in research, policy and practice

Lucy Michael

Introduction

Analyses of hate crimes against students have been a significant feature of the academic hate crime literature in the United States since the early 1990s, with a number of studies examining racial, ethnic, religious, homophobic and gender-related incidents on campus. In contrast, there has to date been little attention to 'campus climate' in the United Kingdom or Europe, despite increasing attention to the safety of international students globally. However, there is good reason to consider students as a unique victim population within hate crime studies. Students on further and higher education campuses tend to undertake their studies between the ages of 16 and 23, meaning that they fall into the age group that experiences the highest number of hate crimes and highest levels of violence in hate attacks (Athwal et al, 2010). Their activities also reflect the characteristics that make young people more vulnerable generally, being frequent users of public space and public transport, where reported hate crimes are most likely to occur, and consumers of alcohol and drugs, which are predictive of violent victimisation (Fisher et al, 1998). They have more frequent and intimate contact with a range of identities and ideas as well as organisations that politicise these (Lyons, 2008), and may be exposed to much greater social diversity than previously experienced (Perry, 2010). They have less day-to-day contact with teaching staff or family, and infrequently report crimes despite high levels of repeat victimisation (Barberet et al, 2004).

This chapter will explore the impact of hate crime research on the development of US and UK policy in this area, and use recent survey findings to examine the gaps in understanding the exact nature of the hate crime suffered by student victim groups in the UK. It will argue that much more research needs to be undertaken within the UK campus context, which builds on the extensive 2010/11 hate crime survey conducted by the National Union of Students, before a fully formed picture of UK campus victimisation can be created and effective policy formulated.

Policy divergence

'Campus climate', and its effect on minority students, has been a concern for US institutions of higher education since the 1990s, when Ehrlich (1994) estimated that up to one million students perceived themselves to be victims of ethnically motivated hate crimes annually. However, Hart and Fellabaum (2008) describe limited publication of commissioned studies in this area, as well as underlying problems such as a lack of attention paid to defining the concept and limited consensus on appropriate variables to be measured. The adoption of the hate crime paradigm in US policy in this area was marked by the publication of two key reports; one which was a general survey of the problem (US Department of Justice Community Relations Service, 2000) and a second that investigated victim groups, offence types and the frequency and impact of hate crimes (Wessler and Moss, 2001).

Official measurement of the problem is a cornerstone of the hate crime paradigm, as it establishes consensus on its existence and problematic nature (Maroney, 1998). US data comes from a range of official sources, including the US Department of Education Campus Security Statistics and Federal Bureau of Investigation (FBI), to whom higher education institutions must report serious crimes in line with the requirements of the Clery (Hate Crime Statistics) Act 1990. Prior to the introduction of this act, the only statistical reports available came from civil rights organisations that noted increases in hate crimes throughout the 1980s (Rankin, 2003). The reporting mechanism drew both resources and attention to the issue. The FBI's annual compilation of hate crime statistics and the International Association of College Law Enforcement Administrators' annual survey of crimes on campuses add to the statistical picture. It is important to note that these reports specifically referenced on-campus events, since the Clery Act required colleges and universities across the US to report campus crime as well as incidents that occur in residential and commercial areas contiguous to campus (Dobbs et al, 2009).

There are, of course, weaknesses in the data available. Only publicly funded institutions are required to report hate crimes to the FBI, and Wessler and Moss (2001) note that the limited number of reporting institutions and the varied research instruments contribute to a disparity in results between surveys. Reporting rates by institutions have been low and unreliable too, possibly due to concerns about institutional reputation (Gregory and Janosik, 2002). In addition, students and staff have been slow to report hate crimes, with Rankin (2003) describing a widespread belief that universities would do nothing beyond the legal requirement to monitor their levels.

The use of surveys to better understand specific student–victim and student–offender groups as well as the context within which hate crimes occur is now well established across the literature (see, *inter alia,* Rayburn et al, 2003; Stotzer and Hossellman, 2012). These surveys have added to contemporary understandings of students' capacity to identify and report hate crimes. Hart and Rennison (2011), however, warn of the inability of this type of study to produce victimisation estimates for subsets of the student population. To supplement these and institutionally reported data, a range of other sources have been used that include specific information on campus location (see Strom, 2001; Hart and Rennison, 2011; Smith and Jones, 2011;).

A key point of divergence between UK and US policy literature lies in the apparent lack of availability of statistical and qualitative data on campus hate crimes in the UK, and this has had a significant impact on the capacity to generate theoretical understandings of the problem. Although the Race Relations (Amendment) Act 2000 requires universities to publish their policies and results of assessment and monitoring annually, there is no obligation to record hate incidents. In the absence of institutional data on hate crimes, published campus climate studies or institutional surveys in the UK, it has been necessary to turn to other sources. To date the British Crime Survey (BCS)[45] has been the most reliable source of information on the overall level of hate crimes, although it excludes those not living in 'normal' households, such as students' halls of residences, making assessment of students' exposure to violence more difficult to establish. Additionally, while the BCS provides figures for student respondents who have been victims of hate crimes, the numbers surveyed are so small that they cannot be representative. Trends over time are even more difficult to examine. While the BCS was able to record significant decreases in both racially motivated crimes (18%) and religiously motivated crimes (26%) in the five year period from 2005/06 to 2010/11 (Ministry of Justice, 2011), no distinct figures are available for the student population.

The first significant policy efforts to address hate crime against students in the UK emerged in 2005, when Universities UK (2005) provided specific advice to individual institutions. These guidelines are not binding, however, and institutions are encouraged to use their own internal processes to mediate and respond to hate incidents on campus, as well as making decisions about the recording of incidents. Later policy documents designed to be used in conjunction with this reflected the changing focus of policy attention towards on-campus student radicalisation risks rather than further investigation of manifestations of campus prejudices (Equality Challenge Unit, 2007; Universities UK, 2011). None of these addressed the lack of specificity within victimisation or offending figures, and instead inadvertently suggested that hate crimes in higher education are rare.

A consistent pattern in these documents is the minimal reference to academic hate crime research or known patterns of hate crime occurrence. Also, the understandings presented generally rely on hate crime statistics and guidance from the Association of Chief Police Officers (ACPO) and Home Office, as well as a range of more general materials on race equality in education and inter-faith relations (see, for example, Universities UK, 2005, 2011; Equality Challenge Unit, 2007). In contrast to the US policy literature, no attempts have been made to construct typologies of campus incidents in the UK, despite their adoption in wider academic research and policy (Burney and Rose, 2002; Iganski et al, 2005, HM Government, 2012).

An exception to this pattern is the Institute for Community Cohesion's review of campus relations (Beider and Briggs, 2010), but it too engages superficially with the available research from the US and relies on a small number of UK-based reports on the experiences of British students of diversity and tolerance (see Sims, 2007). The overwhelming focus of all of these documents is on the balancing of freedom of speech with other rights explicitly framed 'within a human rights perspective' (HM Government, 2012) rather than one of campus safety. There is no reflection, therefore, of the crime prevention work in this area on the identification of problem areas or 'hot spots'.

Other policy documents maintain a near silence on this issue. For example, the government's *Plan to Tackle Hate Crime* (HM Government, 2012) contains no references to further or higher education nor details of how progress may be measured. The picture from UK policy on campus hate crimes that emerges is one in which the impact of hate crime on students is viewed through a narrow perspective and is made from a comparatively low knowledge base.

The absence of national recording systems has not meant that the problem of hate crimes is entirely unmeasured. Universities have worked with the True Vision self-report system introduced by the Metropolitan Police Service and ACPO to encourage the reporting of incidents, and in 2008, university campuses and accommodation were included in the neighbourhood policing plan (ACPO, 2008), to facilitate the identification of 'hot spots' of student victimisation. Data collected from university populations are analysed by force area, however, and include educational campuses within neighbourhood areas (ACPO, 2008, 2012), so that they are mostly indistinguishable from other city areas.

Campaigning groups have pushed hard for the recognition of hate incidents in education, and produced statistical and case study data to draw attention to the problem. These include the Community Security Trust's annual report of anti-Semitic incidents and the FOSIS (2010) report on Muslim student safety on campus, although without systematic collection of incident reports, they offer little in the way of accurate measurement. The most significant data source to date has been produced by the National Union of Students (NUS). This survey, conducted in 2010–11 across 600 further and higher education campuses, is the only large-scale student-victim hate crime survey that has been carried out in the UK to date and represents a significant milestone in this area, collecting both quantitative and qualitative data on frequency, types and locations of attacks, reporting patterns and victim impact. The survey captured a large number of responses (9,229), but was not designed to be representative, as it relied on self-selection among respondents. It cannot therefore be read as an estimate of victimisation in the student population. The results of the survey uncovered a very high level of hate crime against students in all of the categories of protected characteristics. Around a sixth (16%) of respondents reported that they had experienced a hate incident while studying at their current institution while around one-in-twelve (8%) had experienced verbal abuse or threats of violence, while 5% experienced physical abuse. A small number reported being threatened with weapons along with physical abuse. Despite the self-selection of respondents, students displayed very low levels of reporting to other institutions with just 13% reporting incidents to their college or university, and 9% to the police (NUS, 2011a).

In the section below, the survey findings will be explored to examine the extent to which the geography of victimisation is reflected in the model adopted in the UK, and it in turn reflects the present scarcity of measurement and recording in this area.

Fit for purpose? A 'town and gown' model of hate crime

The NUS survey highlights the distance between contemporary policy attention to hate crime against students and the ways in which students experience harassment and violence as they move through campus and other spaces. It is in the discussion of space that policy literatures speak most strongly to the unique position of students on and off campus. While US academic and policy research focuses on the campus and associated spaces, the scholarly focus in the UK has primarily been on the vulnerability of students when they leave the university campus, and reflects the wider construction of students as being at high risk of victimisation (Morrall et al, 2010).

Cox (2011:88) argues that universities, particularly many of the post-war 'redbrick' institutions, display an insularity in campus life which 'serves as a ready focus of the hostility of the surrounding community', even though these communities are often reliant economically on students. These 'hostilities' are complex, being intertwined with class, economic strains and local cultures of racism. Where the university represents privilege and mobility, the town becomes defined in opposition to it as a kind of 'defended neighbourhood', meaning that the campus itself is a symbolic location. These are not always the sites of violence, but they identify who belongs to them and who does not, and are closely linked to 'mission' violence (Levin and McDevitt, 1993). Much like the mosque or the LGB-friendly bar, the campus represents diversity, and moving outside this space may mark out potential victims.

Hate crimes in cities or towns perpetrated by strangers may also be interpreted as random or opportunist violence, although these affect students only insofar as they engage with town commercial centres or choose to live in particular neighbourhoods. This perspective, reflected in hate crime prevention strategies communicated to students by universities and police (British Council, 2007), is not without difficulty however. Contemporary research on student victimisation off campus presents 'studenthood' as problematic (Wattis et al., 2011), regardless of the presence or visibility of protected characteristics, with the campus providing invisibility compared to visibility in the local area. As well as framing students' experiences of higher education within a local crime prevention agenda, it constructs students as 'naïve' or 'careless' with regard to their own safety, which has been most observable in political attention given to international student safety (British Council, 2007).

It also denies the extent to which students already distance themselves from towns and cities and alcohol-related situations, avoiding social activities, leaving home only in groups, staying home after dark or using alternatives to public transport. The low numbers of reported incidents on public transportation and in public places reflect the arduous avoidance strategies revealed by respondents in the qualitative data. There is evidence that 'vicarious victimisation' (Wattis et al, 2011) increases fears around the town centre. The NUS survey finding that 28% of students regularly alter their behaviour, personal appearance or daily patterns because of their victimisation concerns, yet only 16% have actually experienced a hate incident, pointing to a significant level of fear among this population. This may suggest that there is a strong 'ripple effect' creating a sense of vulnerability and social exclusion among students in groups with protected characteristics.

Complete avoidance of risky off-campus environments is, though, extremely difficult. Further qualitative analysis of the NUS data reveals BME respondents' reliance on employment in certain minority ethnic food outlets, LGBT students' desire to engage with LGBT-friendly environments off-campus, and respondents in all categories' reliance on public transport and central commercial areas. This level of fear may also reflect the gap between institutional constructions (or denials) of off-campus risk and the lived experiences of students.

Exploring campus-based incidents

The town and gown model lacks explanatory power when it is employed on the university campus. Higher education has been negatively associated with lower levels of support for racist violence (Bobo et al, 1996) and with lower levels of prejudice towards minority groups (Lyons, 2008). Hate crime is commonly constructed as individualised irrationality or ignorance, and as an exception that is 'backward' (Bettencourt, 2008), and thus it sits easily against the idea of the civilised community that is the campus. Dismantling this concept is essential to understanding how hate crimes can and do occur in higher education, perpetrated by highly educated members of an explicitly diverse community.

It is clear from the NUS survey findings that a significant proportion of hate-related incidents occur on-campus, with 41% of verbal abuse, 31% of physical abuse and 64% of incidents involving written or visual communications occurring in campus buildings or areas (NUS, 2011a). The Community Security Trust (2012; 2013) reports a similar pattern evident in their recorded incidents against Jewish students, and these hold true in all categories of victim (NUS, 2011b; 2012a; 2012b) except disability, where a higher proportion of on-campus incidents of all types are recorded (NUS, 2011c). The picture of hate crimes on campus is clearer when perpetrator characteristics are added. Evidence on student perpetrators is scarce (Franklin, 2000) and the NUS survey relies on victim recognition of the perpetrators as students, which may mean some under- or mis-identification. Nonetheless, respondents to the NUS survey reported that student perpetrators were involved in between 34% and 56% of incidents against each category, and enrolled at the same institution in 71% of these incidents.

As with victimisation patterns off campus, there are some explanatory gaps between the data and adopted concepts of 'student lifestyle'. Fewer incidents, for instance, take place in the commercial or entertainments areas of campus and are concentrated instead in the daytime, reflecting their 'ordinary and commonplace nature' (NUS, 2011b: 26). In fact, learning environments (lecture theatres, classrooms, libraries) appear much more prominently in the NUS statistics, with every group experiencing higher proportions of verbal harassment there than any other location, and property damage or theft (above 20%) also most likely to occur here after 'at or near home'. In contrast, on-campus physical abuse is most likely to occur in areas other than learning environments or the students' union, accounting for 31% of all incidents.

Understanding the dynamics of on-campus violence requires identifying a suitable typology of hate crimes by and against students that can adequately account for the particularities of the university campus. Considering the positions in which students are forced to continuously engage with diversity in intimate spaces (such as student accommodation), or spaces where status may be in question (classroom or nightclub), is crucial to understanding the ways in which students identify hate incidents and make decisions about reporting these. Perry (2010) argues that hate crimes on campus may not only be a way of 'doing difference', but of actualising an identity in uncertain new territory, as starting university may be the first instance in which students are confronted by diversity. Yet there is no observed correlation between levels of diversity in institutions and the frequency with which hate crimes occur, and indeed the opposite may be true (Sims, 2007), although the exact nature of this relationship remains unknown. Of use here may be the review of campus climate studies undertaken by Harper and Hurtado (2007), which points to a range of themes underpinning group tensions and hate crimes, including consensus on institutional negligence, 'race' (or difference) as an avoidable topic, overestimation of minority student satisfaction, and segregation on campus.

There is some overlap here with evidence from the UK of the relationship between everyday segregations and campus racisms. Sims'

(2007) study, situated in one UK university with high diversity, found 'ethnicity and faith lines were seen as ultimately normal though possibly threatening when they positioned to exclude others out of racist convictions' (Sims, 2007: 7). In addition, a significant proportion of respondents to the NUS survey reported regularly adopting 'passing' behaviours on campus as well as off (2011b, 2011c, 2012a). Visibility on campus plays a significant part in the victimisation of certain identities, but particularly where social interactions are enforced over prolonged periods, such as in student accommodation (Valentine et al, 2009) or shared learning spaces such as information commons (Temple, 2007).

Shared accommodation remains one of the locations that is not assessed in depth in US or UK surveys: for example, the NUS survey adopted category of 'at or near home' does not specify if it includes halls of residence, or if these are included in 'other areas of campus'. The distinction between the two will vary by institution, depending on the location of the accommodation and whether it is university-owned. The use of the term 'at or near home' also compounds incidents that occur outside students halls of residence or rented housing with those that occur inside. Further, it is impossible to establish the dynamic of the offence in terms of perpetrator-victim relationships because of the use of the labels of 'Strangers', 'Acquaintances, 'Friends', and 'Neighbours or residents of local area', which appear to be more suited to investigating 'street racisms'.

The collection of accurate data in sensitive areas like this is crucial to the development of greater theoretical understandings of hate crimes against students. Ambiguity in the relationship between perpetrator(s) and victim makes difficult the distinction between reactive and impulsive incidents, and those that are premeditated. At present we know little of the victimisation that occurs indirectly via social media or campus graffiti or signage, which is likely to be premeditated, and could be classified as mission-indiscriminate (adopting Iganski et al's (2005) term), and victimisation in other campus contexts more likely to occur in student accommodation, or in alcohol-related contexts, which might be understood as reactive or impulsive episodes. Significant number of respondents to the NUS survey perceived verbal bullying-like behaviours as 'not serious enough' to report as hate incidents. Highly visible negative public displays such as graffiti, social media messages or property damage appeared to have greater impact.

We also require the means of understanding the impact of everyday experiences of low level harassment, on and off campus, on the recipient. Mason (2005) has argued that the continuing prominence of the image of the stranger undermines our capacity to understand and identify hate crimes in everyday experiences of low level harassment. This is equally applicable in the workplace and the university, and particularly within campus learning environments. Rarely acknowledged, however, are the *multiple simultaneous* victimisations that students may experience as they move between environments populated by fellow students or by strangers. There are acknowledged problems in constructing a complete picture of student victimisations on and off campus, and in longer periods away from campus (Rayburn et al, 2003). Applying a wider net to student surveys, to capture data about past experiences or those away from university, would prove helpful in this regard.

Conclusion

This chapter has explored the patterns of understanding, recording and measurement of hate crimes against students in the policy literature of the US and UK. The results of the 2011 survey, however, demonstrate that our understandings of campus hate crime are lacking in explanatory power, and that future responses require an approach that better captures the dynamic experiences of student perpetrators and victims.

There are several short conclusions to set out here. First, the predominant conception of hate crimes within a framework of 'street racisms' has produced a 'town-and-gown' model for understanding student experiences, which has constructed off-campus spaces as dangerous, responsibilised students for their off-campus victimisation, and marked out the campus as considerably safer. This has been contradicted by survey results showing campus spaces to have significant levels of harassment and violence against all victim groups. Evidence of student avoidance strategies also highlight the extent to which a crime prevention approach can exacerbate the social distance between town and campus populations, even as the widening participation agenda in higher education seeks to close that distance.

Secondly, the gaps in our understanding of on-campus hate incidents and crimes highlight the need for accurate and in-depth investigations to better understand the dynamics of hate crime in UK higher education. The differences in the construction of the problem and responses to it in the UK and US contexts demonstrate the need for comparative studies that test and adapt concepts developed elsewhere, and construct understandings that properly fit the contemporary picture of hate crime in UK higher education. They must be fit for use too with the changing demographic of UK students and the changing landscape of learning and social environments within UK campuses.

Finally, attention must be directed to the most fundamental difference demonstrated here between policy contexts, that students of higher education institutions are recognised as potential perpetrators of violence, and that their attitudes and behaviours may be prompted or facilitated by institutional racisms, and the failings of universities to foster good relations between persons from different backgrounds.

References

Association of Chief Police Officers (ACPO) (2008) *The Application of Neighbourhood Policing to HEIs*, London: Association of Chief Police Officers of England, Wales and Northern Ireland.

Association of Chief Police Officers (ACPO) (2012) *Recorded Hate Crime Data for 2011 for England, Wales and Northern Ireland* [online], London: Association of Chief Police Officers of England, Wales and Northern Ireland, www.report-it.org.uk/.

Athwal, H., Bourne, J. and Wood, R. (2010) *Racial Violence: The Buried Issue*, London: Institute of Race Relations.

Barberet, R., Fisher, B.S. and Taylor, H. (2004) *University Student Safety in the East Midlands*, London: Home Office.

Beider, H. and Briggs, R. (2010) *Promoting Cohesion and Preventing Violent Extremism in Higher and Further Education*, London: Institute of Community Cohesion.

Bettencourt, L. (2008) 'Defeating the Purpose of Multiculturalism: a Case of Hate on Campus', Paper 80, *Ryerson University Theses and dissertations*, http://digitalcommons.ryerson.ca/dissertations/80.

Bobo, L., Kluegel, J.R. and Smith, R.A. (1996) 'Laissez-Faire Racism: The Crystallization of a Kinder, Gentler Antiblack Ideology', in S.A. Tuch and J.K. Martin (eds) *Racial Attitudes in the 1990s: Continuity and Change,* Westport, CT.: Praeger, pp. 15–42.

British Council (2007) *Creating Confidence: International Student Safety Survey*, Manchester: British Council Education UK Marketing.

Burney, E. and Rose, G. (2002) *Racist Offences: How Is the Law Working?*, Home Office Research Study no. 244, London: Home Office.

Community Security Trust (2012) *Antisemitic Incidents Report 2011*, London: Community Security Trust.

Community Security Trust (2013) *Antisemitic Incidents Report 2012*, London: Community Security Trust.

Cox, A. (2011) 'Students' Experience of University Space: an Exploratory Study', *International Journal of Teaching and Learning in Higher Education*, 23 (2): 197–207.

Dobbs, R.R., Waid, C.A. and O'Connor, T.S. (2009) 'Explaining Fear of Crime as Fear of Rape Among College Females: An Examination of Multiple Campuses in the United States', *International Journal of Social Inquiry*, 2 (2): 105–22.

Ehrlich, H.J. (1994) 'Reporting Ethnoviolence: Newspaper Treatment of Race and Ethnic Conflict', *Z Magazine*, June, 53–60.

Equality Challenge Unit (2007) *Update: Promoting Good Campus Relations – an Institutional Imperative*, September, London: Equality Challenge Unit.

Fisher, B.S., Sloan, J.J., Cullen, F.T. and Lu, C. (1998) 'Crime in the Ivory Tower: The Level and Sources of Student Victimization, *Criminology*, 36 (3): 671–710.

FOSIS (2010) *Muslim Students and Safety on Campus: 2010 Briefing*, London: Federation of Student Islamic Societies.

Franklin, K. (2000) 'Antigay Behaviors among Young Adults: Prevalence, Patterns, and Motivators in a Noncriminal Population', *Journal of Interpersonal Violence*, 15 (4): 339–62.

Gregory, D.E. and Janosik, S.M. (2002) 'Clery Act: How Effective Is It – Perceptions from the Field – The Current State of the Research and Recommendations for Improvement', *Stetson Law Review*, 32 (1): 7–59.

Harper, S.R. and Hurtado, S. (2007) 'Nine Themes in Campus Racial Climates and Implications for Institutional Transformation', in S.R. Harper and L.D. Patton (eds) *Responding to the Realities of Race on Campus. New Directions for Student Services,* San Francisco: Jossey-Bass, pp. 7–24.

Hart, J. and Fellabaum, J. (2008) 'Analysing Campus Climate Studies: Seeking to Define and Understand', *Journal of Diversity in Higher Education*, 1 (4): 222–34.

Hart, T.C. and Rennison, C.M. (2011) 'Violent Victimization of Hispanic College Students Findings From the National Crime Victimization Survey', *Race and Justice*, 1 (4): 362–85.

HM Government (2012) *Challenge It, Report It, Stop It: The Government's Plan to Tackle Hate Crime*, March 2012, London: HM Government.

Iganski, P., Kielinger, V. and Paterson, S. (2005) *Hate Crimes Against London's Jews*, London: Institute for Jewish Policy Research.

Levin, J. and McDevitt, J. (1993) *Hate Crimes: The Rising Tide of Bigotry and Bloodshed,* New York: Plenum.

Lyons, C.J. (2008) 'Individual Perceptions and the Social Construction of Hate Crimes: A Factorial Survey', *The Social Science Journal*, 45 (1): 107–31.

Maroney, T.A. (1998) 'Struggle against Hate Crime: Movement at a Crossroads', *NYUL Review*, 73 (2): 564.

Mason, G. (2005) 'Hate Crime and the Image of the Stranger', *British Journal of Criminology*, 45 (6): 837–59.

Ministry of Justice (2011) *Statistics on Race and the Criminal Justice System 2010: A Ministry of Justice publication under Section 95 of the Criminal Justice Act 1991*, October, London: Ministry of Justice, at www.justice. gov.uk/downloads/statistics/mojstats/stats-race-cjs-2010.pdf.

Morrall, P., Marshall, P., Pattison, S. and MacDonald, G. (2010) Crime and Health: a Preliminary Study into the Effects of Crime on the Mental Health of UK University Students, *Journal of Psychiatric and Mental Health Nursing*, 17 (9): 821–8.

National Union of Students (NUS) (2011a) *Hate Crime Interim Report: Exploring Students' Understanding, Awareness and Experiences of Hate Incidents,* London: National Union of Students.

NUS (2011b) *No Place for Hate: Hate Crimes and Incidents in Further and Higher Education: Sexual Orientation and Gender Identity,* London: National Union of Students.

NUS (2011c) *No Place for Hate: Hate Crimes and Incidents in Further and Higher Education: Disability,* London: National Union of Students.

NUS (2012a) *No Place for Hate: Hate Crimes and Incidents in Further and Higher Education: Race and Ethnicity,* London: National Union of Students.

NUS (2012b) *No Place for Hate: Hate Crimes and Incidents in Further and Higher Education: Religion or Belief,* London: National Union of Students.

Perry, B. (2010) 'No Biggie': the Denial of Oppression on Campus', *Education, Citizenship and Social Justice*, November 2010, 5 (3): 265–79.

Rankin, S.R. (2003) *Campus Climate for Gay, Lesbian, Bisexual and Transgender People: A National Perspective,* National Gay and Lesbian Task Force Policy Institute.

Rayburn, N.R., Earlywine, M. and Davison, G.C. (2003) 'Base Rates of Hate Crime Victimisation among College Students', *Journal of Interpersonal Violence*, 18 (10): 1209–21.

Sims, J.M. (2007) *Not Enough Understanding? Student Experiences of Diversity in UK Universities,* London: Runnymede Trust.

Smith, S.S. and Jones, J.A.M. (2011) 'Intraracial Harassment on Campus: Explaining Between-and Within-group Differences, *Ethnic and Racial Studies*, 34 (9): 1567–93.

Stotzer, R.L. and Hossellman, E. (2012) 'Hate Crimes on Campus: Racial/Ethnic Diversity and Campus Safety', *Journal of Interpersonal Violence*, 27 (4): 644–61.

Strom, K.J. (2001) *Hate Crimes Reported in NIBRS, 1997-99,* Bureau of Justice Statistics Special Report, US Department of Justice Statistics: NCJ 186765.

Temple, P. (2007) *Learning Spaces for the 21st Century: a Review of the Literature,* London: Institute of Education.

Tyrer, D. and Ahmad, F. (2006) *Muslim Women and Higher Education: Identities, Experiences and Prospects,* Liverpool John Moores University and European Social Fund, Oxford: Oxuniprint.

Universities UK (2005) *Promoting Good Campus Relations: Dealing with Hate Crimes and Intolerance,* London: Universities UK.

Universities UK (2011) *Freedom of Speech on Campus: Rights and Responsibilities in UK Universities,* London: Universities UK

US Department of Justice and Community Relations Service (2000) *Responding to Hate Crimes and Bias-Motivated Incidents on College/ University Campuses,* Washington, DC: Department of Justice Community Relations Service.

Valentine, G., Wood, N. and Plummer, P. (2009) *The Experience of Lesbian, Gay, Bisexual and Trans Staff and Students in Higher Education,* March 2009, London: Equality Challenge Unit.

Wattis, L., Green, E. and Radford, J. (2011) 'Women Students' Perceptions of Crime and Safety: Negotiating Fear and Risk in an English Post-industrial Landscape', *Gender, Place & Culture: A Journal of Feminist Geography,* 18 (6): 749–67.

Wessler, S. and Moss, M. (2001) *Hate Crimes on Campus: The Problem and Efforts to Confront It,* Hate Crime Series, no 3, Washington, DC: US Department of Justice, Office of Justice Programs, Bureau of Justice Assistance.

TWELVE

We need to talk about women: examining the place of gender in hate crime policy

Hannah Mason-Bish

Introduction

During a recent seminar on hate crime with my first year undergraduates I found myself faced with an all too familiar student query. Having just delivered my lecture on the emergence and problem of hate crime, we sat down to discuss the many different categories that they might include in their own imaginary policy. The inclusion of religion, subculture and appearance led to a heated debate as students observed these to be changeable categories that might be chosen by the victim and not always intrinsic to their character. However, gender was fixed in their minds as a clear cut example of hate crime, which alongside race and sexual orientation, was an aspect of life that was central to daily experiences of discrimination. Of course hate crime scholars can unpick the flaws in the argument of my students, but it has always struck me as curious that in nine years of teaching on the subject, every year students query the exclusion of gender from hate crime policy and ask me why. For them it is obvious, gender is an intrinsic characteristic that cannot be hidden and people are attacked because of it. This discussion is not uncommon with those working outside of academia too who might over a cup of tea, ponder why violence against women is treated differently from violence on the basis of race or sexual orientation.

Aside from my personal experience of discussing gender and hate crime, there are also a number of high profile cases that raise questions about the nature of gender-related violence. In 2008 Levi Bellfield was convicted of the murders of two women and the attempted murder of a third. He has since been convicted of the murder of Milly Dowler. He was described as a 'man with a hatred of women – especially blondes', who had spent many years bullying, attacking and ultimately murdering women (*Independent*, 2011; Drew, 2008). He would often seek out young runaways from care homes or others whose lives made them particularly vulnerable. Yet his deliberate targeting of a particular group passed with very little comment in media reports. A similar serial killer whose victims were selected on the basis of race or sexual orientation would surely have garnered a media examination of racist or homophobic motivation. The notion of gender hatred or gender motivation seems to pass unnoticed by the media and policy makers.

Internationally, gender remains a protected status in hate crime legislation. The recent report by the Office for Democratic Institutions and Human Rights looking at hate crimes in the OSCE region found that gender was recorded as a hate crime group in fifteen states including Belgium, France and Poland (ODIHR, 2012). In the United States, 27 states have enhanced penalties for gender and it was added to federal legislation in 2009 (Anti-Defamation League, 2012). Yet while it is not recorded in Britain, research shows that gender-related hate crimes are happening and victims are identifying them as such. In March 2012, the *British Crime Survey* (BCS) supplement on hate crime and cyber security was published (Smith et al, 2012). Combining the results of the 2009/10 and 2010/11 BCS, it showed that around 0.5% of people had been victims of hate crime in the previous 12 months (Smith et al, 2012: 13). The survey found that there were, out of a total of 260,000 hate incidents per year, around 120,000 incidents that were gender-motivated, with women being more likely than men to have experienced them (Smith et al, 2012: 25). As respondents were able to tick multiple motivations where relevant, it is difficult to ascertain how many were seemingly aggravated by gender alone or in combination with other factors. Nevertheless, the fact that gender was selected more frequently than religion, disability and sexual orientation raises questions that policy and research have been unable to answer. The nature, location and effects of gender motivated hatred remain unexamined. The hate crime academy has also largely ignored or overlooked gender.

This chapter aims to explore how the category of gender has proved controversial for hate crime policy and research. It will begin with a brief outline of the development of the hate crime policy domain and then move on to explore the reasons that provide an explanation for the exclusion of gender. It will then discuss what an examination of gender can add to our understanding of hate crime policy and contribute to scholarship. Importantly, this chapter does not aim to argue for or against its inclusion as a new 'strand' in the hate crime approach. However, the examination of arguments surrounding gender-motivated violence necessarily follows a policy domain that is defined by adding victim groups. Fundamentally, this chapter will show that understanding the lived experience of hate crime for individual victims is a more productive approach. However, the exclusion of gender from hate crime research and practice has meant that the gendered experiences of many hate crimes victims are often overlooked. Instead it is argued that academics and practitioners might want to consider the complex harms caused to victims of hate crime rather than focusing on their membership of a particular identity group.

Gender and hate crime policy

Hate crime legislation in Great Britain encompasses laws that mandate a harsher sentence for crimes aggravated by hostility on the basis of race, religion, sexual orientation and disability. These are accompanied by criminal justice policy that has now agreed a definition of hate crime and the strands that will be monitored. Despite its current exclusion from British hate crime policy, gender has been the subject of some limited debate. For published policy debates on the issue, we have to examine the Scottish Working Group on Hate Crime which was set up as a direct consequence of an amendment to the Criminal Justice (Scotland) Bill which included age and gender as potential hate crime categories. The consultation document included a breakdown of the different groups affected by possible hatred, although one cannot help but note that gender was presented as a 'difficult' group and questions were raised as to why it might not fit within a hate crime definition. For example, the section on gender asked whether, given that half the population is female, a change in the law might 'protect the entire population'. Gender was excluded partly because hate crime has a 'random nature to it … rather than because of any prior relationship between perpetrator and victim' (Scottish Executive, 2004, pt 5.35: 27). A subsequent review found that concerns over evidence gathering, and that a hate crime approach might not pick up on the complexities of violence against women, were also noted as reasons for its exclusion (Burman et al, 2009: 27).

In England and Wales the debate over the exclusion of gender is more difficult to decipher. Peter Tatchell's original amendment to the Crime and Disorder Bill in 1998 had included a wide list of provisions including political opinion, sex, medical conditions and gender identity (Tatchell, 2002: 62). As noted in my own research, when the Association of Chief Police Officers (ACPO) have reviewed their hate crime policy and monitored strands, the category of gender has been subjected to detailed debate but always been excluded in the end. Fundamentally, this has been due to concerns about police officers being able to correctly identify gender hate crime and about the historic treatment of domestic violence and rape (Mason-Bish, 2012). It would be hard to determine which cases of domestic violence are hate crimes and which are not. Instead, the government has said that while gender will not be a monitored strand of hate crime, individual police forces can treat it as a hate crime to respond to concerns of local citizens (HM Government, 2012: 6). These debates about the exclusion of gender or its discretionary inclusion at the local level have existed largely outside of hate crime scholarship.

Where academic debate has provided a contribution is in understanding the purpose of legislating against hate and how it should be defined. There is some consensus that hate crimes are 'message crimes' which send a signal to the victimised group that they are not welcome. As such, society must respond by sending an equally strong message that prejudice will not be tolerated, via a harsh sentencing framework (Dixon and Gadd, 2006: 307). The harm caused by hate crime goes beyond the initial victim to the community, which is the aim of the perpetrator attempting to 're-establish their 'proper' relative positions, as given and reproduced by broader ideologies and patterns of social and political inequality' (Perry, 2001: 10). Generally then, hate crimes are targeted towards groups who have historically had a subordinate position in society. Such an understanding can in part explain the decision of policy makers to protect groups who have a proven experience of victimisation and who also have a long history of being treated unfairly or targeted due to difference. However, deciding who to protect is far from an easy decision and not without consequence.

The silo approach to hate crime policy is arguably one of its defining features and biggest problems. This has developed historically, as legislation in Britain has emerged via social movement activists pushing for change. The racist murder of Stephen Lawrence led to the Crime and Disorder Act 1998 creating specific offences for certain crimes that were racially aggravated, meaning that people convicted of racist hate crimes could be punished more harshly than offenders committing the same offence but without the motivation. This legislation has since been extended to include religious aggravation and in 2003, the government empowered the judiciary to enhance sentences on the basis of hostility towards sexual orientation and disability. The recent decision to create a mandatory minimum 30 year sentence for transphobic murder might be indicative of a future move towards adding gender identity to the list of protected statuses. Great Britain is not unusual in adding groups and re-shaping hate crime policy as time moves on. However, there are a number of problems with such an approach. Critics such as Jacobs and Potter (1998) worried about the 'balkanising' effect of legislation, which would cause resentment between groups excluded and included in hate crime provisions. This has meant that groups left outside of hate crime policy are sent a negative message that their victimisation is not important enough to gain recognition (Mason-Bish, 2012). Jon Garland's (2010: 41) work on attacks against people of the Goth subculture directs us towards a need to focus more on the reasons behind victimisation rather than historical oppression or group membership. This supports the work of Jo Morgan who was concerned about excluding hate crime victims from policy because they lacked political clout or popular support (Morgan, 2002: 32). This creates a victim hierarchy, where those included matter and those excluded, don't. Another problem of recognition presents itself too if we are to question the approach of having separate victim strands. People rarely fit into one box and so to identify hate crimes as separate and neat entities is to underplay the complexity of the victim experience and to risk the reification of identity. This forms the central plank of the chapter because examining gender in relation to hate crime victimisation can actually highlight the need to move away from policy and practice, which has focused on the perceived membership of one identity group.

Considering gender

An examination of gender in relation to hate crime highlights some important assumptions about the framing of violence and a need to understand the historical and cultural context. While undertaking my doctoral research on the emergence of hate crime provisions in Great Britain, I interviewed over fifty 'key informants' who were either campaign activists or senior members of the criminal justice system who were making or implementing policy. It was evident that policy to deal with violence against women (including for domestic violence and rape) pre-dated hate crime policy (Mason-Bish, 2012). As such, women already have their own 'special' laws to deal with the predominant forms of violence against them. This too mirrors the academic field, where research has a long legacy and violence against women might include domestic violence, so-called honour killings, rape, sexual assault, murder, trafficking, sexual harassment and stalking (Kelly and Lovett, 2005: 7). A wealth of scholarly research now exists that explains the continuum of violence against women and how each typology of violence and harm might contribute to wider notions of misogyny and abuse. However, there is very little published discourse evaluating the merits of a hate crime approach, save for a few occasional commentaries. Instead, questions have largely focused on whether domestic violence is a hate crime as this is the predominant crime associated with female victims of crime. During the Scottish Working Group on Hate Crime's consultation process, many responses alluded to this:

> The Unit's view is that domestic violence is abuse of power within a relationship, whereby the man seeks to exert his power over his female partner but does not generally abuse other women. (Scottish Executive, 2004: 27)

This quote touches on a key argument often used to justify the exclusion of gender: interchangeability. Hate crimes, it has been argued, have a terrorising effect because the victim could be anyone who fits within that identity group (Iganski, 1999). However, for victims of domestic violence, the personal relationship might remove that random nature of risk. Critics have argued against this notion, suggesting that a male perpetrator of domestic violence might be a serial offender thus meaning that his victim is interchangeable – they just have to be a woman in a relationship (Taylor, 1996). Such a view also underplays the fear that many women have of rape or sexual assault when living their daily lives and the precautions they take to avoid it.

The issue of personal relationships between the victim and perpetrator has been at issue with other types of violence against women too. Beverley McPhail has noted that this idea has always put female victims of crime in a difficult situation. Marital rape was only recently made a criminal offence in the UK[46] because the personal relationship between a husband and wife often meant that the criminality involved was obscured (McPhail, 2002: 268). Even so, a growing body of scholarly work has examined the relationship between victims and perpetrators and disputed the idea of hate crime as stranger danger anyway (Mason, 2005). Hate crime policy in other areas of victimisation has also shifted to recognise that violence might be perpetrated by a friend, relative or carer and might happen in the context of an intimate personal relationship (Crown Prosecution Service, 2010). Nevertheless, these remain complex aspects of hate crime policy and it has been suggested that for gender-based violence, there are 'particular vulnerabilities on the part of the victim that mark this sort of crime out from other forms of hate crime that are motivated by hatred towards a particular group of people' (Burman et al, 2009: 29). Interestingly though, for arguments around the inclusion of gender in hate crime policy the debate often gets stuck on whether or not domestic violence is a hate crime, rather than as part of a spectrum of gender-based hate crime.

An examination of gender-based violence and hate crime policy also serves to highlight the complex relationships between campaigners, policy makers and researchers. The role of social movement activists has been central to the development of legislative provisions and the victim groups included represent those who have gathered data about their victimisation, lobbied policymakers and been involved with advisory groups (Mason-Bish, 2010). The exclusion of gender is therefore partly due to decisions made by those designing policy but also about campaigners' cynicism over the hate crime approach. During my own research I interviewed a leading campaigner on disability issues who had tried to put forward an amendment which would add gender to the list of protected statuses as well as disability, which was not included at that time. He observed:

> I really needed the support of the Equal Opportunities Commission and I also talked to the leading gender organisations and just couldn't get the support and they just didn't want to take it up. I would be stupid to fight for gender on my own. You can only take the women's movement to the water, you can't make them drink. (Mason-Bish, 2009: 199)

While there may be many violence against women charities and campaigners who do support the inclusion of gender-based violence in hate crime provisions, there has not been a campaign or a further attempt to amend legislation. Rather than being excluded from policy, sometimes groups evaluate the practical outcome of directing resources to new legislation. Scottish group Engender noted that many groups did not support the inclusion of gender because they were:

> sceptical about the potential efficacy of such legislative remedies, or the relative priority of lobbying on hate crimes legislation ... It has underlined the relative difficulty in effecting influence through a show of consensus, when issues relating to gender are complex and multi-faceted. (Engender, 2006: 40)

Even if campaigners were to push for the inclusion of gender-based violence in hate crime provisions, it would be unlikely that a consensus could be reached about which forms of it would be protected. Furthermore, there are questions about whether or not it would lead to a real change in the treatment of female victims of violence and that it would 'not necessarily reduce the scale or impact of such violence, or change its nature' (Burman et al, 2009: 28). Academic Phyllis Gerstenfeld succinctly described the concern that victims of violence against women would be 'subsumed under the larger rubric of bias crime, and thus will be largely forgotten' (Gerstenfeld, 2004: 9). The ability of hate crime legislation to effect real change for victims of violence against women is thus questioned. So a consideration of gender and hate crime policy shows that it is not just about understanding which groups are excluded, but whether some might exclude themselves after an evaluation of pragmatic concerns.

A further problem of the identity group based approach to hate crime shows itself most sharply when considering the issue of numbers. Women are not a minority group, so would protecting them be in the spirit of the law? The Scottish Working Group explained their decision not to include gender in their proposals:

> In the case of gender, given that approximately half the population is male and approximately half is female, a change in the law to highlight motivation of hatred of the victim because they are male or female would be potentially protecting the entire population. (Scottish Executive, 2004, rec 3.21: 11)

Hate crime scholars have certainly been concerned with identifying victim communities and in the characteristics that link victimisation and its negative effects. For Barbara Perry, hate crime victims are subordinates in society who are targeted by a dominant and more powerful group (Perry, 2009). It is not difficult to perceive that victims of gender-based violence are a structural minority, who share a history of oppression and are attacked in sufficient numbers. As the Scottish Executive noted, violence against women 'reveals deep historical, cultural and legal roots in relation to the subordination of women' (Burman et al, 2009: 25). However, more recently hate crime research has moved to look at the concept of 'othering' and the extent to which in the eyes of an offender, the target group is an 'outsider'. Jon Garland's work on the Goth subculture suggests that harassment and violence might not just be about keeping a subordinate in their place but more broadly about a fear of difference (Garland, 2010: 54). Women might not been an obvious group who are outsiders, considering that they make up half of the population. However, it might be that victims of all hate crime have complex memberships of different groups that shift according to time and space. In 2006, Merseyside Police announced that they would be recognising sex workers as potential victims of hate crime (Campbell and Stoops, 2010). Identifying them as targets of hostility and working in vulnerable or risky situations, the police directed resources towards victims and encouraged reporting rates by working with the local community. The gender and lifestyle of the victims in this case leads to an increased vulnerability to attack based on their identity. As Chakraborti and Garland observe:

> they may become a victim because of how that aspect of their identity intersects with other aspects of their self, and with other situational factors and context, to make them vulnerable in the eyes of the perpetrator. (Chakraborti and Garland, 2012: 508)

The hate crime approach has often failed to acknowledge such issues of intersectionality, to which this chapter now turns.

It could be suggested that the omission of gender from policy as a single strand has meant that its effect on victimisation in other areas has been similarly overlooked. In her examination of hate crime policy, Joanna Perry noted that the possible neglect of gender as a hate crime perspective might 'contribute to inadequate crime prevention planning and ineffective responses' (Perry, J., 2009: 15). Hate crime policy is guilty not just of excluding some victim groups, but of not recognising the diversity of groups already included in policy. For example, the banner of 'homophobic hate crime' includes gay men, lesbians and the transgender community into one group when their experiences might also be very different on the basis of gender and other factors. Research has shown that transgender women are 10% more likely to experience harassment than transgender men (Turner et al, 2009: 6). They are also more likely to experience violence and for that to be influenced by their perceived gender transgressions. Research looking at the experiences of disabled people has found that they are at increased risk of hate crime victimisation if they are a woman. (Sin et al, 2009: 20). As such, gender in hate crime can have a compounding effect on victims and make them more vulnerable.

When in-depth research has been carried out looking at the intersection of identity, it has been very illuminating. In her work on how lesbians negotiate public space, Corteen observes that the feelings of safety related to their sexuality cannot be separated from discourse on violence against women and stranger danger (Corteen, 2002: 266). Those people who deviate from gender norms find themselves more likely to experience disapproval, violence or even death (Corteen, 2002: 260). What might come under the rubric of homophobic hate crime cannot be understood without examining the key role that gender plays in experiences of violence towards lesbians. As such, she found that the women would underplay the significance of gender related abuse and blame their sexuality. This might be partly caused by the normalisation of gender abuse and the reinforcement that it is not serious. Furthermore, Corteen (2002: 270) noted that the women interviewed felt more likely to be attacked when they were lacking obvious feminine attributes, such as not wearing a skirt or the right shoes. Negotiating heterosexual space means performing gender roles which might be more likely to lead to the perceived 'othering' so associated with hate crime. How these two aspects of identity interact in the victim's behaviour to prevent hate crime has not been subject to much research. Moreover, Corteen's discussion about the underplaying of gender abuse and how this connects with the perception of hate crime as 'serious' is also an area for further investigation.

Conclusion

The hate crime policy domain in Britain has developed as a response to violence targeted at specific identity groups and a subsequent campaign to make the criminal justice system take action. Policy has been revised, definitions altered and victim strands have been added to the list of protected groups. Gender has been excluded from this largely because violence against women was perceived as already being dealt with elsewhere, under rape and domestic violence policy. This has meant that there has not been a campaign to get gender recognised, as the practical arguments outweigh any conceptual connections that might be made with the hate crime model. However, this has also stymied hate crime research, with the category of gender being under examined. To an extent, academic research on this area has taken its lead from policy developments. Policy makers have also tended to follow the identity group model, meaning that Police and CPS guidance on hate crime has often focused on whether gender is or is not a hate crime.

Yet this chapter shows that considering gender adds a lot to the hate crime debate. First, it questions our conception of hate crime victims as a minority group, feared for their 'difference'. It shows that women might also be in vulnerable situations dependent on other aspects of their identity such as race, disability or sexual orientation. They share a lot with more established and understood hate crime victim categories. Secondly, it illuminates the role of activists and challenges the assumption that categories excluded from hate crime policy are being sent a message that they are irrelevant or not cared about. Thirdly, and possibly most importantly, it serves to highlight the problems of the 'silo' approach to hate crime policy and to force a discussion on issues of intersectionality. The findings from the recent BCS showed that 120,000 victims identified themselves as having been subject to a gender-related hate crime and we can only guess how many are victims of complex, multi-sectional hate incidents. This is where the research agenda needs to move and the work of Corteen (2002) on the gendered experience of lesbians is a good example of such studies. Hate crime research needs to do more here and to understand how victims negotiate space and the performativity of gender.

Where next for policy? At the beginning of the chapter I was clear that it was not an objective to argue for the inclusion of gender as a new strand. Instead, it is about understanding the lived – sometimes gendered – experiences of hate crime victims. To assume that a gay man and lesbian woman have the same experience of hate crime is to ignore the importance of gender. As such we might move towards an approach which identifies 'that *all* vulnerable communities and social groups, irrespective of minority or majority status, can be the subject of hate crime' (Garland and Chakraborti, 2012: 49). This means that policy makers and practitioners should focus less on the victim's perceived membership of a set of identity categories and more on the harm caused by their victimisation. This might hopefully lead to an approach which understands the complexity of the victim experience and which obviates the need for a list of groups. As this chapter has shown, the group-based approach overlooks the reality of victimisation and how aspects of identity intersect and differ across time and space.

References

Anti-Defamation League (ADL) (2012) 'Anti-Defamation League: Combating Hate', www.adl.org/combating_hate/.

Burman, M., Johnstone, J., de Haan, J. and McLeod, J. (2009) *Responding to Gender-based Violence in Scotland*, Scotland: EHRC.

Campbell, R. and Stoops, S. (2010) 'Treating Violence against Women as a Hate Crime', www.rhrealitycheck.org/blog/2010/12/16/draft-treating-violence-against-workershate-crime-liverpool.

Chakraborti, N. and Garland, J. (2012) 'Reconceptualising Hate Crime Victimization through the Lens of Vulnerability and "Difference"', *Theoretical Criminology*, 16 (4): 499–514.

Corteen, K. (2002) 'Lesbian Safety Talk: Problematizing Definitions and Experiences of Violence, Sexuality and Space', *Sexualities*, 5: 259–80.

Crown Prosecution Service (2010) *Disability Hate Crime: Guidance on the Distinction between Vulnerability and Hostility in the Context of Crimes Committed against Disabled People*, London: Crown.

Dixon, B. and Gadd, D. (2006) 'Getting the Message? New Labour and the Criminalization of Hate', *Criminology and Criminal Justice*, 6 (3): 309–28.

Drew, J. (2008) 'The Epidemic of Male Violence against Women', www.thefword.org.uk/features/2008/04/the_epidemic_of.

Engender (2007) 'Measuring Influence', internal memo, unpublished.

Garland, J. (2010) 'The Victimisation of Goths and the Boundaries of Hate Crime', in N. Chakraborti, (ed.) *Hate Crime: Concepts, Policy, Future Directions*, Cullompton: Willan, pp. 40–57.

Garland, J. and Chakraborti, N. (2012) 'Divided by a Common Concept? Assessing the Implications of Different Conceptualizations of Hate Crime in the European Union', *European Journal of Criminology*, 9 (1): 38–52.

Gerstenfeld, P. (2004) *Hate Crimes: Causes, Controls, and Controversies*. USA: Sage.

HM Government. (2012) *Challenge it, Report it, Stop it: The Government's Plan to Tackle Hate Crime*, London: Crown.

Iganski, P. (1999) 'Why Make "Hate" a Crime?', *Critical Social Policy*, 19 (3): 386–95.

Independent (2011) 'Levi Bellfield Hated Blonde Women', 24 June, www.independent.co.uk/news/uk/crime/levi-bellfield-hated-blonde-women-2302339.html.

Jacobs, J. and Potter, K. (1998) *Hate Crimes – Criminal Law and Identity Politics*, New York: Aldine De Gruyter.

Kelly, L. and Lovett, J. (2005) *What a Waste: The Case for an Integrated Violence against Women Strategy*, Women's National Commission. London: London Metropolitan University, www.endviolenceagainstwomen.org.uk/data/files/what_a_waste__the_case_for_an_integrated_violence_against_women_strategy_final.pdf.

Mason, G. (2005) 'Being Hated: Stranger or Familiar?', *Social and Legal Studies: An International Journal*, 14 (4): 585–605.

Mason-Bish, H. (2009) *Hate Crime Policy in Great Britain: Establishing, Expanding and Exploring a Policy Domain*, unpublished PhD thesis.

Mason-Bish, H. (2010) 'Future Directions for Hate Crime Policy', in N. Chakraborti (ed.) *Hate Crime: Concepts, Policy, Future Directions,* Cullompton: Willan, pp. 58–77.

Mason-Bish, H. (2012) 'Examining the Boundaries of Hate Crime Policy: Considering Age and Gender', *Criminal Justice Policy Review,* published online first 4 January 2012.

McPhail, B. (2002) 'Gender-Bias Hate Crimes: a Review', in B. Perry (ed.) *Hate and Bias Crime: A Reader,* New York: Routledge, pp. 261–80.

Morgan, J. (2002) 'US Hate Crime Legislation: a Legal Model to Avoid in Australia', *Journal of Sociology,* 38 (1): 25–48.

ODIHR (2012) *Hate Crimes in the Osce Region – Incidents and Responses Annual Report 2011,* Warsaw: ODIHR, http://tandis.odihr.pl/hcr2011/.

Perry, B. (2001) *In the Name of Hate,* New York and London: Routledge.

Perry, B. (2004) 'The Semantics of Hate', *Journal of Hate Studies,* 4: 121–37.

Perry, B. (2009) 'The Sociology of Hate: Theoretical Approaches', in B. Levin (ed.) *Hate Crimes: Understanding and Defining Hate Crime,* Westport, CT: Praeger, pp. 55–76.

Perry, J. (2009) 'At the Intersection: Hate Crime Policy and Practice in England and Wales', *Safer Communities,* 8 (4).

Scottish Executive. (2004b) *Working Group on Hate Crime Report.* Edinburgh: Scottish Executive, www.scotland.gov.uk/Resource/Doc/26350/0025008.pdf.

Sheffield, C. (1995) 'Hate Violence', in P. Rothenburg (ed.) *Race, Class and Gender in the United States,* New York: St Martins Press, pp. 432–441.

Sin, C.H., Hedges, A., Cook, C., Mguni, M. and Comber, N. (2009) *Disabled People's Experiences of Targeted Violence and Hostility,* London: Equality and Human Rights Commission, www.equalityhumanrights.com/uploaded_files/research/disabled_people_s_experiences_of_targeted_violence_and_hostility.pdf.

Smith, K. (ed.), Lader, D., Hoare, J. and Lau, I. (2012) *Hate Crime, Cyber Security and the Experience of Crime Amongst Children, Findings from the 2010/11 British Crime Survey Supplementary Volume 3 to Crime in England and Wales 2010/11,* London: Crown.

Tatchell, P. (2002) 'Some People are More Equal Than Others', in P. Iganski (ed.) *The Hate Debate: Should Hate Be Punished as a Crime?,* London, UK: Profile Books, pp. 54–70.

Taylor, K. (1996) 'Treating Male Violence Against Women as a Bias Crime', *Boston University Law Review,* 76: 575.

Turner, L., Whittle, S and Combs, R. (2009) *Transphobic Hate Crime in the European Union*, London: Press for Change, www.ucu.org.uk/media/pdf/r/6/transphobic_hate_crime_in_eu.pdf.

PART THREE

Challenging prejudice: combating hate offending

Over the last twenty years or so the focus of much scholarly endeavour in the field of hate crime has been on the complexities of hate-related victimisation, including its nature, frequency and impact across a range of minority communities. This laudable pursuit has helped to develop more nuanced understandings of the process of victimisation and its malign effects. However, until recently comparatively little research has been undertaken into how to combat the prejudice that fuels this behaviour, or how policing policies and practices can be developed that provide an effective and empathetic service for those who are victimised.

Part Three showcases some recent research into new initiatives in the area of challenging offending behaviour which has helped to redress this imbalance. Barbara Perry and D. Ryan Dyck begin this section with an account of how scholars and activists can work in successful partnership in the development and use of an educational resource that challenges homophobic and transphobic prejudice in the Canadian context. Perry and Dyck describe how the resource, including a documentary, proved to be effective in raising awareness of the harms of these forms of hate while also providing a degree of affirmation for lesbian, gay, bisexual, trans, queer audience members. Following this, Gail Mason, Jude McCulloch and JaneMaree Maher reflect on their own research into the effectiveness of the policing of hate crime in Australia via a case study of their research partnership with Victoria Police. The authors emphasise the importance of developing a shared understanding of the nature of prejudice motivated crime between academics and the criminal justice system to the formation of effective policing responses to it. Zoë James then outlines the types of harassment and violence experienced by Gypsies and Travellers; communities that are themselves often marginalised from mainstream discussions of hate crime. Zoë suggests that some of the sedentarist prejudices that influence this hate-related behaviour also inform some of the policing policies that can therefore fail to provide the kind of support needed by victims of targeted violence within those communities.

The last two chapters share some common themes as both examine the effectiveness of different methods of working with hate crime offenders through restorative interventions. The first, by Paul Iganski with Karen Ainsworth, Laura Geraghty, Spyridoula Lagou and Nafysa Patel, outlines the potential of programmes, informed by an in-depth understanding of the hurts of hate crime, to work effectively with those who have committed hate offences and with those who have the potential to. The second, by Mark Walters, draws on his own research to demonstrate how restorative interventions can, in certain instances, develop empathy between offender and victim which can lead the former to realise the impact of their actions on the latter. This in turn can result in the modification of the perpetrator's hate-motivated behaviour, thus reducing the risk of the victim being targeted again in the future.

THIRTEEN

Courage in the Face of Hate: a curricular resource for confronting anti-LGBTQ violence

Barbara Perry and D. Ryan Dyck

Introduction

Current Canadian data (Dowden and Brennan, 2012[47]) and a handful of research projects (Faulkner, 2006/2007; 2006; Burtch and Haskell, 2010; Taylor and Peter, 2011) make it clear that the environment in many Canadian communities remains unsafe for LGBTQ (lesbian, gay, bisexual, trans, queer) people. In light of the isolation and violent victimisation that both documented and undocumented hate crime victims face, it is vital that we develop meaningful strategies both to support the victims of LGBTQ hate crimes and reduce future occurrences. With this in mind, Egale Canada[48] and Dr Barbara Perry partnered to create Courage in the Face of Hate (CFH), which aimed to create safer spaces where story-telling and education could take place among victims of hate crime and hopefully aid in their journey of healing. These sharing activities were also intended to build courage within LGBTQ communities, thus enabling and encouraging victims and witnesses to report crimes to police. Finally, by humanising LGBTQ people in a resultant video, and showing it to students who may not necessarily know an LGBTQ person, we sought to reduce fear and dispel prejudice, with the long term hope of reducing the rates of violence against LGBTQ communities. This chapter aims to lay out the rationale for the project, the strategies we engaged, our experiences in conducting the project, and a summary of our final 'products,' including findings and, of course, the video.

The contexts for anti-LGBTQ violence

Anti-gay and anti-trans hate crime occurs as a result of the heterosexism and cissexism that permeate societal institutions (Herek, 1992). Heterosexism is 'an ideological system that denies, denigrates and stigmatises any non-heterosexual form of behavior, identity, relationship or community' (Herek 1992: 89). Cissexism is the correlative 'belief that transsexuals' identified genders are inferior to, or less authentic than, those of cissexuals' – those whose gender identity is congruent with the sex assigned to them at birth – and the attendant systems of oppression (Serano, 2007: 12). Consider, for example, laws that recognise only opposite-sex marriages and deny same-sex couples the opportunity to adopt children, or receive tax benefits – laws that existed in Canada until as late as 2005. Consider, too, that many employee health and retirement programmes often deny coverage to same-sex domestic partners or to trans individuals; that many religious institutions denounce lesbian, gay, bisexual and trans people, labelling them sick and sinful; and that some jurisdictions across the globe still criminalise sexual behaviour between two consenting adults of the same sex. Anti-LGBTQ hate crimes cannot be properly understood separately from these social and cultural arrangements that perpetuate hetero/cissexism and construct LGBTQ identities as deviant, pathological and predatory.

Thus, it is perhaps not surprising that the school setting is a key environment in which homo/transphobia thrives. Schools are also sites that filter out normative from non-normative, and in this context, hetero/cisnormative from non-hetero/cisnormative. Hetero/cissexist curricula, school yard epithets, and lack of teacher intervention in homo/transphobia all contribute to a climate in which anti-LGBTQ violence is allowed to emerge and flourish. Indeed, myriad sources of data point to the extent to which schools represent unsafe spaces for LGBTQ youth. Educational facilities generally rank among the top three locations for reported hate crime; and school-aged youth (12–17 years) are the most frequent victims and offenders (Dowden and Brennan, 2012). No findings are more telling than those from the first national survey on homophobia, biphobia and transphobia in Canadian schools (Taylor and Peter, 2011). Among the key findings are the facts that 10% of LGBTQ students reported having heard homophobic comments from *teachers* daily or weekly. A total of 43% of trans students and 32% of lesbian, gay and bisexual students reported that school staff members never intervened when homophobic comments were being made. In contrast, 30% of sexual minority female, 24% of sexual minority male and 40% of trans students were unaware of a single member of school staff who were supportive of LGBTQ students. Perhaps it is not surprising, then, that almost two thirds (64%) of LGBTQ students, 78% of trans students and 61% of students with LGBTQ parents reported that they feel unsafe at school. The two school spaces most commonly experienced as unsafe by LGBTQ youth and youth with LGBTQ parents are places that are almost invariably gender-segregated: physical education change rooms and washrooms.

There is also alarming evidence that the situation is getting worse for LGBTQ communities. According to Statistics Canada, there has been an alarming increase in hate crimes based on sexual orientation; in fact, there was an 18.2% increase between 2008 and 2009 (Dauvergne and Brennan, 2011). Further, 74% of these hate crimes are violent in nature, disproportionately higher than for other victim communities. Collectively, the documented patterns of homo/transphobia and hate crime suggested to us a need to intervene, especially among youth, and specifically, within the school setting. Consequently, we developed CFH as a means of sharing the voices and experiences of those most affected by the violence, so that others could understand the impacts of their words and actions.

Goals of Courage in the Face of Hate

CFH arose out of conversations following the 2011 release of the Canadian hate crime data for 2009. As noted above, the latest report showed that anti-gay violence was still rising and that it tended to be more violent than crimes motivated by other identities. What gave our project impetus was that the Executive Director of Egale Canada, Helen Kennedy, was prompted to say, on the publication of the data, that 'We've got to do something'– and she meant it. The data were released at about the same time that Egale entered into a partnership with Dr Barbara Perry. Serendipity! This was clearly a sign that, at last, we would 'do something', and that 'something' turned into this project. We were fortunate to receive funding from three sources: Ontario Victim Services Secretariat; Department of Justice Victim Service Fund, and Ontario Safer and Vital Communities Fund.

Our goals were multi-faceted. Specifically, when seeking funding we proposed the following concrete aims – we would:

1. travel to eight Canadian cities (five cities in Ontario, and three additional cities in Canada) to conduct victim focus groups which would be recorded as part of the video component of our educational modules;

2. create a 30-minute educational video using footage from the victim focus groups and interviews, and distribute it to schools and workplaces across Canada;
3. write a lesson plan that is complementary to the content of the video, with an eye to provincial high school curricula.

Our broader objective was to allow victims of hate crimes to share their stories in a safe space, thereby helping them with their own healing and coping processes. Moreover, while our intent was to directly affect youths' education in the school, we also hoped to enhance public knowledge of the persistence and impact of anti-LGBTQ violence. Thus, the video was disseminated and screened publicly as well. Additionally, as with any research project of this sort, the interviews and focus groups transcripts will continue to be mined for key themes that will enhance our understanding of the processes and effects of victimisation. The goal, in this context, is the development of academic papers and presentations. However, this is only part of the process. We hope also to engage in 'public sociology' whereby we will disseminate findings through public fora and media outlets.

The research

Between November 2011 and July 2012 the CFH team travelled to cities across Canada to conduct interviews and focus groups. The team consisted of Dr Barbara Perry (researcher), Ryan Dyck (Egale, Director of Public Education and Policy), and Matthew McLaughlin (videographer). For the most part, the cities were selected based on what appeared to be high concentrations of anti-LGBTQ violence, according to successive StatsCan reports. In the end, we visited five cities in Ontario (Toronto, Ottawa, London, Kingston, Kitchener-Waterloo), as well as Regina SK, Montreal QC, and Happy Valley-Goose Bay NL. A total of 74 people participated, ranging in age from 14 to 68, with the majority being in their early to mid-twenties. For the most part, the participants were white; in addition, however, there were four Aboriginal, seven black, one Latina, and one south Asian participant. Five people identified as gender queer; 11 as trans; two as drag queens; five as two-spirit; seven as straight; two as bisexual; 24 as gay men; and 14 as lesbian. In total, we conducted eight focus groups of around approximately 90 minutes in length, as well as 33 interviews that lasted anywhere from 45 minutes up to three hours. There was a degree of overlap, in that some focus group participants also agreed to interviews. All of the interviews were videotaped, but few of the focus groups were. We stopped videotaping them when participants suggested that this seemed to be inhibiting participation. Thus, after the second focus group, we used only audio recordings for the focus groups.

The focus groups consisted of three to six participants and revolved around six key questions reflecting their assessment of the local climate for LGBTQ communities, with less attention to individual experiences (obviously, though, these also shone through). We queried group members on their sense of the relative inclusivity and safety of their cities for LGBTQ people, and more specifically, on their perceptions of victims' likelihood of reporting victimisation to police. The intent of this latter topic was to assess the extent to which reported hate crime data might be a reflection of police activity and the relationship between the community and law enforcement. We ended with a discussion of what steps participants felt needed to be taken to ensure the safety and security of LGBTQ communities.

The interviews were much less structured. We generally opened by asking participants to tell us when they first became aware that they were 'not like others' – in essence, these were 'coming out' stories. Following from that, we explored reactions to their expressed sexuality or gender identity, including experiences of homo/transphobia. At some point in the interviews, we also turned toward often lengthy discussions of the impact of social stigma, violence, and other forms of anti-LGBTQ sentiment in their lives. One of the most powerful moments in the interviews came in the concluding minute. We asked each participant to look directly at the camera and, assuming an audience of high schools students, send whatever direct message they cared to make. Many of these were, in fact, featured in the subsequent video.

LGBTQ voices

To provide some context, we will summarise some of key themes to emerge from the interviews and focus groups, although it should be acknowledged that myriad other consistent themes emerged from the study. What we offer here is not an exhaustive account, but simply a sampling from the broader menu. Needless to say, whether in groups or individually, the stories shared were emotionally laden. We were at times overwhelmed by participants' willingness and often eagerness to open up about their experiences and the impacts that these had on them. A few expressed some anxiety about telling their stories, intimating that in so doing they were re-opening old wounds. In such cases, we encouraged people to take their time, and to choose what and whether to reveal. In general, however, participants indicated that they found the interviews cathartic. They represented an opportunity to release some of their anxiety. 'I wanted to take the time to thank you for including me in the Courage in the Face of Hate video project', wrote one participant. 'I am finding the effect of sorting out these memories to forward to you rather therapeutic. I truly believe this is helping me to come closer towards some kind of inner closure and peace.' In the case of focus group participants, it had the added benefit of allowing them to share similar experiences and to remind one another that they were not, in fact, alone. A certain amount of community building was therefore facilitated.

Generally, we opened the interviews by asking participants to describe their personal journeys, to render a narrative about how and when they began to identify sexually or in terms of gender. Almost inevitably, they situated their self-identification in terms of being 'different', of something being 'wrong' with them. Growing up in a hetero/cisnormative culture led them to the conclusion that, because they didn't act/feel/think like others who shared their gender or sex, they must somehow be outside what was 'normal'. According to one gay man, he saw himself, at age six, as 'An oddity, an anomaly. There wasn't anyone else like me. And you just, you just had that sense because you would see yourself and you would see other people and it was a problem – I don't fit, something is different, something is odd, something is not the same.'

Given that many suggested that this self-realisation began to emerge when they were as young as four, five, or six years of age, it is not surprising that they didn't have the language for what they were experiencing: 'I didn't know what or who I was. I just knew I wasn't like the other girls in my class. I didn't know, though, what that difference was' (lesbian interviewee). Interestingly, there were also some generational distinctions in this framing of identity. Older participants, who had come out 50 or 60 years ago, spoke about not having a vocabulary with which to articulate their sexuality, in particular. One gay male who came out in the 1950s suggested that there was limited, if any, public discourse about homosexuality at the time: 'There was a silence. There were no words, there certainly was no "community" that one could turn to for support.' Interestingly, trans people in the current era made very similar observations. Until the last five or 10 years, there has been a similar lack of dialogue about trans identities. Thus, they too have struggled to find the words to describe their lived experience: 'No one talked about trans, what it was. We were just thought of, described as queer too, or at best, cross-dressers. None of the labels we knew seemed to fit how I felt at 15 or 16. I didn't think I was gay, but I wasn't really the "man" I was supposed to be either. What was I? Who was I?' (trans woman).

As a consequence of the anxiety caused by homo/transphobia, many of those whom we spoke to talked about how they felt the need to carefully manage their identities, attempting to look 'less gay' or 'more feminine' or 'more masculine' depending on how they read social expectations of behaviour. Participants expressed the necessity to alter their performance of gender in accordance with what they recognised as the socially established rules for doing gender. They reported changing activities, habits and ways of being in the world. Individuals spoke of their tendencies to self-segregate as a protective mechanism: 'I didn't interact. Very insular. Because there wasn't anyone else that you felt that, that you could connect with' (gay man). A young lesbian shares similar sentiments: 'I was so by myself, I had no friends. Um, I didn't even know who to turn to, what to do.'

The isolation factor had particular and distinct meaning for trans participants. There was frequent reference among trans women, especially, of their lack of trust. They had learned, often very early, that there was nowhere they could turn for support and understanding. According to one trans woman, 'In addition to extreme isolation to the point of the ultimate isolation, which is suicide, is trust. I will say "I", but I mean, I think I can safely say, *we* don't trust anyone. We trust each other, as trans women trust each other, [but] we don't trust anyone and that includes members of the queer community.' Many stated that they had been rejected by virtually everyone in their life, from family, to friends, to therapists, to doctors. There seemed to be no one who was willing or able to provide a secure and accepting environment for them.

Associated with identity management and with issues of trust was a tendency toward hyper-vigilance. Because of the fear that is perpetuated by the looming threat of homo/transphobic speech and action, many participants admitted that they were always on the watch for cues that suggested the potential for harassment or violence. 'You just never know', said one lesbian. 'It could happen anytime, it could be anyone that hassles you.' Again, the fear of victimisation, and thus hyper-vigilance, seemed to be particularly acute among trans women, many of whom spoke of the multiple and complex layers by which they defined 'safety' and lack thereof. One Toronto trans woman spoke at length about her perceptions of safety and what that entailed for her:

'I had to adapt to the experiences of nearly being physically assaulted and my feeling was that I was never safe anywhere and that led to being very reclusive, isolating, which then tied in with severe depression and suicide attempts. So there's the practical issue of safety, but then there's the subjective experience of safety that is radically altered by those experiences you have and without the involved balance, even just harassment, bullying, ridiculing and mocking takes a tremendous toll on us.'

Supportive friends and families and spiritual satisfaction were part of the wider network that helped our participants cope with the lived experiences of homo/transphobia. We were often taken by the strength and resilience that characterised those with whom we spoke. Consequently, the source of this strength often became a topic for further exploration. Almost inevitably, credit was given to their support network of LGBTQ persons, but also allies, as one gay male interviewee suggested:

'I was very fortunate where I had a set of friends who were highly supportive. Very knowledgeable. Accepting. And I would say it would have been that circle of friends who got me through the rough patches, who were, indeed, very supportive; who were not questioning, were very unconditional in the support that they provided.'

Participants characterised their relationship to religion in more ambivalent terms. For many, it was religion that had made their acknowledgement of their sexual orientation or gender identity so problematic. For those raised in staunchly religious families and/or communities, the constant message was that being gay or trans was sinful, unnatural and would condemn them to hell. Ultimately, this frequently meant a rupture in family relationships when they came out. Many have never 'recovered' from the feelings of guilt associated with their identities, due to these religious upbringings. In contrast, many participants would return to a spiritual relationship with some higher power. On the one hand, this might be finding a welcoming faith-based entity. However, another possibility was finding an inner sense of peace and strength through their development of a personal space that allowed them to reconcile the need for spirituality with the need to live as who they were.

Curricular resource: *Courage in the Face of Hate*

The interviews and focus groups were the foundation for a powerful video entitled, appropriately, *Courage in the Face of Hate*. Here we feature the voices and experiences of the people we met on our journeys. To contextualise these stories, we integrated current statistics and relevant graphics to highlight the broader environment of homo/transphobia. This combination of empirical data and emotional evocation will make CFH effective as a documentary and an educational tool.

To provide a framework that would heighten the impact of the video, we also developed a lesson plan to accompany it (http://courage.egale. ca/lesson-plans/). The learning goals associated with the lesson plan asserted that at the end of this lesson, students would:

- be able to identify the potential impact of homophobic, biphobic and transphobic bullying;
- be able to discuss the ways in which individual actions have an effect on more than just the immediate victim of bullying;
- communicate the scope of the effects of bullying and the power of language as a tool of bullying; and
- suggest strategies to challenge homophobia, biphobia and transphobia.

The lesson plan suggested that, prior to sharing the video with students, teachers should allow students to complete an exercise – included with the plan – in which they match up key terms around LGBTQ issues with their respective definitions. Teachers should then discuss with the class the data and statistics on LGBTQ bullying, violence and harassment that are provided with the plan. The groundwork would then be set for viewing the video.

As they watched the video, students would be encouraged to jot down their emotional responses on a handout that also asked them to outline what they had learned from watching it. This exercise was intended to encourage students to attend carefully to the material, but also to explore their own reactions to what they see. A second series of questions aimed to engage students after they have viewed the video by asking them more specifically about issues of loneliness, invisibility and 'acceptance of self' in relation to LGBTQ people.

Extension possibilities were also offered if teachers opted to spend more time working through LGBTQ issues with their students. Both of these extension exercises were 'action oriented' in that they involved activities intended to intervene and facilitate change in their schools, in particular. The first of these asked students to come up with a list of places in the school and the community where help and support actually exist. Teachers would then move the discussion towards creating a list of what needed to be implemented further in the school community to better help deal with issues of homophobic, biphobic and transphobic bullying. If there are computers in the classroom, students could also search for local, regional, or national resources supporting the LGBTQ community. Alternatively, the latter was made a homework assignment.

The second extension activity asked students to consider how they might design a media strategy for confronting anti-LGBTQ behaviours in their school. Examples of strategies that participants could identify included designing and disseminating their own posters/ads (video, paper, etc.), conducting surveys/research to document the problem, writing articles for a school or local newspaper/website, disseminating the message through popular blogs or via Facebook and other social networking forums, conducting an assembly program, organizing an Ally Week or No Name-Calling Week, conducting LGBTQ awareness or anti-bullying trainings for school clubs, youth groups, sports teams, etc. Teachers would discuss with the class which initiatives seemed most practical and potentially effective. If desired, either by vote or consensual decision making, a few ideas were be selected for implementation, which could be carried out over subsequent class periods.

Reaction to Courage in the Face of Hate

For a small project, CFH promises to have dramatic effects in a diversity of communities and contexts. In fact, the video and lesson plan have exceeded our initial goals in the Canadian education sector. Egale Canada delivers LGBTQ Safer and Accepting Schools training programmes to school communities across Canada, and has begun to integrate pieces of the programme into these workshops. In this context, staff members from the Newfoundland and Labrador Department of Education were some of the first to screen the documentary. They immediately requested copies of the DVD and lesson plan for every school in the province, and set out to make CFH a mandatory part of the province's grade 10 curriculum. Yukon has since followed suit, and every secondary school in Ontario has received a copy of the DVD, with extremely positive results.

Some responses in the education sector have been unexpected. While the film and lesson plan were initially designed with a grade 10 audience in mind, reception has been positive from many elementary school educators as well. Perhaps most encouraging, during a workshop with 30 Catholic elementary school teachers in Ontario, nearly all participants stated that they would use the resources in their schools. Requests for the DVD and lesson plan continue to increase in volume from all aspects of the education system across Canada, representing a growing array of demographics.

Reactions to the CFH project have also been positive from a broader community base. Community centres, universities, public and private sector unions, libraries, police services, youth summer camps and community clubs and groups have requested copies of the film and many have hosted screenings for their local communities. The impact of the film in these settings has been overwhelming, from sparking impassioned discussions among non-LGBTQ people around how to be an ally in fighting against homophobia, biphobia and transphobia within their communities, to emotional moments of affirmation within the LGBTQ community itself. As one LGBTQ community member wrote:

> 'My friend and I watched the documentary you guys made to be used in schools. It was absolutely amazing. After I watched it, I felt like I was not alone. I too at 15 was kicked out of my home and was put into foster care because of my sexuality. I was shocked to hear how many other people in the film had that same story. Good work guys. Absolutely a moving and powerful film. How do I get my own copy?'

The participation of one uniformed police officer in the video also sparked reactions in her city, as the local police chief received letters thanking the service for its involvement and for taking a public stand as an ally to the LGBTQ community.

The video itself has also garnered attention from the arts world, both domestically and internationally. It has been screened as an official selection at the Vancouver Queer Film Festival, the Edmonton International Film Festival, the World Film Festival in Montreal, the Indianapolis LGBT Film Festival, the Tampa International Gay and Lesbian Film Festival, and the Reelout Queer Film + Video Festival in Kingston, Ontario. Shortly after its initial release, it was presented twice at World Pride 2012 in London, UK, and a private screening was arranged within a foreign embassy for LGBTQ community members in Sri Lanka. It is generally received – among both LGBTQ and non-LGBTQ viewers – as a moving and impactful portrayal of the experiences, fears and hopes of LGBTQ individuals and communities, as well as an effective intersection of education, activism, cinema and art. Film festivals have recognised it for something deeper than was initially envisioned: not simply a film about hate crime; rather, a film that reaches and poignantly reveals the human impact of homophobia, biphobia and transphobia on individuals, families and communities.

Conclusion

The CFH project poignantly demonstrated a continuing struggle among LGBTQ people in Canada for safety and inclusion. However, what also shone through was the powerful role that allies and communities play in realising this vision. This has been evident both in the interviews and focus groups as well as in the responses we have seen since the completion of the project. This partnership between research and activism, academia and community, education and media, has tremendous potential to activate the 58% of non-LGBTQ youth in Canada who report being disturbed by the discrimination and harassment they witness against their LGBTQ peers – potential allies waiting in the wings.

Perhaps the most pressing outcome of this project has been its confirmation of abhorrently high rates of victimisation experienced by trans people across Canada. Isolation, hyper-vigilance and mistrust are still extremely common themes in the lives of many trans individuals as a result of the violence and discrimination they face. At times, these factors created barriers to outreach and to ensuring trans representation in the CFH project. Moving forward, future efforts to research and address hate and bias motivated violence in Canada will need to place particular emphasis on understanding cisnormativity and drawing attention to the experiences of trans people. Outreach activities will need to rely even more heavily on relationships and community networks in order to mitigate the effects of isolation and mistrust.

Overall, we could not have found a more appropriate term for our small attempt to 'do something'. 'Courage' really was the permeating theme of every interview conducted and of the final documentary film. If subsequent sets of Canadian hate crime data show a decrease in anti-LGBTQ violence, it will have everything to do with Courage.

References

Burtch, B. and Haskell, R. (2010) *Get That Freak: Homophobia and Transphobia in High Schools*, Halifax: Fernwood.

Dauvergne, M. and Brennan, S. (2011) *Police-reported Hate Crime in Canada, 2009*. Ottawa: Juristat. Catalogue No. 85-002-X.

Dowden, C. and Brennan, S. (2012) *Police-reported Hate Crime in Canada, 2010*. Ottawa: Juristat. Catalogue No. 85-002-X.

Faulkner, E. (2006/2007) 'Homophobic Hate Propaganda in Canada', *Journal of Hate Studies,* 5: 63–97.

Faulkner, E. (2006) 'Homophobic Sexist Violence in Canada: Trends in the Experiences of Lesbian and Bisexual Women in Canada', *Canadian Woman Studies,* 25 (1, 2): 154–61.

Herek, G. (1992) 'The Social Context of Hate Crimes: Notes on Cultural Heterosexism', in G. Herek and K. Berrill (eds) *Hate Crimes: Confronting Violence Against Lesbians and Gay Men,* Newbury Park CA: Sage, 89–104.

Serano, J. (2007) *Whipping Girl: A Transsexual Woman on Sexism and the Scapegoating of Femininity,* Emeryville, CA: Seal Press.

Taylor, C. and Peter, T. (2011) *Every Class in Every School: Final Report on the First National Climate Survey on Homophobia, Biphobia, and Transphobia in Canadian Schools,* Toronto: Egale Canada Human Rights Trust.

FOURTEEN

Policing prejudice motivated crime: a research case study

Gail Mason, Jude McCulloch and JaneMaree Maher

Introduction

In 2009, police in the Australian state of Victoria were criticised for their handling of claims of racist violence against Indian students. The criticisms culminated in censure by the United Nations (Flitton, 2010). Media pressure and concern to protect Australia's political relationship with India as well as its reputation as a safe destination for students prompted a plethora of policy and legislative changes across government and private industry. At the same time Victoria Police ('VicPol') was already engaged in a range of initiatives designed to address what they refer to as prejudice motivated crime (PMC).

Early in 2010, VicPol's Chief Commissioner initiated a strategy to address PMC (Victoria Police Diagnosis Paper, 2010). The term prejudice was most likely adopted because the relevant existing Victorian legislation (in the areas of sentencing and racial and religious tolerance) used this term. In 2011 VicPol launched its PMC Strategy. The vision of the Strategy is to develop a 'whole of organisation' response to enable the police to tackle these crimes through sustained, integrated and coordinated capacity building (PMC Strategy, 2010: 3). The Strategy aims to address: low reporting rates; harm to individuals and communities; and gaps in organisational responses, including VicPol's engagement with key community, agency and government stakeholders (Victoria Police, 2010: 2).

This chapter sets out how our research is assisting VicPol to implement this strategy into everyday policing activities. As academics engaged in a research partnership with VicPol, we take a case study approach to describe how our research is responding to the shifting policing environment. In the research process, questions about how the police currently recognise and investigate instances of prejudice motivated crime came to fore. In the second section of the chapter, we set out our preliminary research findings on the collection of relevant evidence for the successful prosecution of PMC, with a particular focus on offence related 'alerts' for investigating police. The recognition by investigating officers that the offence might be a hate crime is crucial in realization of VicPol's PMC vision as well as for the realisation of legislative and social goals for civil conduct in multicultural societies. This case study details a local policing response to the broader social and political pressures that are raised by hate crime. It offers an instance of the trend across Western societies towards 'particularizing protections against abuse' (Feenan, 2006: 157) for groups that are commonly perceived to be marginalised or especially vulnerable, with the broader objective of promoting values of tolerance and inclusion (see Mason, 2009). It demonstrates the importance of building shared knowledge about what constitutes PMC within communities and within police ranks.

Hate crime policing policy in Australia

Prejudice motivated crime is commonly referred to as hate crime. Australia has a diversity of policy and legislative initiatives that promote human rights, equality, multiculturalism and principles of anti-discrimination (e.g. the 2012 national Anti-Racism Partnership and Strategy). There are however few specific hate crime policies.[49] Particular forms of hate crime, such as violence against GLBT communities, have been tackled convincingly in some jurisdictions through government, inter-agency and community partnerships (e.g. NSW Government's *Strategic Framework 2007–2012 – Working Together: Preventing Violence against Gay, Lesbian, Bisexual and Transgender People*). Some of these policing policies have been in place for a number of years (e.g. the New South Wales Police Force Policy on Sexuality and Gender Diversity was issued in 1997). Disappointingly, such policies have not been widely replicated in other Australian jurisdictions. Specific policies addressing the rights and needs of other hate crime target groups have also been slow in emerging. Although the promotion of effective hate crime policing is often identified as a priority in policy documents governing Australian police forces, for example, through systems for recording hate crime, Victoria is the only jurisdiction to have introduced a comprehensive, specific policy statement on hate crime (Mason et al, 2012).

VicPol's PMC Strategy is comprehensive and adopts an integrated approach to building recognition of and responding effectively to hate crime. The Strategy's explicit aims are to increase VicPol's understanding of PMC; to reduce the incidence of PMC; and to increase community confidence to report PMC (Victoria Police, 2010: 3). The Strategy acknowledges existing gaps and issues in VicPol's current responses to PMC. These include: internal education and training; data collection and recording; analytical capability and intelligence; investigative responses; accountability and governance framework for monitoring progress and outcomes; policy formulation; and community engagement (2010: 3). Its overall performance measure is to increase the number of PMC reports to the police that are then recorded in their system (2010: 3). This approach is consistent with good practice in the policing of hate crime internationally, and mirrors approaches adopted in other jurisdictions where the recognition and recording of hate crime is a key element of effective, inclusive policing. A contradiction inherent in the aims of the Strategy is that improvements in community confidence and reporting will necessarily lead to an increase in recorded PMCs. An increase in recording could *prima facie* be taken as evidence of an increase in the occurrence of PMC. VicPol recognises this complication and, as with reforms in the policing of sexual assault or family violence, welcomes any increase in reporting. It is believed that any such initial increases in reporting are likely to stabilise over time so that in the longer term a more precise picture of any decrease in PMC can be captured.

The development of the Strategy occurred in the context of specific incidents of violence against Indian students studying in Victoria, but also drew on recent legislative developments in Victoria that addressed inclusion and prejudice. There are two specific pieces of legislation (in addition to general criminal law, procedure and human rights legislation) that govern the VicPol Strategy. The first, the *Racial and Religious Tolerance Act 2001* (Vic) ('RRTA') was introduced in Victoria with considerable resistance and controversy (Mason et al, 2012). The broader objectives of this statute align with a suite of legislative moves across Australia and in Western countries more generally to enshrine enforceable standards of tolerance in multicultural societies. These instruments aim to directly enhance the protection of citizens in groups understood as vulnerable or marginalised, while promoting the broader objectives of tolerance and inclusion (see Mason, 2009). The Victorian Act provides civil remedies for vilification, or 'hate speech'. A particularly controversial aspect of the RRTA was the creation of criminal offences for serious racial (s24) and religious (s25) vilification, which involve the incitement of hatred through threats of physical harm.[50] Although the Vic Pol Strategy identifies the RRTA as a platform for its approach to prejudice motivated crime, the legislation is rarely used to charge offenders, due to its narrow definition of vilification, high standard of proof and complex procedures (Meagher, 2006).

Thus, while the RRTA may serve symbolic purposes and does shape the broader policy context, it appears to be of limited practical value to the police or prosecutors dealing with PMC (Chapman and Kelly, 2004; Cowdery, 2009; Meyerson, 2009).

The second piece of legislation, enacted in 2009 in response to concern about claims of racist violence against Indian students in Victoria, is based on the proposition that hate crime produces greater negative social outcomes than other crimes. This is because the offence impacts beyond the individual victim, by creating fear within the targeted community and because these offences are sometimes more extreme in character (Mason, 2009, 2012). In 2009, a new section was introduced to the Victorian Sentencing Act 1991 to address these hate crime impacts. Under s5(2)(daaa) of the Act, if a sentencing court finds beyond reasonable doubt that a criminal offence is motivated by prejudice or hatred this will be an aggravating factor in sentencing. The court must have regard to:

> whether the offence was motivated (wholly or partly) by hatred for or prejudice against a group of people with common characteristics with which the victim was associated or with which the offender believed the victim was associated.

These Victorian instruments endeavour to mobilise community awareness of PMC and enhance the capacity of the criminal justice system to respond effectively to hate crime. A report by the Organisation for Security and Co-operation in Europe (OSCE) suggests that unless hate crime motivation is 'explicitly recognised and punished' in legislation (2009: 28) the potential to achieve a deterrent effect and a wider inclusionary impact is lost. In particular, by providing the opportunity for courts to punish more harshly for offences motivated by prejudice or group hatred, the Victorian sentencing legislation seeks to meet the goals of deterrence and inclusion. The OSCE also recognises, however, that hate crime is often difficult to police. As gatekeepers of the criminal justice system, the police determine which cases come before the courts. Unless hate crimes are effectively identified and investigated by the police, sentencing provisions become irrelevant. The PMC strategy is designed to align VicPol's practices more directly with the aims of the sentencing legislation. In the following section, we explore the general and specific challenges faced by VicPol in achieving the objectives of the Strategy.

Challenges of implementing the PMC strategy

Conceptual and practical issues plague the policing and recording of PMC. As Jacobs and Potter have commented, '[a]t first blush it might seem relatively easy to define a species of crime based on prejudice or bigotry' but on closer inspection this is not at all the case: 'What is hate? What is prejudice? What prejudices transform ordinary crime into hate crime? How strong a motivating factor must the prejudice be?' (1998: 9). Although there are several terms available to describe this type of crime – bias crime, hate crime, targeted crime – VicPol adopted 'prejudice motivated crime', as indicated earlier, because it is consistent with the terminology used in sentencing law. Victoria is the only policing jurisdiction in Australia that consistently uses the term 'prejudice motivated crime'. Other Australian jurisdictions (including Tasmania, NSW and Queensland) use this term interchangeably with others including hate and bias crime.

Moves to police hate crime are often contentious and this is the case in Victoria too. The relative newness of this criminal category means that ambiguity and uncertainty surrounds what constitutes a PMC within the community and within the police force too. This ambiguity is compounded because the police do not normally identify motive as part of recording crimes and PMC does not occur as frequently as some other crimes (Jenness and Grattet, 2001: 130; Stanko, 2001: 311; Cronin et al, 2007: 217–1-8). Thus VicPol have not customarily collected the type of data needed to record, track and understand PMC. Moreover, the kinds of evidence needed to convince a court beyond reasonable doubt that a proven offence was motivated by prejudice are difficult to collect and require, as we suggest in the final section of this chapter, higher levels of awareness and response from investigating officers.

Implementation of the PMC Strategy thus presents challenges for VicPol at all levels including the provision of effective corporate leadership, intelligence gathering, integrated training, sensitive and informed investigation, victim liaison, the establishment of inter-agency partnerships and accurate recording. Perhaps the most fundamental challenge is to define and identify the kinds of criminal conduct that amount to a PMC and, in turn, the nature of the evidence needed to detect and establish that an offence is motivated by prejudice for prosecution and/or sentencing purposes. For example, how should the police distinguish between PMC and opportunistic crimes? This task is made particularly complicated in Victoria by the absence of a specific offence that the police can use to charge offenders motivated by prejudice (given the impracticalities of charging offenders under the RRTA as discussed above). Thus the PMC Strategy relies on the *Sentencing Act 1991* for guidance, adopting a definition of PMC that is consistent with the Act but noting that the definition is flexible and can be reviewed as 'new groups and issues' emerge:

> 'A prejudice motivated crime is a criminal act which is motivated (wholly or partly) by hatred for or prejudice against a group of people with common characteristics with which the victim was associated or with which the offender believed the victim was associated. Characteristics include: religious affiliation, racial or cultural origin, sexual orientation, sex, gender identity, age, impairment (within the meaning of the Equal Opportunity Act 1995), or homelessness'. (Victoria Police 2010: 2; see also Victoria Police Diagnosis Paper 2010: 8)[51]

There are several complexities for the police in interpreting and applying this definition in practice. In the Victoria Police strategy:

- There must be a criminal act. In the UK the police are required to record 'hate incidents' as well as 'hate crimes' (Home Office Police Standards Unit, 2005: 9). Hate incidents are any incidents that are perceived by the victim or any other person to be motivated by prejudice or hate towards specified groups while hate crimes must be a breach of the criminal law (Metropolitan Police Service, 2010). While VicPol recognises this distinction and the impact of hate incidents on the target community the strategy adopts a definition of PMC that is limited to criminal offences (Victoria Police Diagnostic Paper, 2010: 11).
- A key element of the Victorian definition hinges on motivation. By way of comparison, the NSW Police Force's 2011 policy statement on Sexuality and Gender Diversity defines homophobic/transgender crime or violence more broadly, as 'hate and fear based on harassment, abuse or violence directed at someone because they are, or are perceived to be, gay, lesbian, bisexual or transgender. It includes physical and non-physical forms of abuse and the fear of violence' (NSW Police Force, 2011: 4). Arguably the use of the phrase 'because' in the NSW definition is broader than the concept of PMC adopted by VicPol as the former includes crimes motivated by homophobia *and* situations where the victim is selected because of their presumed membership of one of these groups.[52]

- The offence may be motivated by either prejudice or group hatred. The use of terms such as 'prejudice' has been critiqued by a number of scholars (Hall, 2005; Iganski, 2008). Jacobs and Potter (1998: 11) argue that it is a 'complicated, broad and cloudy concept'. In highlighting problems, they note:

> If prejudice is defined narrowly, to include only certain organized hate-based ideologies, there will be very little hate crime. If prejudice is defined broadly, a high percentage of intergroup crimes will qualify as hate crimes ... in other words, we can make the hate crime problem as small or large as we desire by manipulating the definition. (Jacobs and Potter, 1998: 28)

The strategy takes a relatively flexible approach to the kinds of prejudice covered, including prejudice based on religious affiliation, racial or cultural origin, sexual orientation, sex, gender identity, age, impairment and homelessness. While race, religious affiliation, sexual orientation, impairment and, to a lesser extent, age are commonly protected in other policing policies through the use of the same or comparable terms, it is less common for sex and homelessness to be explicitly included. As a result of these ambiguities, and limited practical experience because of the newness of this type of approach to offences, research suggests that, like police forces internationally, Victorian police are likely to apply a restrictive definition of PMC, and submit potential PMC to a high level of scrutiny before recording it as such (Cronin et al, 2007: 224). This tendency to underrecord can be clearly seen in the reality that although the majority of PMC are 'everyday' in nature, and may be perpetrated by people known to the victim, policing attention tends to focus on the most extreme incidents, and the most extreme perpetrators (Kielinger and Paterson, 2007: 203). Interpreting the PMC definition, and incorporating it into daily policing activities, thus raises specific challenges that must be addressed if the social and political objectives of hate crime legislative instruments are to be achieved.

International research suggests that it may be possible to overcome some of these issues via implementation of procedures and protocols that inform and influence the discretion of individual police officers (Cronin et al, 2007: 218, 223–4). Officers responsible for initial identification can be encouraged to apply a broad, inclusive definition of PMC, and someone with appropriate experience, expertise and training can later undertake formal classification. Depending on the skills of police responsible for initial identification, a two-tiered system that guarantees effective oversight of initial identification prior to formal recording may be valuable (Cronin et al, 2007: 227–8). Increasing police awareness of communities that commonly experience PMC and the contexts in which PMC occurs would facilitate more comprehensive identification of PMC at first instance, thus ensuring more accurate police recording (Duffin, 2007; Kielinger and Paterson, 2007: 203). These challenges and opportunities have been recognised by VicPol and underpin our research and practice partnership. In the next section we describe our study, the partnership approach and our preliminary findings in relation to investigation and evidence gathering.

Using PMC scholarship to inform implementation

In 2011 academics, led by Professor Sharon Pickering of Monash University, partnered with VicPol to develop a research project on 'Targeted Crime: Policing and Social Inclusion'.[53] Prompted by adverse international attention about hate crime in Victoria, the project was designed to develop an improved understanding within the police of such crime across key communities, using both qualitative and quantitative criminological analysis. It aimed to produce a best practice policing framework to deal with hate crime. However, before the project was funded, VicPol developed their new PMC Strategy, and made effective implementation of this strategy a priority. This required a re-orientation of the research in order to support current police practice, mandated by the Strategy, as well as building knowledge and understanding. The project has been able to refine its methodologies to offer VicPol insight and guidance on the challenge of implementing the strategy while achieving the original objectives of analysing the incidence of hate crime in Victoria. The project thus has several different objectives, necessitating a range of research strategies. Major activities have included: mapping comparable policies in other jurisdictions in order that VicPol is fully aware of other approaches as it works towards optimal implementation of its Strategy; holding focus groups with affected communities enhancing knowledge of the incidences of PMC and strengthening community and police relationships; and evaluating the effectiveness of current PMC training by surveying recruits.

As discussed above, one of the fundamental challenges for VicPol in activating the PMC Strategy is to define and identify PMC in ways that enable the police to build it into their daily activities. While the definition of PMC in the Strategy provides an essential and useful starting point, officers need further guidance on how to understand and interpret it so they can recognise, detect and record PMC in routine policing. As the Strategy's definition of PMC builds on the *Sentencing Act 1991* definition, our project aims to assist VicPol in this task by analysing how courts interpret and apply the same definition.

Thus one strand of our project has examined sentencing decisions and appeals to flesh out the meaning of PMC and the kinds of evidence that may be relied on to support a finding beyond reasonable doubt that an offence was motivated by hatred for or prejudice against a group of people with common characteristics. In addition to Victorian cases, for comparative purposes we drew on judicial interpretations of similar provisions in two other Australian jurisdictions, New South Wales and the Northern Territory,[54] as well as any recognition of PMC under common law (i.e. jurisdictions that have not codified PMC as an aggravating factor at sentencing and pre-reform cases in the three jurisdictions that have). Our study found 25 Supreme, District, County and appeal Court decisions or sentencing judgements where the court considered whether the offence was motivated by prejudice or group hatred. In 20 of these cases such a motive was proved; in 5 cases it was not. In analysing these cases, it was possible to identify the types of evidence that courts have relied on to find that a hate crime has occurred. The research produced a rich body of case law illuminating judicial pronouncements on the meaning of PMC, the characteristics or circumstances of an offence that point to a motive of prejudice and the kinds of evidence that support a finding of a prejudice motivated offence (Mason et al, 2012). While this strand of the project aims to achieve academic outcomes in drawing together and analysing existing hate crime decisions, the identification of the types of evidence necessary to support the finding of prejudice motivated crime can clearly be turned to practical policing objectives. We discuss the relevance and implications of this analysis for policing under VicPol's Strategy below.

Implications of scholarship for policing: PMC 'alerts'

Our analysis of judicial interpretations of PMC under sentencing legislation illuminates the type of evidence that proved useful for establishing prejudice motivation in the cases analysed. Offenders can have more than one motive. The police must bear in mind that courts may still find that a crime is motivated by prejudice even if it is not the only motive. While the courts have not been clear on how partial a prejudice motive can be, our research suggests that the police should ask whether prejudice or hatred makes a substantial contribution to the offender's motive even where it is not the sole motive.

In particular, we pinpoint a number of 'alerts' for the police in initial assessments as to whether prejudice might be involved in a crime and what evidence gathering with regard to prejudice motive is useful. We draw these 'alerts' from decided cases where an offender's prejudiced motive has been held to be an aggravating factor at sentencing and from shortcomings identified in the case law. Grounded in judicial interpretations of PMC, the six 'alerts' are designed to assist members of VicPol to define and identify PMC in order to implement the PMC strategy. While judicial interpretations of sentencing law cannot be directly mapped onto VicPol's strategy – which is wider in its scope and aims – they do provide guidance on the kinds of criminal conduct that are considered, by the highest courts in each jurisdiction, to amount to PMC. These six 'alerts' are:

- *Minority group victims*: the victim in almost all of the cases where the courts have held the offence to be motivated by prejudice or group hatred has come from a minority group (such as a racial or minority ethnic group). However, PMC can also be committed against 'majority' group victims: for example, in one case the court held that an offence motivated by anti-Christian sentiment was prejudice motivated. It is of concern that very few cases of violence against gay or lesbian victims have come before the courts and none involving disabled victims have been raised. As research points to the on-going problem of violence and hostility towards these groups, more needs to be done to assist the police to identify them as possible victims of PMC. Significantly, it has also been held that prejudice against women falls within the definition of PMC (for instance, a case of severely humiliating and demeaning group sexual assault was held to be motivated by gender prejudice).
- *Perpetrator/victim group difference*: in almost all the cases, the victim and the offender come from different social groups: for example, the offender is often from a white Anglo background and the victim is from a minority ethnic background. If a person from a minority group informs the police that he/she has been a victim of crime committed by a member of a majority group, this is *some* indication that the crime may be prejudice motivated. While not enough on its own it should put an investigating officer on alert.
- *Prejudiced or hateful statements by the offender sometime before or after the offence*: this includes statements made directly to the victim or to other witnesses, telephone calls, graffiti or prejudiced material posted by the offender on the internet. Examples of statements include: 'Let's

go and get the black niggers'; 'Bloody Indians. Fuck off'; 'Fucking black cunts'; 'Fuck off. We're full … 100% white. 100% proud.'

It is important, however, to determine the extent to which such statements are probative of the offender's motive as opposed to incidental or additional to the primary motive. If, for example, there is a pre-existing conflict between the offender and the victim (e.g. a dispute over driving or entry to a nightclub) or if the offender is clearly driven by another motive (e.g. financial gain) such statements may not be enough to prove that the offence was motivated by prejudice or hatred against the victim's group.

- *Circumstances of the offence*: the circumstances of the crime may be sufficient to put the police on notice that a crime might be prejudice motivated if, for example, it occurred near a well-known gay area or involved an attack on a synagogue. In one case a prejudice motive was proved as the offender set fire to a mosque. Prima facie such an event suggests the offender was motivated by religious prejudice.
- *The absence of any other motive*: in circumstances where offenders from a majority group attack members of a minority group, and there is no other apparent motive for the attack, this is an alert to investigate closely prejudice motive, especially if the offence is a violent one. For example, in one case a group of white men violently and repeatedly attacked a group of homeless Aboriginal people. The court held that, in the absence of any other apparent motive, the nature and rapidity of the offenders' attack supported the conclusion of a complete lack of respect for, and negative attitude to, the victims because they were Aboriginal.
- *Offenders who chose victims because they are members of a particular group*: if an offender has a history of choosing victims from the same group or if there is evidence that the victim was chosen because of his/ her membership of a particular group this should alert the police to investigate the likelihood of prejudice motivation. Crucially, officers should ask: *why* did the offender choose a victim from this group? Are there sufficient signs that this selection was because the offender wanted to harm a member of this group? It appears that evidence that an offender selected victims who were members of a particular group may not be sufficient on its own to prove a motive of prejudice for sentencing purposes. That an offender attacked, for example, only Indian victims is a good start. But it is probably not enough to prove beyond reasonable doubt that the offender was prejudice motivated against Indians. In such cases, additional evidence of the offender's prejudiced motive will generally be required.

Given the harm that a spate of 'group selection' attacks can have on a vulnerable community, it is important that the police respond promptly, sensitively and thoroughly to the needs of any such community. This is so even if such selection may not in itself be enough to prove prejudice motive and thus aggravate an offender's sentence. One of the aims of VicPol's PMC Strategy is to increase community reporting confidence. This can only be achieved if communities trust that the police will investigate and respond to their concerns seriously.

The police need to be aware of these alerts and use them as an indication of the need to consider evidence of prejudice motive in their investigations. Where any of these alerts exist the police should seek further evidence of prejudice motive. Undoubtedly, a direct admission by an offender that an offence was motivated by prejudice against a group of people will be the strongest evidence in establishing a prejudiced motive. In particular, attention to the notion of hatred for groups is important to establish prejudice motivation. Specific questions in this area can produce relevant evidence. For example, in one case an offender was asked why all of his victims were women. He replied that he 'just hated them'. The investigating officer asked the following question:

POLICE: 'Those particular girls or women in general?'

By asking the offender whether he was motivated to offend by hatred for a *group*, the police officer focused on whether he was motivated to offend by hatred or prejudice against that group. This is crucial in the required evidence.

We found no cases where admissions made to the police about prejudice motivation were used to establish such motivation in court (inexplicably in the above case this evidence was not used to establish a motive of gender prejudice). The seeking of such admissions in police interviews and the use of any such admissions in court provides a rich opportunity for developing police investigations and enhancing prosecutions of PMC.

When alerts are present, apart from tailoring any interviews to obtain evidence about motive, the police should also seek evidence about prejudiced statements made by the offender directly to the victim, or at the time of the offence or in other forums, such as the internet. Statements made to psychiatrists or psychologists may also be used as evidence of prejudice motive. Evidence of the commission of other offences against the same group may also provide evidence of prejudice motive in later similar offences.

In analysing judicial interpretations, our project fleshes out the meaning of PMC and assists VicPol to implement the strategy by identifying common features or circumstances to offences characterised by the courts as motivated by prejudice, as well as the features or circumstances that the courts have held to fall short of PMC. Enhancing members' understanding of PMC alerts can support the implementation of the PMC Strategy in every day policing activities, particularly through integration into practice manuals, recording systems, recruit training and policy documents. Most significantly the alerts direct the police to focus on evidence that can be used to establish PMC. By supporting the PMC strategy the research has the potential to enhance community confidence and contribute to the prevention of PMC.

Conclusion

Condemnation by the United Nations, the potential impact of PMC on the Australian higher education industry, and the level of interest and anxiety expressed in the local and international media about police responses to PMC point to some of the sensitivities and challenges of policing in this area. The VicPol strategy provides a framework for recording, understanding and responding to PMC, while addressing these sensitivities and challenges. VicPol, in partnering with us, is driven by the recognition that the effective implementation of this strategy requires both enhanced organisational knowledge and change in practice. Research such as ours that is built on a sustained and responsive collaboration can assist the police in achieving the objectives of the strategy. The design, and re-design, of the project has built shared understandings between the academics and VicPol of key issues, major areas of interest and, importantly, possibilities for application of emerging knowledge. Partnerships between the police and academics ensure that the research is designed to produce results that are of scholarly and practical importance. Such findings have a greater chance of distribution beyond academic journals to inform policing practice and policy in ways that meet the needs of this dynamic and rapidly shifting terrain.

In this chapter we have sought to provide an example of how case law analysis can provide insight into the manner in which prejudice motivated crime is being defined and interpreted by Australian courts. This analysis is of interest to scholars given the complex nature of hate crime and the criminal justice response. But these insights can, in turn, be mobilised in everyday policing. We hope the identification of evidence found to be sufficient by the courts to support a finding of PMC will assist the police to understand the meaning of the concept of PMC, the 'alerts' that signal that such a crime may have been committed and the kinds of evidence that needs to be gathered to better investigate, prosecute, sentence and, ultimately, prevent, the problem of prejudice motivated crime.

References

Chapman, A. and Kelly, K. (2005) 'Australian Anti-Vilification Law: A Discussion of the Public/Private Divide and the Work Relations Context', *Sydney Law Review,* 27 (2): 203–36.

Cowdery, N. (2009) *Review of Laws of Vilification: Criminal Aspects*, Roundtable on Hate Crime and Vilification Law: Developments and Directions, Sydney Institute of Criminology, http://sydney.edu.au/law/criminology/ahcn/docs_pdfs/Cowdrey_Antivilification_Roundtable_Usyd_2009.pdf

Cronin, S., McDevitt, J., Farrell, A. and Nolan, J. (2007) 'Bias-Crime Reporting: Organisational Responses to Ambiguity, Uncertainty and Infrequency in Eight Police Departments', *American Behavioural Scientist,* 51 (2): 213–31.

Duffin, C. (2007) 'Policing Hate Crime', *Nursing Standard,* 21 (22): 18–19.

Feenan, D. (2006) 'Religious Vilification Laws: Quelling Fires of Hatred?', *Alternative Law Journal,* 31 (3): 153–8.

Flitton, D. (2010) 'UN Panel's Race Crime Rebuke *Age* 10 August 2010 www.theage.com.au/victoria/un-panels-race-crime-rebuke-20100829-13xmw.html

Hall, N. (2005) *Hate Crime*, Cullompton: Willan.

Home Office Police Standards Unit (2005) *Hate Crime: Delivering a Quality Service: Good Practice and Tactical Guidance*, London: Home Office Police Standards Unit and Association of Chief Police Officers.

Iganski, P. (2008) *'Hate Crime' and the City'*, The Policy Press: Bristol.

Jacobs, J. and Potter, K. (1998) *Hate Crimes: Criminal Law and Identity Politics*, Oxford University Press: Oxford.

Jenness, V. and Grattet, R. (2001) *Making Hate a Crime: From Social Movement to Law Enforcement*, Russell Sage Foundation: New York.

Kielinger, V and Paterson, S. (2007) 'Policing Hate Crime in London', *American Behavioural Scientist,* 51 (2): 196–204.

Mason, G. (2009) 'Hate Crime Laws in Australia: Are they Achieving their Goals?', *Criminal Law Journal,* 33 (6): 326–40.

Mason, G. (2012) 'I Am Tomorrow': Violence Against Indian Students in Australia and Political Denial, *Australian and New Zealand Journal of Criminology*, 45 (4): 4–25. Also available as Sydney Law School Research Paper No. 11/93, http://ssrn.com/abstract=1957439

Mason, G., McCulloch, J. and Maher, J. (2012) *Working Paper 1: The Victoria Police Prejudice Motivated Crime Strategy: Contexts, Aims and Comparisons.*

Meagher, D. (2006) 'So Far No Good: the Regulatory Failure of Criminal Racial Vilification Laws in Australia', PLR, 17: 213.

Metropolitan Police Service (MPS) (2010) *Hate Crime Policy*, London: Metropolitan Police Service.

Meyerson, D. (2009) 'The Protection of Religious Rights Under Australian Law', *Brigham Young University Law Review*, 529–53.

Morgan, J. (2002) 'US Hate Crime Legislation: A Legal Model to Avoid in Australia', *Journal of Sociology*, 38 (1): 25–48.

NSW Police Force (2011) *Policy on Sexuality and Gender Diversity 2011-2014: Working with Gay, Lesbian, Bisexual, Transgender and Intersex People*, NSW Police Force.

Organisation for Security and Co-operation in Europe OSCE (2009) *Hate Crime Laws: A Practical Guide*, Warsaw: Office for Democratic Institutions and Human Rights, Organisation for Security and Co-operation in Europe.

Stanko, E. (2001) 'Re-Conceptualising the Policing of Hatred: Confessions and Worrying Dilemmas of a Consultant', *Law and Critique,* 12: 309–29.

Victoria Police (2010) *Prejudice Motivated Crime Strategy*, Corporate Strategy and Governance Department, Victoria Police: Melbourne.

Victoria Police Diagnosis Paper (2010) *Prejudice Motivated Crime Strategy: Diagnosis Paper*, Crime Strategy Group, Victoria Police.

Victoria Police (2011) *Prejudice Motivated Crime Brochure,* Corporate Strategy and Governance Department, Victoria Police: Melbourne.

FIFTEEN

Policing hate against Gypsies and Travellers: dealing with the dark side

Zoë James

Hate crime scholarship in the UK has burgeoned in recent years, providing a voice to victims through research and subsequent policy development that is informed 'from the ground up'. Gypsies and Travellers have been included within this research and policy environment, particularly having been recognised as victims of hate crime by government action plans on hate crime in 2009 and 2012 (Home Office, 2009, 2012a). However, Gypsies and Travellers experience a mixed message from government as other policies that are used to 'manage' their lifestyles act to exclude them and vilify their traditional nomadic ways of living. As a consequence community tensions between Gypsies and Travellers and settled communities are not resolved and Gypsies and Travellers experience hate victimisation (James, 2013).

This chapter examines how Gypsies and Travellers fit within the hate crime agenda and the contradictions this presents in light of their management more generally as a 'problem' population by policing agencies. Initially the chapter contextualises the experiences of Gypsies and Travellers specifically by drawing on hate crime scholarship and Gypsy and Traveller studies. It then goes on to identify the hate victimisation of Gypsies and Travellers and the policing responses to this. Finally, the chapter concludes by briefly considering the underpinning sedentarist notions that inform community tensions and result in hate crimes against Gypsies and Travellers that are not effectively dealt with.

Defining hate crime and managing prejudice

As noted in numerous studies of hate crime, definition of the concept has proved difficult (Hall, 2005; Chakraborti and Garland, 2009) and a lack of consensus serves to stir debate among academics and confusion or dissolution among practitioners (Chakraborti, 2010;

James and Simmonds, 2012). In essence, the aim of defining a crime or incident as a 'hate crime' is to differentiate offences that are committed due to a motivation of 'hostility or prejudice' in order to challenge discrimination and oppression of marginalised groups (Perry, 2001). The notion of hate crime then, and the legislative framework that it informs, provides a message to society that victimisation of people on the basis of their identity is unacceptable.

Despite the laudable intent of the hate crime agenda, the practical application of it within a legal system that is codified is more difficult. As Chakraborti and Garland (2009) note, the law allows sentence enhancement for offences motivated by hostility or prejudice in some instances, but this is not comprehensive for all offences that may be so motivated. The most recent government policy on hate crime (Home Office, 2012a) identifies personal characteristics that may typically be protected under a hate crime agenda and are monitored: disability, race, religion or belief, sexual orientation and transgender identity. However, it also notes that local areas may choose to include other characteristics within hate crime policies in order to reflect local issues and therefore challenge prejudice more widely. Examples given of additional characteristics are age, gender or appearance. There is however, no corresponding legislation that can enhance the sentence of an offender who commits an offence motivated by hostility or prejudice beyond the five monitored characteristics (and even those vary in the robustness of legislation available). Police officers are the most likely state agent to deal with reported hate crimes and senior officers are certainly committed to the goal of tackling discrimination via hate crime resolution. However, police constables are pragmatists, who draw on the parameters of the law to inform their actions (Reiner, 2010). They are therefore less likely to recognise or are confused by the hate crime agenda, which requires a nuanced understanding of a concept that reaches beyond the codified system of law (Hall, 2010; James and Simmonds, 2012).

The aim of providing a broad definition of hate crime is to ensure that individual cases are dealt with by criminal justice processes appropriately. Since Macpherson (1999) identified the failure of police officers to recognise the racist nature of the murder of Stephen Lawrence and the subsequent deficiencies of the investigation of that case, the hate crime agenda has gained pace in order to ensure that police investigations are procedurally appropriate and victims are supported. However, as noted above, police constables that deal with hate crime cases are likely to be led by legal protections, rather than by broad notions of hate crime that will not result in specific legal outcomes (enhanced sentences). The application of hate crime policy to Gypsies and Travellers exemplifies the contradiction between policy and practice due to the diversity of communities represented under the banner of 'Gypsies and Travellers'.

Gypsies and Travellers: race and culture

Gypsies and Travellers have a long history of living in the UK and are made up of a number of distinct communities. Romany Gypsies are recognised as having lived in the UK since the 15th century, Irish Travellers came to the mainland of the UK in the 19th century and Showmen have had ancient charter to hold fairs since the 12th century (Murdoch and Johnson, 2004). Most recently, New Travellers took on a travelling lifestyle in the 1970s (James, 2007). Therefore, the term 'Gypsies and Travellers' refers to multiple communities that includes both racially and culturally defined groups; Romany Gypsies and Irish Travellers are recognised as racial groups within race relations legislation whereas New Travellers and Showmen are not. Despite this, legislation and policy designed to manage the lifestyles of Gypsies and Travellers utilise a broad definition of those communities that refers to, 'Persons of nomadic habit of life, whatever their race or origin' (Office of the Deputy Prime Minister, ODPM, 2006: 9). Contradiction therefore ensues, as Gypsies and Travellers are managed within a broad definition that bases their identity on 'nomadism'. On the other hand, hate crime protections, which utilise sentence enhancement on the basis of racial identity, exclude those Gypsies and Travellers who are not recognised racial groups. The intention of contemporary hate crime policy to allow broader definitions of hate victimisation allows inclusion of culturally defined Gypsies and Travellers, but as noted above, policing agencies are unlikely to embrace such a wobbly concept that does not reflect the codes of legal protection. This is further evidenced by the high proportion of hate crime cases in the crime statistics that are racially motivated (Home Office, 2012b).

The ability of the hate crime agenda to provide comprehensive support and protection to Gypsies and Travellers, and to address prejudicial attitudes more widely, is therefore problematic due to the inability of policing agencies to embrace its aims in application. This is augmented by the policing of the lifestyles of Gypsies and Travellerss under legislation designed to manage 'unauthorised encampments' of Gypsies and Travellers and 'illegal development' of land by Gypsies and Travellers wherein Gypsies and Travellers are perceived 'en masse' as a problem, rather than as communities in need of some protection.

Indeed, research has shown that Gypsies and Travellers are largely considered by policing agencies to be offenders, rather than victims, and are policed accordingly (James, 2013), as will be discussed further below.

Accommodation and victimisation

Multiple governments have attempted to require or encourage local authorities to provide or approve appropriate accommodation for Gypsies and Travellers in their areas since the commons were closed by the Caravan Sites and Control of Development Act 1960. Previously common land had acted as Gypsies and Travellers traditional stopping space and their closure forced Gypsies and Travellers on to land that encroached on sedentarist environments, including towns and cities. Provision of local authority Gypsy and Traveller sites or approval of sites owned by Gypsies and Travellers has been extremely limited as local authorities have resisted requirements, both in legislation and policy, to provide sites (Morris and Clements, 2002). This has resulted in a crisis of accommodation for Gypsies and Travellers that has had multiple consequences for their communities in terms of public perceptions of them, their future accommodation, their consequent welfare and subsequent management as a problem population (Bhopal and Myers, 2008; Cemlyn et al, 2009).

Gypsies and Travellers tend to live in over-crowded accommodation, most commonly on unauthorised encampments. These are often in places deemed inappropriate, such as on the roadside in lay-bys or in public areas like recreation parks (Cemlyn et al, 2009). The inappropriate nature of such spaces for Gypsies and Travellers is largely determined by the general public who complain to local authorities when they see unauthorised encampments that do not conform to their notion of what constitutes a legitimate 'Gypsy' site with a horse-drawn wagon (Holloway, 2005). Gypsies and Travellers in contemporary society are more likely to live in modern vehicles or caravans and unauthorised encampments may appear unkempt due to the lack of facilities, such as rubbish collection, provided to them by local authorities (Greenfields, 2010). Sedentarist communities fear these Gypsies and Travellers and perceive them as 'invaders' (Kabachnik, 2010) who should be removed from their area. Even when Gypsies and Travellers purchase land for development of a site they are rarely welcomed by sedentarist communities and are unlikely to attain planning permission. In 90% of cases planning applications by Gypsies and Travellers are turned down on first hearing, often due to campaigns against such sites by local residents (CRE, 2006).

Legislation allows the eviction of Gypsies and Travellers from unauthorised encampments and illegal developments by local authorities and policing agencies under the Criminal Justice and Public Order Act 1994 (CJPOA) (and as amended under the Anti-Social Behaviour Act 2003) and the Town and Country Planning Act 1990. These laws are accompanied by central and local government policies that place their emphasis on managing community tensions by appeasing sedentary communities, rather than providing for Gypsies and Travellers. So, unauthorised encampments can be evicted under the CJPOA by police within short time frames, if deemed necessary (James, 2004). Further, current government plans to increase the flexibility of Temporary Stop Notices on illegal developments, will mean that Gypsies and Travellers living on their own land without planning permission will be more easily evicted (Milne, 2013). The threat of eviction commonly causes Gypsies and Travellers to move on prior to formal processes being enacted due to their previous negative experiences of forced eviction and fear that such eviction will threaten their homes (James, 2006).

The lack of appropriate accommodation provided to Gypsies and Travellers has been shown by research to have extremely poor outcomes for them in relation to their welfare, their health (Hajioff and McKee, 2000; Parry et al, 2004) and education (OFSTED, 1996, 1999). Additionally, and most importantly in terms of this chapter, Gypsies and Travellers have been found to experience high levels of victimisation, particularly when living on unauthorised encampments (Southern and James, 2006; Home Office, 2009; Greenfields, 2010). Gypsies and Travellers who live in such circumstances are constantly required to move on from their stopping places either due to their inappropriate circumstances, due to their experiences of victimisation or for fear of forced eviction by the authorities. This 'constant cycle' (Cemlyn et al, 2009) of movement and eviction means that Gypsies and Travellers are unable to become part of local communities. They live on the margins of society as 'strangers' who constitute a feared 'other' (Simmel, 1971).

McVeigh (2007) argues that the failure of the state to provide accommodation for Gypsies and Travellers, is due to its assimilationist aims that have been actively pursued by placing Gypsies and Travellers within a discourse of punishment, rather than provision (Bancroft, 2000). Indeed, a number of Gypsies and Travellers have felt compelled to live in housing, despite the cultural dissonance that living in 'bricks and mortar' accommodation causes, not least due to the distance left between families who are used to living closely together on sites (Greenfields, 2010). The move in to housing does not appear to diminish hate motivated victimisation however (Cemlyn et al, 2009), and could be argued to increase its impact, given that families in housing do not have access to traditional support mechanisms and cannot move away from the problem, as they would if mobile (James, 2013).

Hate victimisation of Gypsies and Travellers

The extent of hate crime committed against Gypsies and Travellers is difficult to measure effectively in quantitative terms. Given that, as noted above, Gypsies and Travellers live on the margins of society, there is only a limited knowledge of numbers of Gypsies and Travellers in the UK. In the 2011 England and Wales census a new category of 'Gypsy or Irish Traveller' was introduced and 58,000 people identified themselves in this category, constituting 0.1% of the population. However, by gathering other measures of Gypsy and Traveller numbers in the UK, it is commonly estimated that there are approximately 300,000 Gypsies and Travellers in the UK, making up 0.6% of the population (ODPM, 2006). These figures remain tentative, however, as measures of Gypsy and Traveller numbers have been contested on a number of grounds, not least because the annual 'caravan count' carried out by local authorities tends to count vehicles rather than people and often ignores New Travellers and Showmen (Niner, 2004). Further, Gypsies and Travellers living in housing are rarely incorporated within statistics (though the census may have resolved this somewhat) and Gypsies and Travellers who are on the move or living in more hidden locations are also not counted (James, 2005). The British Crime Survey measures crimes according to households, which would only include those Gypsies and Travellers living in housing. Furthermore, the British Crime Survey does not categorise for Gypsies and Travellers specifically, incorporating them in to a 'white other' category for analysis. No surveys of the victimisation of Gypsies and Travellers have been carried out. Hence, the degree of victimisation is not a 'dark figure' of crime, but rather, an invisible figure.

Knowledge of the hate victimisation of Gypsies and Travellers has needed to be gathered from a range of sources that were not necessarily designed for that purpose. Research and study with Gypsies and Travellers has long recognised their victimisation (for example, see Cemlyn et al, 2009; Morris and Clements, 2002). However, discussion of this issue has been embedded within broader considerations of social exclusion, rather than as specific study. Most commonly, the hate victimisation of Gypsies and Travellers has been conflated with their experiences of discrimination by state agencies. This has occurred for three reasons. First, Gypsies and Travellers place their experiences of victimisation on a continuum that ranges from prejudicial actions against them by members of the public to poor treatment by state officials (James, 2013). Secondly, the failure of agencies to act in support of Gypsies and Travellers when they have reported hate motivated crimes against them has meant that their sense of victimisation has heightened (James, 2011) and they subsequently experience secondary victimisation (Mawby and Walklate, 1994). Finally, scholars of Gypsy and Traveller issues have focused attention on 'anti-nomadism' or 'anti-Gypsyism' (McVeigh, 1997; Greenfields, 2010) that incorporate analysis of all prejudicial actions and sentiment against Gypsies and Travellers. In order to better understand hate victimisation of Gypsies and Travellers here, this chapter will go on to draw knowledge out of existing research on crimes committed against Gypsies and Travellers that have been hate motivated. It will then consider how the police specifically manage these experiences and the interaction therein.

Most recent research exploring Gypsies and Travellers experiences of victimisation has been carried out through secondary analysis of surveys designed to assess the accommodation needs of Gypsies and Travellers. In 2004 the New Labour government attempted to resolve the accommodation crisis for Gypsies and Travellers by requiring local authorities to assess their accommodation needs alongside broader measures of housing need under the Housing Act 2004. The Gypsy and Traveller Accommodation Assessments (GTAA) that were subsequently completed informed Regional Spatial Strategies (RSS), which provided evidence for provision of sites in local areas (the RSS were abandoned in 2010 by the Coalition government). The GTAAs varied in quality and consistency, despite the identification of good practice and they have largely failed to result in provision of sites (Brown and Niner, 2009). They do, however, provide the most comprehensive 'snapshot' of Gypsies and Travellers lives available and as such are an excellent research resource that does not require further invasion in to the lives of Gypsies and Travellers who express research fatigue (Robinson, 2002).

The GTAAs that followed best practice guidance gathered some information on the victimisation of Gypsies and Travellers. This was rationalised as necessary in GTAAs due to the impact of victimisation on Gypsies and Travellers movement and choice of dwelling, as had been noted by earlier research (Morris and Clements, 2002; Cemlyn et al, 2009). Greenfields (2010) utilised analysis of three GTAAs to consider anti-Gypsyism, including hate crime (though she does not refer to it as such). My research on hate crime (James, 2011, 2013) similarly utilised GTAA research findings that were gathered from a random sample of all GTAAs completed in England. These pieces of research clearly identify patterns of victimisation of Gypsies and Travellers that are motivated by hate and are not appropriately dealt with by the police or other support agencies.

The pattern of hate victimisation of Gypsies and Travellers is similar to other groups who experience victimisation motivated by hate. Offending, harassment and anti-social behaviour against Gypsies and Travellers was found in research to be perpetual, manifested in multiple incidents and crimes that were commonly minor but also included serious offending (Greenfields, 2010; James, 2011, 2013). Greenfields (2010: 63) research found that over 95% of Gypsy and Traveller respondents to the GTAAs she analysed reported having experienced incidents of 'racism and discrimination from surrounding populations'. Gypsies and Travellers found to be most at risk of hate crime lived on unauthorised encampments, often on the roadside (James, 2011). Abusive behaviour towards Gypsies and Travellers living in such circumstances was often committed by passers-by, apparently in the normal course of their day (Greenfields, 2010).

As is known from other research, repetitive minor offences or incidents against individuals or groups can have a cumulative impact (Bowling, 1999) that can also affect the wider community (Noelle, 2002). Gypsies and Travellers interviewed in GTAAs often reported hate crimes against other members of their community that had caused them to be fearful. The tradition of storytelling among many Gypsy and Traveller communities can exacerbate such fears as tales of abuse and harassment are passed between generations and a sense of 'safety' is only attained by close proximity to family (Greenfields, 2010). The lack of appropriate accommodation provided to Gypsies and Travellers, their forced movement through eviction and their assimilation in to housing breaks down those family ties, but their safety remains tentative as hate crimes do not diminish when Gypsies and Travellers live in housing and they increase when they live on unauthorised encampments, as previously noted.

The types of incident committed against Gypsies and Travellers that were reported in GTAAs included name calling and abuse, criminal damage of vehicles (homes), stone throwing and physical assault (Greenfields, 2010). One GTAA referred to their being an 'endemic level of hostility towards Gypsies and Travellers' (James, 2011: 141). Additionally that research noted that experiences of bullying, harassment and crimes against Gypsies and Travellers were reported as having occurred on sites, in housing, in school and at work. It is unsurprising then, that Gypsies and Travellers commonly do not identify themselves as such for fear of further abuse (Cemlyn et al,

2009). Neither is it surprising that Gypsies and Travellers living on unauthorised encampments cite harassment and abuse from sedentarists as one of the core reasons for moving away from their previous location, alongside their fear of eviction (James, forthcoming).

Clearly then, hate crimes against Gypsies and Travellers are commonplace and range in seriousness. The potential seriousness of hate crime against Gypsies and Travellers may be best described by reference to a particular case. In 2003, a 15 year old Irish Traveller boy, Johnny Delaney, was brutally kicked and beaten to death. The teenagers who carried out the murder made racist comments while they assaulted Johnny, including referring to him as 'only a … Gypsy' (Greenfields, 2006). The police did treat the case as a racist incident, but the court did not enhance sentence on the basis of the hate motivation. The failure of the court to recognise the motivation for the murder of Johnny Delaney may be explained by the normalisation of hate crime against Gypsies and Travellers. Again in 2003, the Firle Bonfire incident exemplifies the societal acceptance of the demonization of Gypsies and Travellers. As part of their annual bonfire night celebrations, the small village of Firle in Sussex, England, burnt an effigy of a Gypsy caravan. The effigy was a large cardboard construction of a caravan that contained the image of a family, two adults and two children, and had a licence plate of 'P1 KEY'. This incident led to one complaint from a villager to the authorities, who was then herself subjected to threats and intimidation by other villagers for having complained. The Commission for Racial Equality intervened in the case, that appeared not be being pursued by the police effectively, but ultimately no conviction was sought by the Crown Prosecution Service against the organisers of the event. Greenfields (2006) questions the likelihood of such cases against any other minority community being dealt with similarly and she suggests that the lack of action denotes the low status given to Gypsies and Travellers by the state.

Policing hate against Gypsies and Travellers

Hate crime scholarship has identified that victims of hate crime rarely report incidents against them to the authorities and multiple efforts have been made to enhance reporting rates, particularly through third party mechanisms that do not require reporting directly to the police (for example, Hall, 2005; Chakraborti, 2010; Christmann and Wong, 2010). The reluctance of hate crime victims to report to the police may be due to the minor nature of the offending against them, which they deem not serious enough to warrant police attention, it may be because they fear reprisal, because they do not think the police will take the offending against them seriously, or because they do not trust the police to deal with it effectively (Hall, 2005). Further, the failure of police to recognise the cumulative impact of multiple hate crime incidents experienced by individuals or groups has been argued to have an effect on the willingness of victims to report hate crimes to them (Bowling, 1999).

Gypsies' and Travellers' hate crime reporting behaviour reflects that of other hate crime victims. The main reason cited for their lack of willingness to report hate crimes to the police is the lack of trust Gypsies and Travellers have in them. This lack of trust is twofold. First, similar to other minority communities and particularly black communities (Bowling, 1999), the over-policing of Gypsies and Travellers as offenders has resulted in their unwillingness to engage with the police. This sense of over-policing is largely in relation to the management of Gypsies and Travellers lifestyles, particularly their mobility. The crisis of accommodation for Gypsies and Travellers has resulted in them living in places that are illegal and allow the police to evict them and, if deemed necessary, to remove their vehicles. Given that the removal of Gypsies' and Travellers' vehicles would result in them becoming homeless, it is unsurprising that they fear eviction more than any other state action (James, 2005). Policies designed to encourage reporting of hate crime via multiple agencies in order to circumvent communities concerns regarding policing, are not necessarily effective for Gypsies and Travellers however.

Similar to other families living in poverty, Gypsies and Travellers experience 'policing beyond the police' (Donzelot, 1997) within a plural policing environment. Public agencies that are designed to provide welfare to Gypsies and Travellers, including health, education and local authorities, have been found to act in a policing role when working with Gypsies and Travellers as they gather information on them that is shared and utilised to enforce eviction (James, 2007). Additionally, research has shown that private agencies commissioned to provide sites for Gypsies and Travellers also work closely with public agencies in order to police Gypsy and Traveller communities (James and Richardson, 2006). The large scale eviction of Gypsy and Traveller sites by multiple agencies epitomises the fears of Gypsies and Travellers. The eviction of the Dale Farm Traveller site in Essex, England in 2011 is a case in point; over 100 police officers in full riot gear, using public order policing methods, including the use of Tasers, forced entry to the unauthorised development in order to facilitate private bailiffs to carry out the eviction for the local authority.

The third sector is therefore the final port of call for many Gypsies and Travellers to attain support. However, notwithstanding some excellent support provided in some areas (such as, in England, Friends, Families and Travellers in Sussex or Leeds Gypsy and Traveller Exchange) their services are rarely set up in a flexible fashion that can support communities on the move. Research commissioned by the Citizens Advice Bureaux (James and Simmonds, 2012), showed that there were multiple barriers to Gypsy and Traveller engagement. Race Equality Councils often fill the breach for Gypsies and Travellers in need of localised support. However, these services are provided within the confines of determinants of race, and their willingness to engage with New Travellers particularly is variable.

Gypsies and Travellers therefore do not trust the police, nor do they trust other agencies associated with them. Their existence on the margins of society and their increasingly insular lifestyles as a consequence of over-policing has augmented their lack of trust and their subsequent unwillingness to report hate crimes. Furthermore, when they *do* report hate crimes, they are rarely dealt with effectively. Greenfields (2010) research found that Gypsies and Travellers who reported hate crimes to the police were often ignored. Additionally, my research showed that Gypsy and Traveller reports of hate crime to the police were not dealt with appropriately (James, 2011). In some instances policing agencies were found to have prejudiced attitudes towards Gypsies and Travellers that exacerbated their other negative perceptions, leaving Gypsies and Travellers feeling unprotected and unsafe (James, 2013; Greenfields, 2010). Neighbourhood policing policies that attempt to engage more effectively with diverse communities are sometimes effective in working with Gypsies and Travellers living on authorised sites (James and Richardson, 2006). However, the geographically bounded nature of this policing approach does not cohere with the mobility of Gypsies and Travellers whose settlement in an area is generally addressed by police response officers as a problem to be solved, i.e. moved on (James, 2007).

Conclusion

This chapter has considered how Gypsies and Travellers fit within the hate crime agenda, in policy and in practice. It initially outlined the problem of defining hate crime by examining its application to different groups of Gypsies and Travellers, some of whom are not protected by legislation. In doing so, it identified the implementation gap between policy and practice in policing as police officers are loath to utilise actions that do not end up with a 'result'. Hall (2005) has previously noted the lack of 'will' in policing to effectively engage with the hate crime agenda and this chapter affirms this point. The chapter went on to outline the importance of accommodation issues in determining the victimisation experiences of Gypsies and Travellers and their designation by authorities as a 'problem', in need of management or assimilation and thus their prevailing identity as offenders, rather than victims. The accommodation crisis faced by Gypsies and Travellers underpins their lived experience, their failure to be embraced within society and the community tensions this augments. The principles of sedentarism that order contemporary western society are subverted by Gypsies and Travellers, who utilise space and place differently, in ways that are deemed inappropriate by the sedentary norm (Kabachnik, 2010, 2012). Gypsies and Travellers are therefore misunderstood and feared by sedentary communities. In the portentous words of Star Wars' Yoda, 'fear leads to hate, hate leads to anger and anger leads to the dark side' (Lucas, 1977) and hence, the fears of sedentary communities have been shown here to result in the commission of crimes against Gypsies and Travellers that are motivated by hate. Tragically, such crimes are commonplace and normalised within society to the point that policing agencies do not respond to them appropriately and Gypsies and Travellers have no faith in the services designed to protect them as citizens.

Policy development in the arena of hate crime has effectively engaged with research identifying Gypsies and Travellers as victims, as noted in the introduction to this chapter. Such engagement with research is vital in providing a policy environment that is meaningful to managers and practitioners who work with hate crime victims. However, as has been identified here, there are gaps in implementation, due to the diverse, complex nature of hate crime victimisation and the communities affected by it. It is therefore necessary for those carrying out research with Gypsies and Travellers to engage with policy makers effectively, and such research should be disseminated in light of policy development in other areas in order that policies designed to protect and support Gypsies and Travellers are not negated by policies designed to manage them.

References

Bancroft, A. (2000) 'No Interest in Land': Legal and Spatial Enclosure of Gypsy-Travellers in Britain, *Space and Polity,* 4 (1): 41–56.

Bohpal, K. and Myers, M. (2008) *Insiders, Outsiders and Others: Gypsies and Identity,* Hatfield: University of Hertfordshire Press.

Bourne, J. (2002) 'Does Legislating against Racial Violence Work?' *Race and Class,* 44 (2): 81–5.

Bowling, B. (1999) *Violent Racism: Victimisation, Policing and Social Context,* Oxford: Oxford University Press.

Brown, P. and Niner, P. (2009) *Assessing Local Housing Authorities' Progress in Meeting the Accommodation Needs of Gypsy and Traveller Communities in England,* London: EHRC.

Cemlyn, S., Greenfields, M., Burnett, S., Matthews, Z. and Whitwell, C. (2009) *Inequalities Experienced by Gypsy and Traveller Communities: A Review.* London: EHRC

Chakraborti, N. (2010) 'Future Developments for Hate Crime Thinking: Who, What and Why?', in N. Chakraborti (ed.) *Hate Crime: Concepts, Policy, Future Directions,* Cullompton: Willan.

Chakraborti, N. and Garland, J. (2009) *Hate Crime: Impact, Causes and Responses,* London: Sage.

Christmann, K. and Wong, K. (2010) 'Hate Crime Victims and Hate Crime Reporting: Some Impertinent Questions', in N. Chakraborti (ed.) *Hate Crime: Concepts, Policy, Future Directions,* Cullompton: Willan, pp. 194–208.

CRE (Commission for Racial Equality)) (2006). *Common Ground: Equality, Good Race Relations and Sites for Gypsies and Irish Travellers,* London: CRE.

Donzelot, J. (1997) *The Policing of Families,* London: The John Hopkins Press Ltd.

Greenfields, M. (2006) 'Gypsies, Travellers and Legal Matters', in C. Clark and M. Greenfields (eds) (2006) *Here to Stay: the Gypsies and Travellers of Britain.* Hatfield: University of Hertfordshire Press.

Greenfields, M. (2010) 'Settlement and Anti-Gypsyism: 'If You Know Someone Hates You Before You Start, You Puts up the Barrier'', *Romani Mobilities in Europe Conference,* University of Oxford.

Hajioff, S. and McKee, M. (2000) 'The Health of the Roma People: a Review of the Published Literature', *Journal of Epidemiology and Community Health,* 54: 864–9.

Hall, N. (2005) *Hate Crime,* Cullompton: Willan.

Hall, N. (2010) 'Law Enforcement and Hate Crime: Theoretical Perspectives on the Complexities of Policing "Hatred"', in N. Chakraborti (ed.) *Hate Crime: Concepts, Policy, Future Directions,* Cullompton: Willan, pp. 149–68.

Holloway, S.L. (2005) 'Articulating Otherness? White Rural Residents Talk about Gypsy-Travellers', *Transactions of the Institute of British Geographers,* 30 (3): 351–67.

Home Office (2009) *Hate Crime – The Cross-Government Action Plan,* London: Home Office.

Home Office (2012a) *Challenge it, Report it, Stop it: The Government's Plan to Tackle Hate Crime,* London: Home Office.

Home Office (2012b) *Hate crimes, England and Wales 2011/12,* www.homeoffice.gov.uk/counter-terrorism/uk-counter-terrorism-strat/.

James, Z. (2004) *New Travellers, New Policing? Exploring the policing of New Traveller communities under the Criminal Justice and Public Order Act 1994,* PhD University of Surrey.

James, Z. (2005) 'Eliminating Communities? Exploring the implications of policing methods used to manage New Travellers', *International Journal of the Sociology of Law,* 33(3): 159–168.

James, Z. (2006) 'Policing Space: Managing New Travellers in England', *British Journal of Criminology,* 46 (3): 470–85.

James, Z. (2007) 'Policing Marginal Spaces: Controlling Gypsies and Travellers', *Criminology and Criminal Justice: An International Journal,* 7 (4): 367–89.

James, Z. (2011) 'Gypsies and Travellers in the Countryside: Managing a Risky Population', in R. Yarwood and R.I. Mawby (eds) *Constable Countryside? Policing, Governance and Rurality.* Aldershot: Ashgate.

James, Z. (2013) *Offenders or Victims?: An exploration of Gypsies and Travellers as a Policing Paradox,* in C. Phillips and C. Webster (eds) *New Directions in Race, Ethnicity and Crime.* Abingdon: Routledge.

James, Z. (forthcoming) *Policing Gypsies and Travellers: Managing identity and controlling nomadism,* Bristol: The Policy Press.

James, Z. and Richardson, J. (2006) *Controlling Accommodation: Policing Gypsies and Travellers,* in A. Dearling, T. Newburn and P. Somerville (eds) *Housing and Crime,* Chartered Institute of Housing.

James, Z. and Simmonds, L. (2012) *Exploring Prejudice: Mapping Hate Crime in the South West,* Plymouth University.

Kabachnik, P. (2010) 'Place Invaders: Constructing the Nomadic Threat in England', *The Geographical Review,* 100 (1): 90–108.

Kabachnik, P. (2012) 'Nomads and Mobile Places: Disentangling Place, Space and Mobility', *Identities: Global Studies in Culture and Power.* DOI: 10.1080/1070289X.2012.672855.

Lucas, G. (1977) *Star Wars* [DVD], USA: Twentieth Century Fox.

Macpherson, W. (1999) *The Stephen Lawrence Inquiry,* London: HMSO.

Mawby, R. and Walklate, S. (1994) *Critical Victimology,* London: Sage.

McVeigh, R. (1997) Theorising Sedentarism: The Roots of Anti-Nomadism, in T. Acton (ed.) *Gypsy Politics and Traveller Identity,* Hatfield: University of Hertfordshire Press.

McVeigh, R. (2007) 'The "Final Solution": Reformism, Ethnicity Denial and the Politics of Anti-Travellerism in Ireland', *Social Policy and Society,* 7 (1): 91–102.

Milne, R. (2013) *More Flexible Stop Notice Regime for Traveller Sites Proposed,* www.planningportal.gov.uk/general/news/stories/2013/Jan13/10012013/100113_2.

Morris, R. and Clements, L. (2002) *At What Cost? The Economics of Gypsy and Traveller Encampments,* Bristol: The Policy Press.

Murdoch, A. and Johnson, C. (2004) 'Introduction', in C. Johnson and M. Willers (eds) *Gypsy and Traveller Law,* London: Legal Action Group.

Niner, P. (2004) *Counting Gypsies and Travellers: A Review of the Gypsy Caravan Count System,* London: Office of the Deputy Prime Minister.

Noelle, M. (2002) 'The Ripple Effect of the Matthew Shepard Murder', *American Behavioural Scientist,* 46 (1):27–50.

Office of the Deputy Prime Minister (ODPM) (2006) *Gypsy and Traveller Accommodation Assessments: Draft Practice Guidance,* ODPM: Gypsy and Traveller Unit.

OFSTED (1996) *The Education of Travelling Children: A Survey of Educational Provision for Travelling Children,* London: OFSTED Publications Centre.

OFSTED (1999) *Raising the Attainment of Minority Ethnic Pupils,* London: OFSTED Publications Centre.

Parry, G., Van Cleemput, P., Peters, J., Moore, J., Walters, S., Thomas, K. and Cooper, C. (2004) *The Health Status of Gypsies and Travellers in England,* Report of Department of Health Inequalities in Health Research Initiative Project 121/7500, London: Department of Health.

Perry, B. (2001) *In the Name of Hate: Understanding Hate Crimes,* New York: Routledge.

Reiner, R. (2010) *The Politics of the Police,* Oxford: Oxford University Press.

Robinson, V. (2002) "Doing Research" with Refugees and Asylum Seekers', *Swansea Geographer,* 37: 61–7.

Simmel, G. (1971) *On Individuality and Social Forms: Selected Writings of George Simmel.* Chicago: University of Chicago Press.

Southern, R. and James, Z. (2006) *Devon-wide Gypsy & Traveller Housing Needs Assessment,* Plymouth: University of Plymouth.

SIXTEEN

Understanding how 'hate' hurts: a case study of working with offenders and potential offenders

Paul Iganski, with Karen Ainsworth, Laura Geraghty, Spiridoula Lagou and Nafysa Patel

All crimes leave a hurtful residue for the victims. But some crimes inflict more pain than others. This is not just or always even a matter of physical pain. Physical assaults against the body are relatively few considering all the different crimes committed. It is the rather more frequent emotional wounds to the hearts and minds of victims left behind after the event. Victims try in different ways to heal these wounds. For their part, many offenders do not foresee the extent of the injuries they cause. A few offenders do of course act intentionally to inflict particular hurts. But in many instances offenders act on impulse without much forethought. And in many other instances their acts are expressive reactions to situations in which they find themselves and in which they lash out when they feel they have been wronged.

In jurisdictions where verbal expressions can constitute criminal acts, such as in the United Kingdom, these types of offences account for a majority of so-called 'hate crimes': so called, because it is rare that offenders truly hate their victims. Most 'hate crime' scholars would agree that. Accepting that the matter is rather more complex than the perpetrators of 'hate crime' simply hating their victims opens-up the potential for working with offenders to prevent damage they might inflict on a future occasion. Some practitioners working to rehabilitate 'hate crime' offenders work on the principle that if empathy for the victim can be engendered within the perpetrator's own heart and mind, if they can be brought to appreciate the full consequence of their actions, then those who do not truly 'hate' might think twice before acting again in the way they had done so before. And likewise if potential perpetrators can be brought to understand the full consequences of what they might do, then they too might think twice before they do it. This chapter unfolds the development of the type of understanding about the hurts of 'hate crime' that is used in working with offenders and potential perpetrators. Two case studies are offered from evaluations of projects in the north west of England to illustrate how understanding about the hurts of 'hate crime' can be used in working with offenders and potential offenders.

How 'hate' hurts

While most victims of crime experience some mental and emotional disturbance, an accumulation of research evidence now clearly shows that on average 'hate crime' victims are more likely than victims in other crimes to report such impacts. Awareness of that differential has informed the legislative and policy response to the problem, and it has also shaped practitioner interventions as this essay will demonstrate. Knowledge of the effects and consequences of 'hate crime' began to be developed in a number of pioneering studies across the 1990s in the United States (cf. Barnes and Ephross, 1994; Hershberger and D'Augelli, 1995; Otis and Skinner, 1996). While the research during this period provided a significant step in understanding the potential harms to individual victims caused by 'hate crime', the research findings were limited in indicating whether 'hate crimes' hurt more than parallel crimes. This was inevitable given that the research aimed to explore and understand in-depth the nature of the impacts on the victims and hence studies consisted of small purposive samples of research participants without matched samples of victims of other crimes. This style of research, which has important value for informing the support needs of victims, has continued and a body of evidence has now accumulated from research in a number of countries which unravels in-depth the harms and impacts of 'hate crime' (for some more recent studies see Dzelme, 2008; Victim Support, 2006).

On the matter of whether 'hate crimes' hurt more than parallel crimes, towards the end of the 1990s Herek et al (1999) compared a purposive sample of lesbians and gay men who had been victims of 'hate crime' with a sample who had been victimised on other grounds than their sexual identity. The 'hate crime' victims recorded statistically significant higher scores on measures of depression, traumatic stress, and anger. And at the beginning of the last decade, Jack McDevitt and colleagues (McDevitt et al, 2001), carried out a mail survey of a purposive sample of victims of assaults reported to the Boston Police Department and victim advocacy agencies. The survey included victims of both 'hate crime' and parallel crimes. The survey questionnaire was designed to measure the psychological post-victimisation impact of 'intrusiveness' and 'avoidance' reactions according to Horowitz's

Psychological Scale utilising a 19 item scale. A number of the items presented statistically significant differences between victims of 'hate crime' and victims of parallel crimes, with the former reporting stronger reactions on measures of depression, nervousness, lack of concentration, unintentional thinking of the incident and thoughts of futility regarding their lives (McDevitt et al, 2001).

A further step forward in the evidence was taken by analyses of British Crime Survey (BCS) data for England and Wales, initially for racist crimes (Iganski, 2008), using BCS sweeps for 2002–03, 2003–04, and 2004–05. The analyses were later extended to British Crime Survey sweeps of 2007–08, 2008–09 and 2009–10, to develop understanding of the impacts and consequences of other types of identity crime in which victims are targeted because of their religion, sexual orientation, disability, or age, in research initiated and commissioned by the Equality and Human Rights Commission (EHRC) (Botcherby et al, 2011; Nocon et al, 2011). This body of research overcame methodological limitations of earlier studies by using large random samples of victims, multivariate analyses, and multiple controls, applied to the British Crime Survey data. The BCS (now known as the Crime Survey for England and Wales) asks approximately 45,000 respondents about their experiences of crime in the previous twelve months. The survey enables up to six incidents to be reported by each respondent. For each reported incident respondents are asked whether they think the incident was motivated by the offender's attitude towards their sexual orientation, gender, age, disability, religion or belief, or whether it was racially motivated. This definition is similar to that used by the police in England and Wales when coding crimes as 'hate crimes'. For up to three incidents reported by individual victims, if they report more than one incident, the BCS asks 'Many people have emotional reactions after incidents in which they are victims of crime. Did you personally have any of these reactions after the incident?' Generally, higher proportions of victims in incidents believed to be motivated by the offender's attitudes towards their identity report having an emotional reaction, compared with victims in incidents believed to have been motivated by other reasons. The difference holds even when controlling for major categories of crime. Respondents are asked about the extent of their emotional reaction, and the difference in the proportions reporting 'very much' is wider still between victims in incidents of identity crime and otherwise motivated crime. Again, this holds even when controlling for crime type. Victims are also asked to indicate actions taken by themselves or their household to try to prevent the crime happening again. Victims of 'hate crime' are over three times more likely to report avoiding walking in or going to certain places than victims in otherwise motivated crimes.

More recently, the UK Home Office's first ever statistical report of British Crime Survey data on 'hate crime' (from the 2009/10 and 2010/11 surveys combined) similarly shows that victims of 'hate crime' as a group are more likely to report a range of emotional impacts compared with victims of parallel crimes (Smith et al, 2012: 22), and confirms the findings from the earlier analyses of BCS data.

Applying understanding about the harms of 'hate crime' in redemptive interventions with offenders

Some practitioners working with programmes to rehabilitate 'hate crime' offenders recognise that many offenders are not fully aware of the consequences of their actions at the time they offend, and hence interventions which might help to develop insight into the harms offenders inflict might potentially inhibit future offending. Given such understanding, a number of rehabilitation programmes explicitly seek to foster victim empathy (Iganski, 2012). The principle of empathy for the victim also lies at the heart of restorative justice interventions. The restorative justice model goes beyond victim–offender mediation to promote involvement of the victim, the offender, and the community in the justice process. Such victim–offender mediation has been used in an increasing number of contexts and appears to be increasingly used in the case of 'race-hate crime' – as has begun to be captured in the scholarly literature (Walters and Hoyle 2010, 2012). This essay focuses on some other ways in which victim empathy is promoted with offenders and potential offenders.

For a programme working with offenders, in 2007, Lancashire Constabulary initiated a Hate Crime Awareness Programme designed and delivered by Smile Mediation Ltd, a limited company and charity. Smile provides community, workplace and family mediation, as well as the Hate Crime Awareness Programme, with the services delivered by trained specialist volunteer mediators. The origins of the programme lie in recognition of the need for interventions with 'hate crime' offenders as an alternative to the management of cases by the courts. Such a need is founded on a belief in the limitations of the courts in reducing re-offending, and a belief in the potential effectiveness of non-punitive interventions. The programme is founded on an understanding that many 'hate crime' offenders are not fully aware of the consequences of their behaviour and hence early intervention that helps them to develop insight might potentially inhibit re-offending more effectively than would criminal prosecution.

Offenders attend the Smile Hate Crime Awareness Programme as a condition of a community sentence or as a requirement of post-custody supervision. 72 racially aggravated offenders, who committed offences under Section 5 of the 1986 Public Order Act, have been referred by Lancashire Constabulary to the programme since 2007. A substantial proportion of 'hate crime' offences dealt with by the police involve verbal abuse – expressive acts, rather than physical violence or threats. It is offenders in these types of incidents who are referred to the programme.

A common denominator to these types of incidents is that the offender often feels they have been wronged or slighted in some way and seemingly retaliates to impose an informal justice on the victim and repair the damage to respect the offender feels. The offender's retaliation might be regarded from their point of view as cancelling out the wrong they had suffered by inflicting the same hurt or a greater hurt than they felt themself. Hurting back is a common defence against hurt that has been felt. The words expressed in retaliation are intended to wound. As a mediator suggested, "they are picking on what they see as weakness in somebody to hurt them for whatever that might be. And I think in life people do that. If you want to hurt somebody you try to find their weak point". Such 'weak points' are socially constructed, and social constructions of difference, with negative connotations attached to some differences – skin colour, ethnicity, religion, disability, sexuality, age, gender, body shape, social class, for example – provide well known 'weak points'. They are well known because arguably they are lying in the minds of many, and for some people they might even be present in everyday discourse. To use the words of one of the programme participants: "…everybody on our estate speaks like that. That's the language they all use, we all use it, never known any different."

The feelings of hurt may not solely be generated by the instance of conflict in which the about-to-be racially aggravated offender finds him or herself. Past hurts, or 'baggage', to borrow a word from one of the mediators interviewed, might compound the hurt of the particular incident. The retaliation might then also be targeted well beyond the person inflicting the hurt in the immediate moment to past moments of hurt as well to impose an informal justice and right the wrongs of the past – although such a process will commonly occur beneath the surface of the offender's conscious cognition. In addition to compounding incidents, offender 'baggage' is also seen to be commonly complicit in the emergence or the occurrence of the initial incident which then becomes racially aggravated. While the expressed racial abuse has an instrumental purpose in that it is intended to hurt, arguably many offenders would not anticipate the full extent of the hurt inflicted by their words.

Given such understanding, the key principle underpinning the Smile programme concerns the fostering of victim empathy: a belief that if the awareness of offenders can be raised about the impacts and the consequences of the words they use, then with such insight they might think twice before repeating their behaviour. The programme also works with a premise, founded on the experience of the mediators, that most offenders referred to the programme are not committed 'haters', motivated in their actions or in things they say, by deeply held racist views that they consciously target to maximise the hurts they inflict. Instead, offenders' words are seen to be expressive rather than instrumental with their racist thoughts lying below everyday cognition, springing to the surface with the right trigger, rather than consciously motivating their behaviour. Consequently, although programme participants are referred by the police for racially aggravated offences, racist ideas and racial prejudice are not the main targets of the programme's intervention. Instead, given the understanding concerning offender-impulse and victim-impact underpinning the programme as just discussed, the programme mostly aims to better enable participants to empathise with the victims of their offences, handle the 'baggage' that provided the antecedents to their offence, and manage their emotions and especially their anger in situations of stress so that they might be less likely to lash-out when hurt.

The programme is designed to be delivered jointly by two mediators in a two-hour session with offenders on an individual basis, with a shorter follow-up session six weeks later. On a few occasions it has been delivered with small groups of offenders. A key component of the session involves a focus on 'How hate crime hurts people'. In a sequence of questions offenders are first asked in the face-to-face session with two mediators to think broadly about the consequences of their actions ('Who do you think gets hurt in a hate crime?') and then they are asked to focus specifically on the victim ('How do you think the victim is hurt?'). To spark their thinking offenders are asked to put themselves in the position of the victim, and also imagine their family in the victim's position ('How would you feel if you had been bullied, had your property damaged, or your family threatened because of your race/colour of your skin, your sexual orientation, disability, gender?' 'What would you like to say to the person/people who had done this to you?'). The wider potential impact of 'hate crime' beyond the person targeted (cf. Noelle, 2001, 2009; Perry and Alvi, 2012) is also explored. As one of the mediators explained, "…we use the ripple effect to say what this effect can have right up to the community level of distrust … and also the effect it has on the victims".

Participants are asked to complete an empathy questionnaire from which a 'victim empathy score' is calculated at the beginning of the session and again at the end of the session. Almost all participants show an improvement between the two scores. Participants complete the empathy questionnaire again in a follow-up meeting six weeks after the intervention and the results are more mixed. For some, the increase in empathy is consolidated and marginally further improved, while in other instances there is a decline in victim empathy.

An independent evaluation was commissioned in 2012. The evaluation research applied a 're-offending test' in which a group of 'Smile offenders' who had participated in the Smile intervention more than 18 months prior to the research was compared with a matched, or 'control', group. This consisted of racially aggravated offenders dealt with by the courts and selected from Lancashire Constabulary's records of offenders who had been charged or cautioned for a racially aggravated offence under Section 5 of the Public Order Act 1986 since the inception of the Smile programme in 2007.

The re-offending test showed that when considering re-offending of any type, less than half, or 45%, of the Smile programme participants included in the re-offending test, were charged with an offence on a future date after their completion of the Smile programme. This is a smaller proportion than the three quarters of offenders from the control group who were subsequently charged with an offence on a future date after being dealt with by the courts for a racially aggravated offence. Significantly, none of the participants in the Smile programme was charged with racially aggravated offences on a future occasion following completion of the programme. By contrast, 4 of the 42 matched offenders from the control group were charged with a racially aggravated offence on a future occasion after they had been dealt with by the courts for the earlier racially aggravated offence for which they were selected for the control sample. While this result was at the margins of, and just below, statistical significance, it provided *prima facie* evidence that the Smile programme might be more likely to reduce the potential for future racially aggravated offending when compared with the disposal of offenders by the courts. At the time of writing the evaluation is being extended to include more cases.

Understanding the harms of 'hate crime' for preventative interventions with potential offenders

Preventative activities with potential 'hate crime' offenders, also in the north west of England, were undertaken by the Preston and Western Lancashire Racial Equality Council Race Hate Awareness and Prevention (PWLREC-RHAP) service. The service was funded by the Big Lottery Fund from 2007 to 2013. It provided a vital independent service to which victims of 'hate crime' could turn if they preferred an alternative to making a report to the police, or if they were dissatisfied with the way that they were handled when they did report to the police and other relevant authorities. It was highly active in raising awareness about 'hate crime' and received national recognition for its awareness raising activities (The service now continues independently as the Independent Hate Crime Hub). From the establishment of PWLREC-RHAP in 2007 up to August 2012 when an independent evaluation of the service was undertaken, it delivered a total of 52 'hate crime' awareness sessions in 41 schools, colleges or other facilities for young people, involving approximately 4,114 students and teachers. In some instances the sessions have been delivered in response to incidents that have occurred in schools or elsewhere. The sessions are flexible and they have also been adapted in partnership working with the police, council and community groups, for delivery to groups of adults – including local community groups, victim support volunteers, and take-away, pub and night club door supervisors. The session, developed by the two PWLREC-RHAP case workers and delivered jointly with a police officer, uses multi-media and engages the participants in interactive activities and group work.

The primary objective of the session is to explore the impact of 'hate crime' victimisation on victims' lives so that the participants will have an understanding of what 'hate crime' is, and what the impacts and consequences are for victims. The aim is that such understanding will potentially serve as a preventative measure by making the participants more aware of the consequences of their actions if they abuse, ridicule, harass, or are physically violent against somebody because of some aspect of their identity. Case studies, along with powerful video images of victims of 'hate crime', are used in the sessions to evoke an emotional response and empathy for victims among the participants. The images presented in the sessions in schools include an animated depiction of the murder of Stephen Lawrence produced by the Holocaust Memorial Day Trust.[55] The use of animations might be less shocking than the real-to-life images used in presentations to older participants – but they generate an impact nevertheless. A short film is also shown – *The Sophie Lancaster Story*[56] – which powerfully conveys the impact of the murder of Sophie Lancaster in a park in Bacup, Lancashire in 2007, who was attacked along with her boyfriend, because of their Goth appearance.

One of the teachers interviewed for the evaluation of the RHAP 'hate crime' awareness session reported the impact that they saw the session had on the young people participating:

> 'I think they are very shocked by the content ... because it is hard not to have a lump in your throat. Even the young men, I can see them thinking '... don't look at me because I might just cry.'

Another teacher also clearly conveyed the emotional impacts on the students:

> '...To actually see the impact of hate crime was quite powerful ... I looked across at the students towards the end – my own emotions had been pulled by the video – and I looked across and I could see a lot of them were affected by the video, by the power of the message that was getting across ... In that session, more than [any other] in comparison, I think the impact was the key thing ... By the end of the session I think people walked out of the classroom feeling that their eyes had been opened. It had made them think – I even saw some of them shed a tear...'

The presentational style that has been developed for the 'hate crime' awareness session has been cleverly designed to engage and capture the interest of young participants and serves as a model for educational work with young people. As one of the respondents interviewed for the evaluation said:

> 'They have come up with a package that is engaging and they can keep their audience going for an hour and a half, you know capture their audience. Capturing young people for an hour and a half is very, very difficult and their faces when they watch the victims' montage, our young people you can see the shock in their faces. This is real. This isn't something that has been made up...They've actually spoken to victims of hate crime and that's why our young people were more shocked about that "Oh my god, I didn't realise

that bullying someone just because of their sexuality could
lead to them doing this to themselves" and it was so real.'

It appears to be commonly accepted by educators that the fostering of
empathy for those who are victimised, along with promoting values of
civility and kindness, is an effective way of working to tackle bullying
and hate. The PWLREC–RHAP sessions evoke empathy among
participants and the dramatic scenes of 'hate crime' victimisation
clearly convey the message that hate hurts. The impact on participants
in the sessions is clearly evident from feedback comments provided
by session participants.

At the end of the session PWLREC–RHAP distributes badges to the
participants and also invites them to have their photograph taken for
inclusion in a montage depicting opposition to 'hate crime' on a 'Say
No to Hate' poster, which is then displayed in the school or college.
The badges and the poster cleverly leave triggers that will potentially
remind participants about the messages in the sessions.

Conclusion: healing the hurts of 'hate crime'

Understanding of the emotional and psychological impacts of 'hate
crime' is critical for the provision of sensitive but effective support to
victims. Many practitioners working to support victims have developed
such understanding from their own practice, and sometimes their own
experience. Such understanding has been enhanced by an accumulation
of research evidence that has drawn out in-depth the particular harms
felt by 'hate crime' victims and how such harms can be magnified in
comparison to similar but otherwise motivated offences. Understanding
of the harms is not only vital for supporting victims but it can also
be applied to interventions with offenders and also for preventative
work with potential offenders, as this essay has illustrated. In the
separate jurisdictions of the United Kingdom, and in a number of
jurisdictions elsewhere (in the United States and Canada, for instance),
prejudiced motivations of offenders are taken into account, either as
an aggravating circumstance, or in the prosecution of specific offences,
for the determination of greater penalties for those convicted in cases
of 'hate crime'. The wielding of greater punishment in such cases
provides offenders with justice for their crimes. Greater punishment is
an acknowledgement of the greater hurts inflicted by 'hate crime' when
compared with otherwise identical crime which occurs for another
reason than the victim's skin colour or some other characteristic of
their identity. There is no one type of offender of course, and there are

many offenders who do think before they act and who do intend to inflict some hurts and are fully culpable for their actions. But it is also likely that many will not anticipate the extent and depth of hurt they inflict – especially when their crimes are expressive acts of the type prosecuted as public order offences.

The diversion of such offenders into rehabilitative interventions arguably offers as much justice for victims and offenders than disposal by the courts with a fine. It opens-up the opportunity to work with offenders to help redeem themselves from the prospect of future offending and by consequence reduce future victimisation. Offenders might also potentially be offered the opportunity and support to tackle their own emotional and social deficits which often provide the contexts for offending. The evaluation of the Smile project in Lancashire provides *prima facie* evidence that such an intervention may well reduce re-offending, and while there is much to be investigated and confirmed in the longer term concerning the efficacy of such an intervention, in the mean-time it potentially offers a more humanistic approach to managing some 'hate crime' offenders than simple disposal by the courts. Likewise, while the efficacy of utilising understanding about the 'hurts of hate' crime in awareness raising work has yet to be fully determined, it too provides a humanistic approach to seeking to prevent 'hate crime' occurring.

References

Barnes, A. and Ephross, P.H. (1994). 'The Impact of Hate Violence on Victims - Emotional and Behavioural Responses to Attacks', *Social Work,* 39 (3): 247–51.

Botcherby, S., Glenn, F., Iganski, P., Jochelson, K. and Lagou, S. (2011) *Equality Groups' Perceptions and Experiences of Crime,* Manchester: Equality and Human Rights Commission.

Dzelme, I. (2008) *Psychological Effects of Hate Crime,* Riga: Latvian Centre for Human Rights.

Herek, G.M., Gillis, J.R. and Cogan, J.C. (1999) 'Psychological Sequelae of Hate-Crime Victimization among Lesbian, Gay, and Bisexual Adults', *Journal of Consulting and Clinical Psychology,* 67 (6): 945–51.

Hershberger, S.L. and D'Augelli, A.R. (1995) 'The Impact of Victimization on the Mental Health and Suicidality of Lesbian, Gay, and Bisexual Youth', *Developmental Psychology,* 31: 65–74.

Iganski, P. (2008) *Hate Crime and the City,* Bristol: Policy Press.

Iganski, P. (2012) *Taking Stock – Programmes for Offenders of Hate,* Belfast: NIACRO.

McDevitt, J., Balboni, J., Garcia, L. and Gu, J. (2001) 'Consequences for Victims: a Comparison of Bias and Non-Bias Motivated Assaults', *American Behavioral Scientist,* 45 (4): 697–713.

Nocon, A., Iganski, P. and Lagou, S. (2011) *Disabled People's Experiences and Concerns about Crime,* Manchester: Equality and Human Rights Commission.

Noelle, M. (2001) 'The Ripple Effect of the Matthew Shepard Murder: Impact on the Assumptive Worlds of Members of the Targeted Group', *American Behavioral Scientist,* 46 (1): 27–50.

Noelle, M. (2009) 'The Psychological and Social Effects of Antibisexual, Antigay, and Antilesbian Violence and Harassment', in P. Iganski (ed.) *Hate Crimes (Volume 2). The Consequences of Hate Crimes,* Westport CT: Praeger: 73–105.

Otis, M.D. and Skinner, W.F. (1996) 'The Prevalence of Victimization and its Effect on Mental Well-Being among Lesbian and Gay People', *Journal of Homosexuality,* 30: 93-122.

Perry, B. and Alvi, S. (2012) 'We are all Vulnerable': The *In Terrorem* Effects of Hate Crimes' *International Review of Victimology,* 18 (1): 57–71.

Smith, K., Lader, D., Hoare, J. and Lau, I. (2012) *Hate Crime, Cyber Security and the Experience of Crime among Children: Findings from the 2010/11 British Crime Survey,* London: Home Office.

Victim Support (2006) *Crime and Prejudice. The Support Needs of Victims of Hate Crime: A Research Report,* London: Victim Support.

Walters, M. and Hoyle, C. (2010) 'Healing Harms and Engendering Tolerance: The Promise of Restorative Justice for Hate Crime', in N. Chakraborti (ed.) *Hate Crime: Concepts, Policy, Future Directions,* Cullompton: Willan, pp. 228–48.

Walters, M. and Hoyle, C. (2012) 'Exploring the Everyday World of Hate Victimization through Community Mediation', *International Review of Victimology,* 18 (1): pp. 7–-24.

SEVENTEEN

Restorative approaches to working with hate crime offenders

Mark Austin Walters

Introduction

For some considerable time now, legislatures across the Western world have sought to respond to the proliferation of hate crimes by increasing the punishments of offenders. The use of penalty enhancements seems intuitive given the severity of harms caused by hate-motivated offences (Iganski, 2008; Smith et al, 2012). The criminalisation of hate also promotes an important symbolic message to society that hostilities demonstrated towards racial, religious, sexual orientation, disability and transgender groups (among others) are wholly unacceptable (Iganski, 1999). Yet while a punitive approach to tackling hate offenders has its merits, there are several limitations to this approach that require attention. First, the law does little to support the healing of hate victims – beyond perhaps appeasing a visceral desire for an offender to receive his 'just deserts' (Dixon and Gadd, 2006). Furthermore, it can be argued that the punishment and labelling of offenders as 'hate offenders' does little to challenge individuals' hate-motivated behaviours (Jacobs and Potter, 1998; Dixon and Gadd, 2006). In fact, some academics have gone so far as to suggest that hate crime laws may actually antagonise (would-be) offenders who see certain groups as receiving unequal protection from the state (Jacobs and Potter, 1998).

The lack of victim support and offender edification offered by retributive hate crime laws suggests that a new or additional approach is needed when tackling hate-motivated offences (Burney, 2003: 36; Perry, 2003: 44). With this in mind, a growing number of academics have begun to explore the effectiveness of using a restorative approach to tackling the phenomenon (see, Shenk, 2001; Umbreit et al, 2002; Gavrielides, 2007; Walters and Hoyle, 2010; 2012). This chapter adds to the small but growing knowledge base on restorative justice (RJ) for hate crime by focusing on the potential benefits that restorative practices may yield in relation to transforming the behaviours of hate crime offenders. Drawing on empirical research undertaken for the author's doctorate, the chapter explores the ways in which restorative practices have been used to challenge effectively and modify the hate-motivated behaviours of offenders, while simultaneously protecting participants against re-victimisation (Walters, 2012a).

Part I: What is restorative justice?

There is currently no universally agreed definition of 'restorative justice' (RJ). Instead, the term is often said to embody a set of established values and principles that are now commonly applied to various criminal and noncriminal justice practices (Gavrielides, 2007). Gerry Johnstone and Daniel Van Ness, for example, state that regardless of whether RJ is deemed to be a practice, theory or ideology, the same concepts of 'encounter', 'repair' and 'transformation' are embraced by most, if not all, 'restorativists' (2007: 16). While it is fair to say that a general consensus exists among restorativists as to the applicability of these concepts to restorative practices, differences inevitably emerge as to the extent to which each concept should be utilised. The purpose of this chapter is to focus on the third concept of 'transformation' as outlined by Johnstone and Van Ness. This is not to underplay the intrinsic importance of reparation and emotional healing which RJ frequently elicits (see Walters and Hoyle, 2010, 2012; Walters, 2012a. 2012b). However, there is scant discussion within the study of hate crime that explores the effects that restorative practices may have on offenders of hate crime. As such it is on the potentially reforming effects of RJ that this chapter will focus.

A variety of criminal justice practices now exist which incorporate restorative principles. In the United Kingdom (UK), at least, these practices are a relatively new addition to the criminal justice milieu. During the 1970s community mediation centres opened with the purpose of resolving neighbourhood conflicts. These centres still use both direct and indirect meetings between the stakeholders of a crime, or those embroiled in anti-social behaviour, in order to resolve conflicts and repair the harms that have been caused. The aim of mediation is to explore both the causes and consequences of an incident/conflict. Of utmost importance to the process is that participants are given a voice through which they are able to explain how their lives have been affected. Mediators frequently prepare a contract, signed by the parties, outlining the undertakings that the parties have agreed to.

Although RJ principles had been utilised for some time within the third sector, it was not until the Youth Justice and Criminal Evidence Act 1999 (now consolidated in the Powers of Criminal Courts [Sentencing] Act 2000) created the Referral Order that RJ was put on a legislative footing in the UK. The order is a mandatory sentence imposed on first time young offenders (10–17 year-olds) who plead guilty to an imprisonable offence. Offenders are required to attend Youth Offender Panel (YOP) meetings along with their parents (where the offender is under the age of 16). Victims are also invited to attend and may bring along parents or other family members for support. The offender is asked to sign a contract with the panel. The Ministry of Justice states that there are two core elements that each contract should contain:

a) reparation to the victim and/or the wider community, and
b) a programme of interventions, delivered or organised by the youth offending team, which addresses the factors likely to be associated with any reoffending. (Ministry of Justice, 2012: 36)

In some cases additional restorative justice meetings are carried out – typically referred to as 'family group conferences'.[57] These are direct meetings set up between the offender and victim and their family supporters. Alternatively, restorative meetings are carried out indirectly (known as shuttle mediation). In these latter cases practitioners facilitate meetings between the victim and offender separately. In either direct or indirect meetings the aim is to explore the reasons behind why the offence was committed, the harms that it has caused to the victim and other stakeholders, the means by which the offender will repair the harms he or she has caused, and the reintegration of the offender into the community.[58]

Part II: Engendering tolerance of 'difference': the importance of empathy

If restorative practices are to bring about genuine transformations in hate crime offenders, practitioners will be required to facilitate dialogue which exposes, and effectively challenges, the prejudices that are causal to hate incidents. Such a sensitive task is likely to be of greater effect where stakeholders, rather than the state, hold the offender to account. Within restorative practice it is not the role of the facilitator to chastise the offender for his or her hate-motivated actions.[59] Rather, the function of the facilitator is to create the conditions whereby all participants are encouraged to articulate their experiences of harm and identity-based prejudice (Walters and Hoyle, 2010). Effective communication between participants is crucial if victims are to receive emotional reparation and all participants are to gain greater insight into each other's cultural and identity backgrounds.

Braithwaite's (1989) thesis on reintegrative shaming helps us to further explain how RJ can bring about offender edification. The theory explains that social condemnation – that which is expressed indirectly through participation in a restorative practice and directly by other stakeholders of an offence – helps to *shame* the offender who in turn may experience a sense of *guilt* for his or her actions. Harris et al (2004: 193) assert that 'shame in this view occurs when one feels disapproval in the eyes of others (imagined or real disapproval)' while on the other hand the feeling of 'guilt occurs when one disapproves of one's own behaviour (disapproval by one's own conscience)'. For shame and guilt to occur the offender must be aware that others are disapproving of his or her behaviours. This occurs where the stakeholders of a crime collectively convey their condemnation of the offender's actions.

Intrinsic to the shaming process will be the emotion of *empathy*. Empathy is the ability of people to transpose themselves into the feelings of another (Jackson, 2009). It can involve individuals placing themselves into another situation and comprehending the other's circumstances. The value of empathy is that by placing oneself into another's situation, one becomes more concerned for the other person's welfare. Someone who experiences empathy will be likely to feel emotional anxiety on hearing about another's experience of pain and suffering (Jackson, 2009). It is through these very powerful emotions that restorative dialogue entices offenders into experiencing a sense of shame – for the offender now understands first-hand the pain and suffering they have caused. If such an emotional connection is successfully achieved it is likely that the offender will also experience a sense of guilt; that is a sense of self-disapproval that ultimately acts as a catalyst for attitudinal change.

The formation of emotional connections during RJ can provide a powerful engine for behavioural change. Yet whether this can be successfully achieved in cases involving hate, prejudice and bigotry is far from certain. It is likely that the cultural and identity differences that exist between the stakeholders of such incidents will result in an 'empathic divide' between the participants (Haney, 2004: 189–210). Participants may find it difficult to understand the lives of others who come from different social or cultural backgrounds (Harris et al, 2004: 194). Stakeholders may hold different beliefs and values, and will typically socialise in different groups (Smith, 2006). Dialogue may further be inhibited by variations in communication style. Cross-cultural communication can easily be misinterpreted where participants speak different first languages and/or use contrasting modes of paralanguage and non-verbal expression (Umbreit and Coates, 2000).[60] This may mean that participants of cross-cultural dialogue will struggle to form the empathic connections which become central to engendering genuine transformations (Smith, 2006). The route to empathy in hate crime cases therefore lies not just with an exploration of physical and/or emotional harm, but with a potentially more arduous process of *humanising* the victim's 'difference'.

Overcoming cultural and communicational barriers to empathy

Differences in cultural values and communication styles are clearly inhibitive to the restorative ideal (Daly, 2002). This does not mean, however, that empathic divides cannot be bridged. Unlike other conventional justice measures, restorative interventions are malleable to the needs of participants. The restorative principle of *inclusivity* means that restorative practitioners will aim to provide opportunities for all stakeholders to participate in dialogue that is focused on experiences of emotional and physical harm (Albrecht, 2010). Practitioners who are trained in RJ should be responsive and reactive to the needs of all participants. They may need to explore innovative ways of ensuring that participants can communicate during meetings. This may simply involve other family members and/or community supporters attending meetings in order to translate and clarify proceedings. Victim advocates may also be included in cases where the victim is unable to articulate their experiences of harm. In cases where participants are unable to communicate verbally due to mental impairments, practitioners may find that using drawing boards, or practising with the victim beforehand as to what they would like to say, helpful in ensuring they are included in the process (Holland, 2011).

The flexibility and inclusivity of restorative practice certainly helps to bridge the emotional gaps that frequently pre-exist victim–offender dialogue. Victims and other community stakeholders who are able to articulate the pain and suffering they have endured directly to the offender create genuine opportunities to challenge offenders' hate-motivated behaviours – even in cases where parties begin the process feeling no empathy for each other at all. That said, there will inevitably be cases where one or more of the parties simply refuse to open themselves to the differences that stand before them. And no matter how dedicated the practitioner and how willing the victim, some offenders will themselves be too emotionally damaged to respond positively during restorative encounters. Though this may sound defeatist it is important to remember that RJ is not a panacea that will transform all hate crime offenders. More accurate is to assert that RJ provides a more meaningful opportunity to engender emotional and behavioural transformations. This is especially true when restorative dialogue is compared to conventional interventions aimed only at stigmatising and punishing offenders.

Part III: Challenging prejudice

'Low-level' prejudice

Having explored how RJ can engender transformations through the power of emotions, such as empathy, shame and guilt, it is now helpful for us to look more specifically at the varying degrees of prejudice which are connected to an offence (see generally, Jacobs and Potter, 1998). Research into the aetiology of hate crime has found that very few 'hate crime' offenders are motivated by an ideology of hate (Levin and McDevitt, 2002; Iganski, 2008). More common is for offenders to hold what we might call superficial, or 'low-level', prejudices towards certain groups of people. These prejudices are often based on little other than fallacious stereotypes that have been perpetuated within society about a group's morality or social worthiness (Levin and McDevitt, 2002). A high proportion of incidents also involve a multitude of contextual factors (Iganski, 2008). For instance, hate incidents frequently arise between neighbours where, for example, noise pollution caused by a neighbour playing his music too loudly has led to an altercation between two individuals (families) (Walters and Hoyle, 2012). In other cases incidents may be directed towards service providers such as shop assistants, waiters or taxi drivers whom the offender sees as somehow 'wronging' them (Ray and Smith, 2002; Gadd et al, 2005). Altercations between individuals in these types of situations can quickly escalate, especially where large amounts of alcohol have been consumed (Walters and Hoyle, 2012). Most of these cases are the product of both anger and frustration about a particular situation, but are also exacerbated by superficially held prejudices that are expressed in the 'heat of the moment' as a way of demeaning the victim in the most potent way possible (Gadd, 2009; Walters and Hoyle, 2012).

It is in cases involving low-level prejudices that restorative justice will yield its greatest potential in challenging and modifying the behaviour of hate crime offenders. Inclusive dialogue will help offenders to appreciate not only the impact that hate speech has on an individual but also the effects that such language has on other community members. The victim's story becomes crucial to challenging negative stereotypes, which in turn may have a positive influence on an offender's future conduct. While it is important not to overstate the potential benefits of RJ in this regard, it is not far-fetched to suggest that offenders who are directly faced with the consequences of their actions will be more likely to appreciate the immorality of their behaviour than those who have the proverbial book thrown at them. Restorative dialogue allows each of the participants to describe the impact of the incident, thereby exposing each other's individuality, as well as the sociocultural idiosyncrasies that make them 'different'. In doing this, the negative stereotypes that partly give rise to expressions of hatred ultimately dissipate as each of the participants observe one another's humanity as well as the suffering which such acts have caused.

Incorporating moral learning into restorative agreements

Direct dialogue can in itself be a powerful engine for attitudinal change. However, restorative practitioners can further enhance the edification of offenders by building additional measures of 'moral learning' into reparation agreements/contracts (Schweigert, 1999). In many cases victims will want the offender to learn more about cultural and identity difference in order to reduce the likelihood of him or her reoffending (see, Victim Support, 2006). There are various ways that moral learning can be achieved. For example, Theo Gavrielides (2007) refers to a case in the United States where an offender had made several death threats to members of an Islamic cultural centre shortly after 9/11. The offender and representatives from the centre were involved in two mediation meetings during which the offender apologised. As part of the reparation contract the offender agreed to attend lectures on Islam while continuing counselling for his anger issues (Gavrielides 2007: 206–7).

Within the author's own study, various examples of moral learning were incorporated into the restorative process. In one case, an offender, who had been convicted of racially and religiously aggravated harassment and sentenced to a referral order,[61] was asked by the victim to undertake a research study into the effects of anti-Semitism. The project was set up and supervised by an offender manager, herself Jewish. The offender completed the project and presented a report back to the victim and his family. The report included detailed information on the deleterious harms caused by the rise of Nazism in Europe during the 20th century. At the end of the document the offender provided some reflections on his behaviour and the impact that this had on the victim:

> ... I feel that I understand why incidents involving racial abuse against Jewish citizens and [other] races are taken so seriously. As I have been ... reading about ... the holocaust ... [and] I understand the hurt and pain the victim and his family must of felt when I said what I said to him as it was obviously a terrible time for there [*sic*] race ... it is not just him that it relates to but a whole race of people and that's not what I intended to do.
>
> On reflection of my actions I now feel that I will be able to use language more appropriately towards over [*sic*] people and not to talk about peoples religions and believes [*sic*] in such a way... as it is unacceptable because of the pain it causes to the people it happens to....

Offenders who deny prejudice

Effectively challenging prejudice in cases where the offender has been convicted of an offence such as 'racially aggravated harassment' is made easier where the offender has admitted that he or she has demonstrated hostility and accepts responsibility for this. However, practitioners must be aware that many offenders will continue to deny the hate element of their offence despite having been either accused or convicted of demonstrating hostility during the commission of an offence (Burney and Rose, 2002).

Denials will be most common in cases where multiple social and circumstantial factors form the basis for the offence (Chakraborti and Garland, 2012). The multifarious dynamics of many hate incidents provide ample opportunity for offenders to deny that they are, for example, racist or homophobic (Walters and Hoyle, 2012). In other cases, offenders may admit to having said 'those words' but remain resolute about the fact that they were not meant as an act of prejudice (Gadd, 2009). Offenders who vehemently deny that they are prejudiced certainly make discussing the causes and consequences of 'hate' challenging (Gadd, 2009). It will be important in such cases for facilitators to explore *all* the relevant casual factors of the case (including hate) if the parties are to find a resolution that is agreeable to all. This may mean that both victim and offender take some responsibility for any previous actions which have led to the escalation of the conflict (Walters and Hoyle, 2012).

Unlike most other criminal justice practitioners, restorative facilitators are well equipped to facilitate complex dialogue on sensitive issues such as (among others) racism, anti-religion, homophobia or disablism. The role of the restorative facilitator is not to supervise the offender (as probation officers do) or to chastise them (as the courts do). Instead, the facilitator's role is to support the formation of positive emotional connections between the stakeholders of an offence (Walters and Hoyle, 2010). As explained above, the resulting social condemnation that is conveyed via restorative processes helps to challenge the morality of the offender's actions. This can be done whether the offender accepts responsibility at the beginning of the process for his or her prejudiced actions or not. What is important is that the process includes discussion on the direct impacts of prejudice as well as discussion on what it is like for the victim to be 'different'. In fact, the author has made a number of observations of RJ meetings whereby an offender has admitted to an offence or incident but has denied s/he is prejudiced (Walters, 2012b). In each of these cases practitioners were still able to facilitate discussion on the issue of hate and its impacts (see, Walters, 2012b). Typically, offenders go on to promise that they will not engage in any 'further' racist, anti-religious, homophobic, and/or disablist behaviours (Walters and Hoyle, 2012). Such promises hint at the acceptance of responsibility, even where there is no *outright* acknowledgement by offenders that they had initially acted in a biased way.

Deep-seated prejudice

The examples provided above support the assertion that restorative practices can effectively challenge and modify the superficial prejudices evinced by *some* offenders of hate crime. However, it remains less clear whether RJ can positively affect offenders who are motivated by deeply seated hatred. Research suggests that a small minority of offenders will make it their 'mission' in life to eradicate certain minority groups; those they see as a direct threat to the purity of society (Levin and McDevitt, 2002). Some offenders will have grown up in an environment extremely hostile towards certain identity groups; people who are perceived as 'invading' *their* territory and taking *their* jobs and state welfare benefits (see for example, Ray and Smith, 2002; Gadd et al, 2005; Garland and Treadwell, 2012).

The emotional dynamics of deeply felt hatred are extraordinarily complex and multifaceted (Gadd, 2009). There is no one simple explanation as to why people 'hate' others. For some offenders, their conduct may have little to do with actual feelings of hatred but instead be the result of an internalised emotional struggle about their place in the world. For instance, Ray and Smith (2002) assert that many racist hate incidents are the result of an unacknowledged shame that is rooted to a perpetrator's own social and economic disadvantage. Unconscious feelings of shame frequently surface as conscious feelings of anger, which are then projected onto those who are seen as the cause of their problems. The prospect of effectively confronting these issues, and what for many offenders is likely to be years of learnt animus, becomes a highly sensitive and complex task. As a result of this, it is unlikely that a short-lived restorative intervention will make any meaningful impact on an offender's own internalised struggles or their world views. This is not to suggest that positive outcomes cannot be furnished through the application of restorative dialogue in cases involving deeply seated hate. Rather one must simply remain realistic about its transformative effects.

Part IV: Protecting victims

Before concluding this chapter it is essential that I highlight the risks that are involved in bringing together the stakeholders of hate crime and how these concerns can be protected against. The fact that hate crimes have profound emotional and physical impacts on victims and other community members (see, Iganski, 2008) means that practitioners must remain alive to the risks of further compounding participants' experiences of victimisation. Critics of RJ have noted that in cases where the offender holds a dominant position over the victim, there is the potential for the restorative process to become simply another means through which the victim is subjugated (see for example, Stubbs, 2007). Bringing community members together via a process of direct dialogue aimed at challenging bigotry has the potential to do the very opposite. The fear is that victims' revelations might be perceived as being provocative, thereby eliciting a hostile response from the offender and his or her community supporters (Smith, 2006).

The importance of preparation and ground rules

The possibility of revictimisation during restorative encounters should not be underestimated. Such a concern must remain at the forefront of practitioners' minds when preparing participants for restorative dialogue. Preparation of the parties should entail practitioners talking through the incident/s with each of the parties. Participants should be asked to explain how and why the incident occurred and how it has affected them. It is at this point that practitioners may wish to hold 'mini conferences' with the offender (without the victim), during which the facilitator can ascertain how the offender was feeling about his or her actions, while further exploring the extent to which prejudice gave rise to the offending behaviour. Facilitators will also need to ensure that the parties are willing to participate with the right motives. Lengthy discussions with offenders should uncover whether they are willing to accept responsibility for their actions or whether they wish to repeat their hostilities. Participants who are well prepared and voluntarily wish to participate in meetings will have digested the purpose of the restorative process, and at this stage be ready to discuss the harms that have been caused as well the means through this these might be repaired.

In addition to preparing each of the participants, facilitators should lay down firm ground rules at the beginning of direct meetings. Participants should be asked to speak to each other respectfully, not to use abusive language or gestures and to refrain from pointing or shouting at other participants. The facilitator may also wish to highlight the fact that the participants will be discussing sensitive issues and that small rest periods may be required if any participant feels the need to break for a moment. If at any time a party diverges from these rules the facilitator should politely remind that individual what they have agreed to at the start of the meeting.

Including appropriate supporters

Finally, facilitators who invite other community members (supporters) into the dialogic process must endeavour to include individuals who provide appropriate social condemnation for the wrongs committed (Braithwaite, 2002). This becomes problematic in cases where offenders' supporters, especially parents, are the primary source of their prejudices. In such cases the facilitator must determine whether the inclusion of an offender's parent will antagonise the victim and/or help to neutralise his or her wrongdoing. Such a scenario may be avoided if facilitators encourage the attendance of other positive role models, such as teachers, sports coaches or other well-meaning relatives.

Still a dichotomy arises in such circumstances. Without parental input, young offenders will not be engaging with the 'community' that has greatest influence over them. If offenders are to be reintegrated into a community that does not support their prejudiced attitudes, practitioners may well need to include offenders' parents in the hope that dialogue on harm, prejudice and identity 'difference' helps to challenge the negative views of both offender and his or her parents. Greater reliance on ground rules will be required in order to reduce the likelihood of parents voicing any animosity against the victim's identity during meetings.

Conclusion

Restorative approaches to hate crime provide a powerful mechanism through which an offender's prejudice motivated conduct can be socially condemned and potentially transformed. Restorative dialogue creates the platform from which offenders are directly confronted with the harms of their actions. Such communication subjects participants to emotions that few other justice interventions can elicit. It is through the formation of emotional connections between offenders and victims that damaged relationships can be transformed, ultimately reducing the likelihood that incidents will be repeated. Furthermore, the flexibility of restorative practice allows facilitators to incorporate additional forms of moral learning into reparation agreements. As we have seen in this chapter, this can be achieved through the use of small research projects that look deeper into the impacts of hate crime and that allow offenders to further reflect on the wrongfulness of their actions. There will be a myriad of other methods through which moral learning can be achieved. This, of course, will be for victims, their supporters and restorative practitioners to determine.

Although RJ offers an approach to hate crime that effectively challenges prejudice, potentially modifying offender behaviour, practitioners must remain mindful of the risks that direct forms of communication pose to the welfare of victims. These risks can be minimised by facilitators administering adequate preparation, setting strict ground rules and inviting appropriate community supporters to participate. Yet for all its potential, RJ is by no means a panacea for the prevention of hate crime. There will inevitably be cases where offenders' prejudices run so deeply into their world views that restorative dialogue will only ever be of limited transformative effect. What this chapter aims to convey is that for a high proportion of hate crime cases, a restorative approach will provide a more intelligent means through which communities can attempt to challenge, condemn and ultimately transform the behaviours of hate crime offenders.

References

Albrecht, B. (2010) 'Multicultural Challenges for Restorative Justice: Mediators' Experiences from Norway and Finland', *Journal of Scandinavian Studies in Criminology and Crime*, 11: 3–24.

Braithwaite, J. (1989) *Crime, Shame, and Reintegration*, Cambridge: Cambridge University Press.

Braithwaite, J. (2002) *Restorative Justice and Responsive Regulation*, New York: Oxford University Press.

Burney, E. (2003) 'Using the Law on Racially Aggravated Offences', *Criminal Law Review*, 28–36.

Burney, E. and Rose, G. (2002) *Racist Offences: How Is the Law Working?*, London: Home Office.

Chakraborti, N. and Garland, J. (2012) 'Reconceptualising Hate Crime Victimization Through the Lens of Vulnerability and "Difference"', *Theoretical Criminology*, 16 (4): 499–514.

Daly, K. (2002) 'Mind the Gap: Restorative Justice in Theory and Practice', in A. von Hirsh, J. Roberts, A. Bottoms, K. Roach and M. Schiff (eds) *Restorative Justice and Criminal Justice: Competing or Reconcilable Paradigms?*, Oxford: Hart Publishing.

Dixon, B. and Gadd, D. (2006) 'Getting the Message? "New" Labour and the Criminalization of "Hate"', *Criminology and Criminal Justice*, 6 (3): 309–28.

Gadd, D. (2009) 'Aggravating Racism and Elusive Motivation', *British Journal of Criminology*, 49 (6): 755–71.

Gadd, D., Dixon, B. and Jefferson, T. (2005) *Why Do They Do It? Racial Harassment in North Staffordshire*, Keele: Centre for Criminological Research, Keele University.

Garland, J. and Treadwell, J. (2012) 'The New Politics of Hate? An Assessment of the Appeal of the English Defence League Amongst Disadvantaged White Working Class Communities in England', *The Journal of Hate Studies*, 10 (1): 123–41.

Gavrielides, T. (2007) *Restorative Justice Theory and Practice: Addressing the Discrepancy*, New York: Criminal Justice Press.

Haney, C. (2004) 'Condemning the Other in Death Penalty Trials: Biographical Racism, Structural Mitigation, and Empathic Divide', *DePaul Law Review*, 53: 1557–90.

Harris, N., Walgrave, L. and Braithwaite, B. (2004) 'Emotional Dynamics of Restorative Conferences', *Theoretical Criminology,* 8 (2): 191–210.

Holland, B. (2011, June) *Making Restorative Approaches Inclusive for People with Special Needs.* Paper presented at Oxfordshire Restorative Justice Network, Worcester College, University of Oxford.

Iganski, P. (1999) 'Why Make Hate a Crime?', *Critical Social Policy,* 19 (3): 386–95.

Iganski, P. (2008) *Hate Crime and the City,* Bristol: The Policy Press.

Jackson, A.L. (2009) 'The Impact of Restorative Justice on the Development of Guilt, Shame, and Empathy Among Participants in a Victim Impact Training Program', *Victims and Offenders,* 4 (1): 1–24.

Jacobs, J. and Potter, K. (1998) *Hate Crimes,* New York: Oxford University Press.

Johnstone, G. and Van Ness, D. (2007) 'The Meaning of Restorative Justice', in G. Johnstone and D. Van Ness (eds) *Handbook of Restorative Justice,* Cullompton: Willan.

Levin, J. and McDevitt, J. (2002) *Hate Crimes Revisited: America's War on Those Who Are Different,* New York: Basic Books.

Ministry of Justice (2012) *Referral Order Guidance,* London: Ministry of Justice.

Perry, B. (2003) 'Where Do We Go From Here? Researching Hate Crime', *Internet Journal of Criminology,* 1–59.

Ray, L. and Smith, D. (2002) 'Hate Crime, Violence and Cultures of Racism', in P. Iganski (ed.) *The Hate Debate,* London: Profile Books.

Schweigert, F.J. (1999) 'Moral Education in Victim Offender Conferencing', *Criminal Justice Ethics,* 18 (2): 29–40.

Shenk, A. (2001) 'Victim–Offender Mediation: The Road to Repairing Hate Crime Injustice', *Ohio State Journal on Dispute Resolution,* 17: 185–217.

Smith, K. (2006) 'Dissolving the Divide: Cross-Racial Communication in the Restorative Justice Process', *Dalhousie Journal of Legal Studies,* 15: 168–203.

Smith, K. (ed.), Lader, D., Hoare, J., and Lau, I. (2012) *Hate Crime, Cyber Security and the Experience of Crime among Children: Findings from the 2010/11 British Crime Survey: Supplementary Volume 3 to Crime in England and Wales 2010/11,* London: Home Office.

Stubbs, J. (2007) 'Beyond Apology? Domestic Violence and Critical Questions for Restorative Justice', *Criminology and Criminal Justice,* 7 (2): 169–87.

Umbreit, M., and Coates, R. (2000) *Multicultural Implications of Restorative Justice: Potential Pitfalls and Dangers,* Center for Restorative Justice and Peacemaking, University of Minnesota.

Umbreit, M., Coates, R., and Vos, B. (2002) *Community Peacemaking Project: Responding to Hate Crimes, Hate Incidents, Intolerance, and Violence Through Restorative Justice Dialogue,* Minnesota: Center for Restorative Justice.

Victim Support (2006) *Crime and Prejudice: The Support Needs of Victims of Hate Crime: A Research Report,* London: Victim Support.

Walters, M. (2012a) 'Hate Crimes Hurt More: Can Restorative Practices Help Repair the Harms?', DPhil Thesis, Oxford University, available at the Bodleian Library.

Walters, M. (2012b) 'Hate Crimes: Promoting the Values of Dignity and Respect for Young Victims through Restorative Justice', in T. Gavriliedes (ed.) *Rights and Restoration within Youth Justice,* Canada: de Sitter Publications.

Walters, M. and Hoyle, C. (2010) 'Healing Harms and Engendering Tolerance: the Promise of Restorative Justice for Hate Crime', in N. Chakraborti (ed.) *Hate Crime: Concepts, Policy, Future Directions,* Cullompton: Willan: 228-248.

Walters, M. and Hoyle, C. (2012) 'Exploring the Everyday World of Hate Victimisation through Community Mediation', *International Review of Victimology,* 18 (1): 7–24.

Conclusions

Jon Garland

Clouds on the horizon

The study of hate crime has grown in size and significance during its relatively short 'lifespan'. From the birth of the concept in the 1960s in the United States through to the present day, scholarly interest in the causes and consequences of hate crime has grown to such an extent that there are now a number of key texts that are into their second or third editions, accompanied by a plethora of edited collections, specialist journals or dedicated editions thereof, as well as numerous articles. The range of topics covered has also expanded, from initial investigations into the causes and consequences of acts of 'hate' that mainly focused around 'race' and racism, through to those that have examined a wide variety of 'emerging' groups whose victimisation is characterised by attacks on their core identities. These studies have also crossed a number of academic disciplines, including criminology, political science, psychology, forensic science, history, law and sociology, spawning a seemingly ever-rising number of conferences, workshops and symposia that attract delegates from across the globe.

Accompanying this rise in academic interest in hate crime has been a recognition of the social significance of the phenomenon across statutory, voluntary and private sectors, from key actors within the political and criminal justice spheres through the media and then 'down' to those at a grassroots level, including activists, campaigners and community volunteers. Work across and within all of these different levels, both nationally and internationally, has been influenced by a desire to challenge manifestations of prejudice and bigotry, through legal and political interventions, police initiatives and a vast array of community and organisational campaigns. Yet, as my co-editor of this book, Neil Chakraborti, mentions in the Introduction to this volume, there have been concerns that this growth in interest in hate crime has, at times, seemed like so much 'hot air' as it has not produced the types of outcomes or benefits that it should have, given the resources dedicated to it. In both the practitioner and scholarly domains, there has been a danger that the activity in and around hate crime has developed into something of a self-sustaining 'industry' that lacks the capacity to make a meaningful difference to the lives of victims of these offences.

Of course, in many ways this is a simplistic and overly harsh assertion, as there have been many important developments in the last twenty years or so that have helped to improve understandings of hate crime victimisation and perpetration, as well as how to challenge its motivations, prevent its occurrence and deal with its consequences. In the UK context, for example, there have been noticeable improvements in the recognition of the harms of hate crime among law and policy makers, police officers, prosecutors and the judiciary, much of this mirroring or following on from theoretical developments in academia. Third sector organisations have also played a significant role in combating the prejudice behind hate-related harassment and/or helping victims deal with its after effects. Much of this laudable work has been reflected in many countries across the globe, something that undoubtedly would not have happened if it were not for the advent and expansion of this 'industry'.

The range of topics and issues within the present volume also underscores the positive side of academic and practitioner work in the field of hate crime, and represents, in many cases, how those two worlds can co-exist in a mutually beneficial way. The thoughtful (and, at times, dryly amusing) contribution of Paul Giannasi summarises very neatly how many of those outside of the academy can judge its output as being in many ways irrelevant to their day-to-day work, seeing it rooted in so much high-brow intellectualism that has little basis in the practicalities of their pressurised roles. This chapter also shows, though, how such attitudes can change, and how even those in the 'hard-bitten' world of policing can grow to appreciate the contributions that researchers can make to developments in policy and practice out there in the 'real world'.

However, to lay the blame for the separate and parallel existence of the spheres of policy and practice in one hand, and academia on the other, solely at the feet of the former is to ignore the role that the latter has (sometimes unwittingly) played in fostering this problematic situation. Indeed, the unhelpful attitude of some academics, who have, at times, either seen little relevance in dealing with those working outside of their 'ivory towers' or held rather patronising and condescending views of them, has contributed equally to the atmosphere of mutual enmity that has, unfortunately, often clouded relations between themselves and practitioners. In essence, often neither 'side' has particularly valued or rated the other or their potential to contribute to their own endeavours, and thus, all too often, they have existed apart, creating, as Chakraborti mentions in the Introduction, an 'implementation gap' between the two.

Yet, as this book illustrates, there has been something of a rapprochement between the spheres in recent times; a thaw in relations between researchers, policy makers and practitioners which has prompted a number of progressive programmes that have made a practical difference 'on the ground'. This does not mean that all is 'rosy in the garden', however; all too obvious barriers still exist that hamper inter-domain working. Some of these are longstanding in nature, while others have appeared more recently, reflecting the challenges that all who work in this rapidly evolving area face. Indeed, this constant evolution poses ongoing problems for academics and practitioners that test not just the utility of their own work but their professional relationships with each other too. It is to a number of these challenges that this chapter now turns.

Key challenges in the contemporary 'hate debate'

Some of the most pressing issues facing those working within the hate crime field, such as the global rise in Islamophobia over the last decade or so, are fairly recent phenomena whose multiple facets are still relatively unexplored (Mythen et al, 2009). The chapters by Zempi and Treadwell in this volume contribute to this growing body of work by suggesting new ways that academia can inform criminal justice and third sector responses to incidents of Islamophobic harassment as well as the policing of the marches and demonstrations of the openly Islamophobic English Defence League (EDL). Both academics' own separate studies of the targeted harassment of Muslim women who wear the veil (see Chakraborti and Zempi, 2012) and of the motivations and characteristics of many of those involved in the EDL (see Treadwell and Garland, 2011) are excellent examples of research that is positioned right on one of society's contemporary faultlines. This work is becoming ever more relevant in the wake of the terrorist incidents in Boston and London in 2013, and the resultant backlash against Islamic communities.

Interestingly, though, comparatively little research has been undertaken into the views of young white people who express prejudiced views against Islam, and this is one of the reasons that Hardy's chapter in this book is so significant. Hardy highlights the difficulties that many of those involved in academia have in attempting to comprehend what may lie beneath the surface racist hostility of marginalised and 'lost' white youths whose everyday, lived experience of urban multiculturalism serves to fuel their prejudice. By ignoring these views, or by writing them off as merely the opinions of the bigoted, will, Hardy argues, only increase those young people's sense of alienation and exacerbate the problem.

This approach underscores a priority for hate studies more generally: that it must now progress and develop by, where necessary, examining the views held by those who traditionally have had a lack of engagement with middle-class academia or its associated 'intelligentsia', who, in turn, often have little or no regard for them either. Yet if the hostile views of 'lost' white communities are to be meaningfully challenged, and policy devised to combat their development, then they must first be researched by those with a genuine commitment to understanding them. Perhaps some of those within academia will need to confront their own prejudices in order to do so.

While contemporary issues such as these pose fresh challenges for academics and practitioners, other more longstanding problems endure. For example, almost since it was first used over forty years ago the term 'hate crime' itself has caused a degree of consternation, not least because many of the incidents that we think of as hate crimes are neither crimes nor motivated by hate (Chakraborti and Garland, 2009). It also has the propensity to mislead or be misunderstood, as it gives the impression that the only manifestations that 'count' as hate crimes are those that are extreme in nature, involving violence that is perpetrated by someone with 'hateful' convictions, such as a neo-Nazi (Iganski, 2008). Having said that, and despite the growth in popularity of 'bias crime' in the US, hate crime is still the term that is most widely used by those that work in the field and recognised by members of the public (Chakraborti, 2010).

Furthermore, another, and perhaps more significant, difficulty remains with hate crime: there is often little shared understanding between academics and practitioners regarding *what it actually is*. In the former domain, the most cited definition is that provided by Barbara Perry (2001, 2009) who argues that it is best understood as a phenomenon perpetrated by dominant societal groups against those who are weaker and marginalised, in order to maintain society's precarious hierarchies and to reinforce boundaries and established hegemonic ideologies. For police officers, prosecutors and the judiciary, however, these restrictions simply do not apply: *anyone* can be the victim of hate crime if they have been targeted because of an aspect of their identity, whether from a majority or minority community. Even though this clash of ideas has been debated frequently within academic circles, there has not yet been a resolution to the problem. This may illustrate wider differences between the practitioner and academic domains. While the latter debate and discuss this definitional problem at length, the former seem relatively unconcerned – they simply work to the operational guidance used within the criminal justice system with little regard for academic quandaries.

Interestingly though, in the UK hate crime context one of the most significant developments of the last few years has been the decision in 2013 by Greater Manchester Police (GMP) to recognise and record attacks against 'alternative' subcultural groups, such as goths, emos and punks, as hate incidents (Price, 2013), thereby further challenging long-held academic notions of how a hate crime victim group is understood. This decision was influenced by the prominent campaigning by Sylvia Lancaster and colleagues in the Sophie Lancaster Foundation (whose work is discussed in the interview with Sylvia earlier in this volume), an organisation that has been striving to achieve this kind of recognition of the targeted harassment of 'alternatives' since its inception. That the Foundation can achieve this kind of impact is testament to the abilities of those involved, and charts the transition of Sylvia (as she herself acknowledges) from a 'naïve beginner' in the field of hate crime into someone who is now internationally respected as an articulate spokesperson in the broader campaign against bigotry.

Importantly, the Foundation's achievement exemplifies how campaigners, the police and academics can work successfully together. As Sylvia reflects in that earlier chapter, the work of the Foundation has been both influenced and legitimised by theoretical developments around hate crime driven by the editors of this volume (see Garland, 2010; Chakraborti and Garland, 2012) as well as benefiting from the support provided by other contributors, such as Nathan Hall and Paul Giannasi, from the academic and practitioner domains. It is this 'synergy' between the different spheres, fostered in an atmosphere of mutual respect and the genuine desire to make a difference, that offers a way forward for others seeking to engage in this type of work.

However, the success of the campaign has highlighted some of the more uncomfortable conceptual and practical difficulties with hate crime that pose challenges to a number of different actors and audiences. The first of these relates to the dilemma now faced by the police and others within the criminal justice system concerning how they react to GMP's recognition of 'alternatives' as a hate crime victim group. Do they wish to appear progressive and thus follow suit, thereby widening the 'net' of hate crime victim groups still further, or do they resist this temptation and risk accusations of being out of touch with new developments and innovative ways of thinking? Additionally, if only a handful of other constabularies follow GMP's lead then this may add further complication to the status of 'alternatives', as they may find that their victimisation is recognised as hate-related in one area but not in another perhaps just a few miles down the road. While it could be argued that this situation exists already, in that police forces are free to collate victimisation statistics for groups other than just those covered by hate crime legislation, it was surely not the intention of GMP or the Sophie Lancaster Foundation to exacerbate further the 'patchwork' nature of the status of victim groups.

A similar quandary lies with campaigners and spokespeople for those hate crime victim communities already recognised as such within legislative provision, hate crime policy and academia. Should they embrace these developments, seeing them as a step forward in the quest for wider inclusion of groups previously marginalised from the hate debate, or reject them, as they regard this net-widening as a potential threat to their own established positions? (see Mason-Bish, 2010, for some insightful thoughts into how this 'competitive' process between groups can evolve).

A further dilemma poses more questions for victim groups and academia; for, if members of 'alternative' subcultures are to be included under the hate crime victimisation 'umbrella', does this then undermine the very basis of the original idea of the concept, which was to recognise the shared suffering of historically marginalised and disadvantaged groups, such as Black or gay communities, who have endured decades – indeed centuries – of prejudice and discrimination? Can the inclusion within this framework of goths and other 'alternatives', who are commonly from more privileged, white, middle-class backgrounds (Hodkinson, 2002), be justified?

These types of issues are reflected in the situation that other groups, whose identity is also targeted, find themselves in. For example, as Rosie Campbell outlines in her earlier chapter, there are strong arguments for recognising sex workers as hate crime victims, not least because they are a similarly stigmatised and socially excluded out-group that regularly experiences prejudice, harassment and violence. Yet, and like goths, older people, those who are homeless and other groups on the margins of the hate debate, sex workers find their claims challenged by those who argue that hate crime victim status should be the sole preserve of those whose targeted characteristics are immutable. Sex working, they suggest, confers an identity that *can* be changed (as, in theory, sex workers can seek alternative employment), and therefore the impact of attacks on them is not as severe as that felt by minority ethnic communities when they are targeted, for example (see Chakraborti and Garland, 2011, for a summary of these debates).

This type of discussion has typified the contentious way, over the years, that some groups have become acknowledged as 'hate crime victims' while others have not. Furthermore, these inclusion/exclusion arguments have been an unfortunate bi-product of the development of a conceptual and legal framework of hate crime that has developed in a piecemeal fashion over the years, 'granting' hate crime victim status to one group and then another. This process has undoubtedly been divisive, with some communities wondering why they have been excluded seemingly at the expense of others (Jacobs and Potter, 1998).

Also, crucially, the central conundrum of this debate – where the line is drawn between recognised and unrecognised groups – is more or less unsolvable, and throws into stark relief the limits of the 'victim group' framework. As the editors have suggested previously (Chakraborti and Garland, 2012), perhaps there is an opportunity to develop a new conceptual framework around hate crime that emphasises the targeting of the victim due to an aspect of their identity, regardless of whether they have recognised hate crime 'victim status' or whether they are from a majority or minority community. This would mean that one of the most significant aspects of the original hate crime concept – that an attack on someone's core characteristics hurts more than other types of crime – is retained while rendering redundant the kind of complicated 'inclusion/exclusion' arguments that have dogged the hate crime debate for so long. Such a conception would also chime more readily with practitioners' own ideas of hate crime and would facilitate the necessary theoretical space for the investigation of other topics, such as the targeted victimisation suffered by majority communities, that hate crime scholars have traditionally been reluctant to tackle. Whether this sits very well with those who champion what they consider to be the original purpose of the idea of hate crime – to highlight the victimisation of disadvantaged and marginalised communities – is, however, a moot point.

Conclusion: the case for connecting policy and research

Despite the rather gloomy picture painted in the summary of contemporary challenges above, there is much to be optimistic about with regards to ongoing efforts to combat the impact, causes and consequences of hate crime. This book highlights many of the reasons for this optimism, as it showcases a range of innovative work already being undertaken in this area as well as the new lines of inquiry coming from it.

As we have seen, though, the path to achieving better co-operation can be a rather rocky one, as the priorities of the work of academics (to shed new light on problems and generate fresh theoretical angles) can differ from those of practitioners such as the police (to find working solutions as speedily as practicable). This 'clash of understandings' is epitomised by Nathan Hall's wry anecdote in this book regarding the occasion when Deputy Assistant Commissioner Grieve gave him the time they shared a lift to the ground floor, all of 30 seconds, to inform him of the 'headline' findings from Hall's research. Such a way of working is an anathema to many academics, although Hall admits he learned a valuable lesson in 'cutting out unnecessary waffle' that others in his profession could heed too. It also brought home to Hall how keen practitioners can often be to learn from academics.

As Nutley et al (2002: 134) suggest, 'successful implementation [of research findings] involves a focus on *local* ideas, practices and attitudes' that practitioners can relate to (emphasis in original). In other words, practitioners need to know how research can benefit them in their own local context, rather than having findings presented to them in a more abstract way that academics are often prone to do. Scholars therefore need to deliver their outputs in ways that are relevant to practitioners who must, in turn, be open-minded enough to take on board the findings from such projects. This kind of mutual understanding can be generated by the involvement of key stakeholders throughout the research process who are enthusiastic, committed and feel supported by strong leadership that guarantees organisational buy-in (Nutley et al, 2002). This work can take place via informal and formal networks and the use of multi-agency steering groups that inform the research process throughout all its stages.

Encouragingly, this book is evidence that many such projects have already been undertaken in the field of hate crime and that these *have* delivered tangible and worthwhile outcomes. They have entailed the long-term commitment of academics and practitioners working in tandem to achieve shared aims. They offer hope that, whatever label we may use for hate crime and however differently we may sometimes conceive of it, we all share the common goal of tackling the prejudice that lies behind it and developing more effective ways of helping those most affected by it. With that as a basis, we can be confident of making significant future progress in tackling hate crime together.

References

Chakraborti, N. (2010) 'Crimes Against the 'Other': Conceptual, Operational and Empirical Challenges for Hate Studies', *Journal of Hate Studies*, 8 (9): 9–28.

Chakraborti, N. and Garland, J. (2009) *Hate Crime: Impact, Causes and Responses*, London: Sage.

Chakraborti, N. and Garland, J. (2011) 'Hate Crime' in W.S. DeKeseredy and M. Dragiewicz (eds) *The Handbook of Critical Criminology*, London: Routledge: 303–15.

Chakraborti, N. and Garland, J. (2012) 'Reconceptualising Hate Crime Victimization through the Lens of Vulnerability and 'Difference', *Theoretical Criminology*, 16 (4): 499–514.

Chakraborti, N. and Zempi, I. (2012) 'The Veil under Attack: Gendered Dimensions of Islamophobic Victimisation', *International Review of Victimology,* 18 (3): 269–84.

Garland, J. (2010) 'The Victimisation of Goths and the Boundaries of Hate Crime', in N. Chakraborti, (ed.) *Hate Crime: Concepts, Policy, Future Directions,* Cullompton: Willan, pp. 40–57.

Hodkinson, P. (2002) *Goth: Identity, Style and Subculture*, Oxford; Berg.

Iganski, P. (2008) *Hate Crime and the City,* Bristol: Policy Press.

Jacobs, J. and Potter, K. (1998) *Hate Crimes: Criminal Law and Identity Politics*, Oxford: Oxford University Press.

Mason-Bish, H. (2010) 'Future Challenges for Hate Crime Policy: Lessons from the Past', in N. Chakraborti (ed.) *Hate Crime: Concepts, Policy, Future Directions*, Cullompton: Willan, 58–77.

Mythen, G., Walklate, S. and Khan, F. (2009) '"I'm a Muslim, but I'm Not a Terrorist": Victimisation, Risky Identities and the Performance of Safety', *British Journal of Criminology,* 49 (6): 736–54.

Nutley, S., Walter, I. and Davies, H.T.O. (2003) 'From Knowing to Doing: A Framework for Understanding the Evidence-into-Practice Agenda', *Evaluation*, 9 (2): 125–48.

Perry, B. (2001) *In the Name of Hate*, New York and London: Routledge.

Perry, B. (2009) 'The Sociology of Hate: Theoretical Approaches', in B. Levin (ed.) *Hate Crimes: Understanding and Defining Hate Crime,* Westport, CT: Praeger, pp. 55–76.

Price, S. (2013) 'Violence against Goths is a Hate Crime', *Guardian* 4 April , www.guardian.co.uk/commentisfree/2013/apr/04/violence-against-goths-hate-crime?CMP=twt_gu.

Treadwell, J. and Garland, J. (2011) 'Masculinity, Marginalisation and Violence: A Case Study of the English Defence League', *British Journal of Criminology*, 51 (4): 621–34.

Notes

[1]   This may include characteristics such as the group affiliation of the victim; the imbalance of power between perpetrator and victim; the relevance of context, structure and agency to the process of hate crime; or the notion of acts of hate being 'message' crimes designed to create fear within the victim's broader community (Chakraborti and Garland, 2009: 150).

[2]   The term 'adventures' is used loosely here and should not be interpreted in the 'Dr Indiana Jones' sense.

[3]   Apologies to my academic colleagues.

[4]   In 2012 I addressed a second ACPO hate crime conference at the launch of the Cross-Government Hate Crime Action Plan, this time in a joint presentation about the legacies of Lawrence with John Grieve and Neville Lawrence; an occasion that remains (alongside addressing the conference to mark the tenth anniversary of the Lawrence Inquiry in 2009) the proudest of my career.

[5]   Further details can be found at www.sophielancasterfoundation.com.

[6]   The five 'strands' or characteristics protected by specific hate crime legislation in England and Wales are those pertaining to 'race' and ethnicity, faith, sexual orientation, disability and gender identity.

[7]   The strapline of the Foundation's campaign is 'Stamp Out Prejudice, Hatred and Intolerance Everywhere' – S.O.P.H.I.E.

[8]   Whitby, a coastal resort in Yorkshire in the north of England, has long been associated with goth subculture due to the town featuring in Bram Stoker's novel *Dracula*.

[9]   'Never Take Us Down' specifically addresses the issue of the victimisation of 'alternatives'. Bloodstock is an annual rock and metal music festival that has a specific stage named after Sophie.

[10]   Cherie Blair is a practising barrister and QC. At the time Sylvia met him, Jack Straw (Labour MP for Blackburn) was Secretary of State for Justice in the then Labour government while Michael Gove (Conservative MP for Surrey Heath) was Shadow Secretary of State for Children, Schools and Families.

[11]   Helen Newlove is a community campaigner who was appointed Victims' Commissioner in 2012, while Brooke Kinsella is an active anti-knife crime campaigner. Both were prompted to act following the murders of close family members.

[12] Julian Kynaston is the founder of Illamasqua, a leading cosmetics brand.

[13] *Dark Angel* is a short animated film (produced by Propaganda and featuring the music of Portishead) that dramatises the murder of Sophie Lancaster – see www.youtube.com/watch?v=qW2ve6_BkRA.

[14] Those convicted of Sophie Lancaster's assault and murder appealed against their sentence lengths: just one had their sentence subsequently cut.

[15] Herbert was, along with Brendan Harris, convicted of Sophie's murder.

[16] *Black Roses*, written by author and poet Simon Armitage, uses poetry and the 'voices' of both Sophie and Sylvia to dramatise the events surrounding Sophie's death to moving and beautiful effect. The play was first broadcast on BBC Radio Four on 11/03/11 and staged at the Royal Exchange Theatre, Manchester, in the following year.

[17] Julie Hesmondhalgh is an actress best known for her portrayal of Hayley, a male-to-female transsexual character in popular television drama *Coronation Street*.

[18] Merseyside is a county in the North West of England, home to the major city of Liverpool.

[19] My PhD research field work was carried out during 2010–11 and involved interviews with 40 police officers, 22 sex workers and 11 service providers and commissioners. The research examined Merseyside police's policy of treating crimes against sex workers as hate crime.

[20] I make intentional reference to the play *Unprotected* produced by the Everyman Theatre, Liverpool about street sex work in Liverpool based on interviews with sex workers, project workers, police, parents of murdered sex workers, residents, councillors and clients of sex workers. This went on to win the prestigious Amnesty International Award at the Edinburgh Fringe Festival.

[21] In December 2006 the town of Ipswich, in the east of England, became a focus for global press attention when the bodies of five women were found over a short period. Anneli Alderton, Paula Clennell, Gemma Adams, Tania Nicol and Annette Nicholls had been murdered between 30 October 2006 and 10 December 2006. All the women had been involved in street sex work in the town. Steven Wright, who lived in the local area, was found guilty of their murders and received a life prison sentence.

[22] 'Ugly Mugs' is a colloquial term for people who present a danger to sex workers and commit crimes against them. The Prostitutes Collective of Victoria, Australia, were the first to set up an Ugly Mugs scheme (in a context of underreporting to the police) so sex workers could be warned about people harassing and committing crimes against them. In the late 1980s Ugly Mugs Schemes were adopted by local sex work support projects in the UK where they now act as third party reporting schemes coordinated by projects to provide a mechanism for sex workers to be warned about dangerous individuals through alerts, to report crimes against them to projects, and to encourage information sharing and formal reporting to the police. In the UK a National Ugly Mugs pilot scheme, funded by the Home Office and coordinated by UK Network of Sex Work Projects (UKNSWP), was launched in 2012 (https://uknswp.org/um/).

[23] Peter Sutcliffe, also known as the Yorkshire Ripper, is one of the UK's most infamous serial killers. In 1981 he was found guilty of murdering 13 women and attempting to murder seven other women, a number of his victims were sex workers. The murders took place over a five year period between 1975 and 1980, with the majority perpetrated in the county of Yorkshire in the north of England. He had attacked women prior to these murders starting with the assault of a woman working as a street sex worker in 1969. He is currently serving a life prison sentence.

[24] A suspect was charged in June 2011, his trial took place in January 2012 and a not guilty verdict was given, so this case officially remains unsolved.

[25] All names used for sex worker interview participants are pseudonyms.

[26] The majority of UK studies of female street sex work and survival/street male sex work samples find high levels of problematic drug and alcohol addiction and other markers of social disadvantage. High levels of problem substance use are not found among sex workers in research studies of other sectors off-street where only a minority are found to have such issues (Jeal and Salisbury, 2007). Similarly, the high levels of homelessness found among street sex workers are not found among off street sex workers.

[27] Merseyside Police's new strategy on prostitution, 2014 reaffirms the policy.

[28] This chapter is written in the author's personal capacity and not in her role as hate crime officer for the OSCE Office for Democratic Institutions and Human Rights. Any views expressed are the author's own and do not necessarily reflect those of the OSCE.

[29] As of 21 November, 2012, Mongolia became the 57th OSCE participating State.

[30] For example, Azerbaijan, Greece, Iceland and Ukraine, among others.

[31] See The International Covenant on Civil and Political Rights, the International Convention on the Elimination of all Forms of Racial Discrimination (CERD), Article 4 of the UN Declaration on the Elimination of All Forms of Intolerance and of Discrimination Based on Religion or Belief

[32] Along with the notable exception of Alke Glett, see also the SOVA Centre for Information and Analysis, www.sova-center.ru/en/, which produces monthly reports of hate crimes along with a separate analysis of Russia's use of anti-extremism laws.

[33] The analysis focuses on South Yorkshire as a result of the author's ongoing, active involvement in Sheffield's LGB&T academic, community voluntary and statutory sectors. This includes being an advisor for the South Yorkshire Police LGB&T Independent Advisory Group, a member of the South Yorkshire Hate Crime Scrutiny Panel (operated by Stop Hate UK) and a part of the South Yorkshire LGB&T Multi-Agency Network (comprising of various public authorities). She also helped to establish and advertise a dedicated LGB&T domestic abuse helpline service for the Sheffield Domestic Abuse Helpline.

[34] A pseudonym has been adopted to protect the interviewee's anonymity.

[35] This legislation currently only applies to England and Wales.

[36] At the time of writing the development of this initiative is ongoing. However, if it is successfully implemented, it will be interesting to review any impact this has on members of LGB&T communities in South Yorkshire.

[37] Police authorities have been replaced by police and crime commissioners. The future of the IAGs was under consideration at the time of writing.

[38] Eid is a Muslim holiday that marks the end of Ramadan, the Islamic holy month.

[39] Victim Support is a locally based organisation, backed up by a national infrastructure. It has evolved from a federation of 77 independent local charities to a single national charity in 2008 (Victim Support, 2012).

[40] This study explores the lived experiences of veiled Muslim women as victims of Islamophobia in public places in Leicester and elsewhere. The research methodology comprises of individual and focus group interviews with victims, individual interviews with statutory and voluntary service providers, and also, an ethnographic approach which includes wearing the full veil in public places in Leicester.

[41] The findings indicate that Muslim women have been targets of increasing anti-Muslim hostility in public places while children as well as elderly Muslims have also been verbally and physically attacked. In particular, Muslim women who wore the *niqab* were more likely to be physically attacked on the streets. There have also been hate calls recorded to the MAMA line itself.

[42] Analyses of cases received so far indicate a clustering of attacks in London, the West Midlands and Greater Manchester area, including Luton. In line with these cluster areas, the MAMA (2012) findings point to a direct or indirect link between Islamophobic attacks and the English Defence League. According to available data, there has been an English Defence League involvement in about a quarter of the cases recorded to date.

[43] 'Islamaphobia [sic] a threat to democracy ... oh the irony', blog posted in March 2010, available online on the EDL website (www.englishdefenceleague. org) to registered site users.

[44] Of course, the extent to which the EDL opposes militant Islam or Islam generally varies, with commentators suggesting that the reality is that it is the latter that is more commonly targeted by the organisation.

[45] Since 2012, the British Crime Survey has been renamed the Crime Survey for England and Wales.

[46] Until 1991, rape legislation had an exclusion clause, which meant that marital rape was not a criminal offence.

[47] Since 2006, the Canadian Centre for Justice Statistics has published an annual report on police reported hate crime in Canada. CCJS is a division of Statistics Canada, the nation's key statistical agency, which conducts the Census, as well as an array of surveys on diverse social, economic, demographic, and cultural issues.

[48] Egale is Canada's only national lesbian, gay, bisexual and trans (LGBT) human rights organisation. It seeks to advance equality, diversity, education and justice.

[49] Australia is a Federation comprised of 8 States and Territories. Each jurisdiction has its own criminal laws and government agencies, including the police. There are also Federal laws and agencies.

[50] Comparable provisions operate in the Australian jurisdictions of New South Wales, Queensland, South Australia and the Australian Capital Territory. These provisions are similarly under-utilised.

[51] The first part of this definition is a direct reproduction of s5(2)(daaa) *Sentencing Act 1991* (Vic) and the second part which includes examples of characteristics is taken from the Explanatory Memorandum of the Bill which inserted s5(2)(daaa) into the *Sentencing Act 1991*:see *Sentencing Amendment Bill 2009* Clause 3.

[52] However, it should be noted that the NSW definition refers only to harassment, abuse or violence which may limit its application. Vilification is also defined in the NSW policy following the legislative definition.

[53] The academic team is comprised of: Sharon Pickering, Monash University; Gail Mason, University of Sydney; Jude McCulloch, Monash University; JaneMaree Maher, Monash University; Lorraine Mazerolle, University of Queensland; and Rebecca Wickes, University of Queensland. ARC Linkage Project LP100100585. Under the Linkage scheme the Australian Research Council provides the opportunity for academics to partner with 'industry' to undertake applied research.

[54] *Crimes (Sentencing Procedure) Act 1999* (NSW) s21A(2)(h); *Sentencing Act 1995 (NT)* s6A(e).

[55] See: http://hmd.org.uk/resources/films/hmd09-the-hate-game

[56] See: http://youtu.be/vzAj4WsF3VE

[57] The author spent 18 months researching several hate crime cases that were referred to the Oxford YOP; see Walters (2012a).

[58] More recently, police services across the country have begun to introduce restorative cautions (sometimes referred to as restorative disposals) as a means of disposing of minor offences, often in cases where prosecution is not deemed viable.

[59] Though facilitators may need to explore with the offender the appropriateness of certain hate-motivations if other stakeholders are not willing to challenge them on this.

[60] In some cases facilitators may need to use interpreters in order to ensure that all participants are included in dialogue.

[61] The offender had persistently targeted the victim for being Jewish.

Index